CUSTOMERS

SIXTEEN GLANCES THROUGH THE LENSES
OF A BATHROOM COMEDIAN

JOHN LESLIE

authorHOUSE®

AuthorHouse™
1663 Liberty Drive
Bloomington, IN 47403
www.authorhouse.com
Phone: 1 (800) 839-8640

Published by AuthorHouse   12/27/2018

ISBN: 978-1-5462-7228-1 (sc)
ISBN: 978-1-5462-7227-4 (e)

Library of Congress Control Number: 2018914721

CONTENTS

DEDICATION

FIRST AND FOREMOST, I would like to give thanks to the Almighty. Without him, none of this would have been possible.

Secondly, I would like to shower thanks and appreciation on my dearly beloved elders—those going through purgatory at this moment, and the ones still enjoying each new day the good Lord has blessed them with here on this earth. These loved ones include my grandmother, Delmathia Stibble, "Aunt Dell" (who died in 2016); my granduncle, Stanley Watson, "Uncle Sun,"(1996); Daphne Johnson, "Aunt D" (1997); Ms. Iris Watson (1973); Percival John Men (1985); Carmen Walker, "Auntie C"; Carroll Walker, "Uncle C"; Alvin Brown "One son"; Isolyn Douglas; and my dear mother, Kathleen "Little Miss" Watson.

Thirdly, I would like to give special thanks to my loving family: to my kids, Bianca "Binky," John "Junior," Patrick "Pat," Elijah "Eli," Gabriela "Gabby," and Angel "AJ"; the best cousin anyone could hope for, Linval Leslie; the other cousins I grew up with, Carlton Leslie, Michael "Mikey Dread" McQueen, Jeanette "Deserine" Francis, Elorine Francis, Janet "JJ" Watson, Jacinth Smiley, Cally Smiley, Kenneth Smiley, Shanet Smiley, and Oran "OJ" Walker;

also to my brothers, Dolphin "Ben" Black, Noel Black, and Carlton Men; and to my sisters, Marsha (2016), Rowena, and Merna.

I want to thank some of the best friends anyone could ask for: Karen Grant, Stafford "GG" Mullings, Hong "Rose" Gagnon, Richard "Rick" Gagnon, Derick Nieves, Harry Wheeler, Shannon "PID" Johnson, Bettina Tyree, and Rachel Alves.

Finally, I want to thank all of my fans, especially those in the military circle, who have wholeheartedly supported me since my first project, *The Bathroom Comedian*. I have nothing but love and gratitude for you all.

CHAPTER 1

WHEN REALITY BIT ME

O N APRIL 1, 2011, I was forcefully but not physically pushed out the door of the only comfort zone I had known for the better part of my adult life (twenty-five years, five months, and three days) into the United States Air Force. I use the word *forcefully* because even though I knew the end for me was near, when it came prematurely, I was not ready, prepared, or wanting to go. So as it stands, if the air force was to make that we-made-a-mistake call tomorrow, I would be back in my uniform and in my old office before the phone was back on the hook.

Believe me. I am dead serious about this. If you allow me a few minutes of your time, I will give you an idea of how profoundly serious I am.

Since that fateful day and on any given day of the week, I always have at least three companions riding in my vehicle with me: the good Lord, my military, camouflaged backpack, and my military uniform, which is still in the plastic cover from the last time I picked it up from the dry cleaners. If you cannot already guess, at least one of my companions always prompts people who get inside or look into my vehicle to ask a question—one that I will assume is mostly triggered by my uniform or backpack.

First of all, if they could see the good Lord, they would ask me, "Why is he riding with you and not with me? Why is he always hanging out with you and not with someone else? What's the deal, ah? Do you guys have something going on?"

To which I would answer, "Yes, he likes me more than he likes the rest of you guys."

However, because they can't see the good Lord, they look at my uniform instead and say, "I thought you were retired," or, "I thought you been done retired" (by the ones from the real ghetto).

To their assumption of course, I always reply, "Yes, but ..." then leave it at that—just sit there with a smile in my heart and watch the puzzled looks on their faces. I smile because I know in my heart that I will never be fully retired. I will only give up hope of going back on active duty on one condition: when Don Knotts, starring in the *Shakiest Gun in the West,* has a steadier aim than I do. Until then, I will forever hold out hope.

Still, the reality of that call coming to end my last few months of suffering is as sure as me leaping from earth to the moon. One reason why is that on the cover of my latest copy of *Air Force Times,* it says ten thousand officers face early separation. This newly announced number is in addition to the thirty-three thousand mostly enlisted folks (myself included) who have been forced out over the last eighteen months. Therefore, I can say without a doubt that I will not be receiving a call that will make me act like Clark Kent.

Even though we enlisted folks have always been told, "You are the backbone of the services," we are always the first to be forced out when the upper echelons need to crunch numbers, cut the budget, or buy expensive equipment that Congress has not approved. We are the last to be recalled, if ever. We only have a one in ninety-nine chance of this happening and only if we are in critical-career fields. Even this is unlikely because most critical-career fields are usually undermanned, and the possibility of being forced out of one in the first place is remote. Therefore, I would be hoping against hope.

However, this idea of being a backbone, which has been drilled into my head over the years, is hard to let go of. It is no way to treat your backbone. Many have said time and time again, "Lift with your legs and not your back. You need to protect your back. Be careful before you mess up your back. Where is your back brace? Why aren't you wearing a back brace? You know you can't function without your back. You must really have a strong back." So if we are supposedly its backbone, why has the air force treated us like this? Anyhow, it must answer for this.

Like the air force, I was at the crossroads of a predicament. Upon retirement, I sat down to calculate my expenses against my new projected income, and reality sat with me. Yes, it literally came into the room and sat down at the table beside me, and the chart below will show you why.

Monthly income Before Retirement: Living on Base

Salary:	$4,450
Housing:	$1,764
Food:	$323
Total:	**$6,537**

Expenses

Rent:	$1,764
Food:	$1,000
Bills: Credit Cards, phones cable and internet:	$2,800
Total:	$5,564

Personnel living on bases/posts do not have to pay for water, sewage, electric, gas, garbage, or anything else that people who live off base have to pay for. It is something we take for granted—and most of the time abuse. Once we are on the outside, it becomes painfully clear how good we had it. We start wishing for do-overs. Yes, even the most wicked of us will try to seek religion in our darkest moments. Most of the government's generosity is wasted by my hardheaded, unappreciative kids who still have not learned. Even now, they show that they do not care about conserving energy or a dime. They leave every downstairs light (including the garage's and the backyard's) and television on. They simply walk away without a thought.

When I was on base, I had roughly eight hundred to a thousand dollars left over each month to squander, and to me that was living peacefully. Not many on the outside could say that. Then retirement came and forced me to join the ones I used to call "the other people." I am one of them now because I had to move off the base and find a place to live. I was also shocked by the initial cost that came with such an adventure.

Finding a new domicile caused me to immediately shell out more than $6,000: deposit, first month, and half the rent; moving vehicle rental; and other fees to get things started in or transferred to the new place. If I was going to try to plug some of my many abruptly opened financial doughnut holes, which was something that had to be done quickly. I now had a new financial forecast.

Income Before Retirement: Living on Base

Retirement pay:	$2,275
9/11 GI Bill (school allowance):	$1,380 (for thirty-six months)
VA disability payment:	$00.00 (paperwork was still being processed)
Total:	**3,655** (thus far until June 6, 2011)

Expenses

Rent (leased house):	$2,000
Food:	$1,000
Bills:	$2,800 (Reality bites right here with bills.)
Added bills (gas, electric, water, sewage, etc.)	$600
Total:	**$6,400**

Seeing the dysfunctional dichotomy above—or as others would classify it, the great disparity of the continental divide—my reality walked away from the table and left me sitting there all by myself. Within seconds of reality hitting, my calculator began to scream at me. However, please bear in mind that I was using a knockoff of a Texas Instrument calculator. Nevertheless, even if I was using a Russian made one—wait, everything is built in China these days. Well then, even if I was using a Chinese calculator, it would have screamed the same thing: "Boy, you are screwed! You need another $2,745 each month to make ends meet. Therefore at this venture, you have to do something because it will be four to six months before you and your family are living on the street."

Furthermore, my calculator said to me, "Look. I just saw that online business, which you've been dreaming about and aching to start, go up in smoke. Listen to me, son. You do not have that much left in your savings.

"When your Veterans Administration compensation kicks in in about six months to a year and if they award you anything at all, it probably won't be much. I actually foresee nothing more than 70 percent, for a grand total of about $1,200 a month—at best. My senses say 60 percent, but I'll be generous and grant you 70 percent so as not to hurt your feelings, but again, that's only if you're lucky. Yes, it is something you will receive for the rest of your life, if Congress doesn't change its mind like it has been doing with everything else, except for higher taxes put on the richest people.

"If or even when it does kick in, it still won't be enough. It will only put that much more in your coffer. Remember, you will have burned through almost half of your 9/11 GI Bill housing allowance, leaving you with only two years before you're back here again. So it's best that you do something now. Therefore, think fast because you're at a crossroads, and those who enter before knowing where they are going get run over. So a word to the wise: You'd best not enter unless you're sure what direction you should go."

At that point, I wisely decided to grab the bull by its horns before it gored me in the ass. Doing so caused the following events to transpire in succession, not because I wanted to—if I had had my way, I would still have been on active duty—but because reality was making sense as it started to bite.

I ran upstairs like I had indeed been gored in the ass, kicked my boys off their computer (long story and not enough time), and started to search for several companies the military had said were military-friendly-hire jobs. I only filled out one application, not because that was the only job I wanted to do, but because this company's application website was the easiest to navigate.

Being computer illiterate, the slightest glitch throws me for a loop and sends me running to one of my kids for help. They are glad to provide this help, but I know that deep down they get annoyed when I ask the same question time and time again. The thing that gets to my kids most of all, is when I turn on the computer, it takes a little while for it to get up to speed, and I run to them for help because I think something is wrong. I am pretty sure it drives them bananas, which is not intentional by any means. Still, from the look on their faces at times, I am just thankful that I am not a mind reader. If I was, I would definitely need to turn off my mind-reading skills during those times.

As a grown man, I should not admit these things, but I am so bad at operating a computer that even my little one knows more about it than I do—and she's only seven. A few weeks ago, I was trying to get into my Yahoo! account, which my seventeen-year-old set up for me, when I somehow opened up a website called Porn-Hub. I haven't the foggiest idea how it happened or what keys my fat fingers hit, but I could tell something had gone wrong. From out of the wild blue yonder and instead of Yahoo! saying, "You've got mail," nude women were popping up on my computer screen screaming fake pleasure through the speakers at me.

Anyhow, the good Lord must have been looking out for me because a few days after I submitted my application, the store's resource manager called my house. I was not home at the time, but as soon as I got home from school that night, my kids gave me the message. At first, I was a thrown off course because normally my kids do not give me my messages (My mom can verify that fact). So for them to part with this information was very unusual, to say the least.

To me, it meant one of two things: Either they sensed the impending emergency, which I had yet to explain, or they wanted me out of the house. Still, I happily took the message, and I returned the human resource manager's phone call first thing on the following morning.

We chatted for about three minutes as if we knew each other and set up an interview for Friday at 1:00 p.m. However, she neglected to tell me that everyone had to go through a minimum of three interviews just to make the final cut. So I got off the phone thinking that I was going there to wow her with my military (air force polished) charm. Therefore, my hardest decision was what I should wear to the interview, and so the process began.

I had several part-time jobs while serving my twenty-five years in the military, but those interviews had been done during my lunch breaks, so I had been in uniform. I liked doing that because I had found that people gave me more respect when I had been in uniform—any kind of uniform (an issue I will get into more later).

Anyhow, I was a little perplexed as to what I should wear. I had spent the last two and a half decades dressing the same way (military), and now I was finding it very hard to move on with the rest of my dressing life (civilian). I would have loved to reach into my closet and to pull out the first military outfit that touched my hand, but I couldn't very well do that. On my application, I had said that I was retired, and while talking to the resource manager, I had reiterated that it had taken effect on April 1, 2011.

So I would have to figure out another way to make myself look presentable and respectable. Because I lived in a house full of jurors, I turned to my family members for their input.

After discussing my dilemma with my family, the decision was made that I should wear something casual. The sealing argument was, "You are going to interview for a job at a home-improvement store, so there's no need to dress fancy. Everyone there is always dressed casually—some are even downright sloppy."

After I thought about it, I came to conclusion that they were correct. Therefore, I dressed in nice blue jeans, a white polo shirt, and my blue and brown Timberland shoes and then took I of for my interview.

CHAPTER 2

ARE YOU KIDDING ME?

I ARRIVED AT THE store's parking lot at 12:55 p.m. and ran like my ass was on fire through the store, paying particular attention to the directions the resource manager had given to me to get to her office. The journey took me two and a half minutes, and when I arrived, the conference/ training room was empty of any human presence.

Shortly thereafter though, one of the store's assistant managers approached me and introduced himself. He did not know me from Adam, and I did not know him from Joe Blow, but as faith would have it, we were destined to meet again three more times. But for now, he told me to have a seat until the resource manager came back.

While sitting there for what felt like forever even though it was only fifteen minutes, I read just about all the posted signs that were on the walls. I even read some of them twice because the information was tantalizing and I wanted to absorb it and think about the possibilities. I barely looked at others with only a glimmer of interest. I was never one to clamor over other people's bar graphs and charts when I had no idea where they had gotten the statistics and numbers.

My likes and dislikes of their wall displays continued for about fifteen minutes. At 1:15 p.m., the resource manager walked in and interrupted my solace. My back was to the open door, and as she blew by me to enter her office, she asked if I was whom I was supposed to be, and I replied, "Yes, ma'am."

After apologizing for being late, she added, "You don't need to call me ma'am. Just call me Susan. Around here we use first names."

"Yes, ma'am," I replied immediately, like a true twenty-five-year polished US Air Force veteran.

She produced a wry smile and then turned to shuffle through the papers on her desk. I assumed she was trying to find my application among the pile of rubble she had neatly stacked on the far right side of her desk. As I later witnessed, I was not the only interview she had scheduled for that afternoon. Moreover, the moment she turned her attention to the papers, I thought, *Dude, she's overly dressed compared to all the others workers that I've seen here.*

As I was thinking this, the store manager, Bill, appeared in front of the resource manager's office door from out of nowhere. Bill nodded a hello to me immediately upon arriving there. However, before a word was exchanged between Susan and Bill, I heard her say, "I went to the event at the university and did not feel like going home to change."

"I was wondering," he replied in his brash voice.

"I have three interviews this afternoon," she replied. Then she immediately added, "Will you be available?"

"Just let me know when you are ready for me," Bill said as he prepared to walk off. Before Bill left the doorway, he looked at me and asked, "Is this one of them?"

Susan told him that I was, and Bill pivoted in my direction. He came over to the table where I was sitting and extended his hand. I jumped up from my chair and clasped his hand.

He said to me, "Hi, I'm Bill, the store manager. How are you? Are you looking for a career with us?"

I introduced myself and added, "Yes, sir, I am." and at that point, Susan handed Bill a stack of paper she was holding in her right hand.

"Well, good luck. Hopefully, I'll see you later," Bill said before he was paged over the intercom and had to depart.

I did not know what Bill meant at the time by "Hopefully, I'll see you later," as if there was a possibility I might be sent home before having my interview with him. After all, his resource manager had scheduled an interview with him and me. In fact, he had just confirmed it when he stated, "Just let me know when you are ready for me." However, the process of how things worked there would become clearer to me as the day wore on.

The resource manager spread the stack of papers out in front of me and gave me instructions on what to do. She also said that I should give her a shout if I had any questions. Then she went back to her office to shuffle through some more papers. I will also happily add that she did not ignore me while she was getting her papers in order. She would occasionally ask if all was going well.

Around 2:30 p.m., the resource manager called me into her office and said, "I have a copy of your online application that I've printed out. I will go over it with you, along with the paperwork you just filled out. Then I will give you the first of three interviews."

I momentarily stopped focusing on what she was saying and onto the voice in my head, which was saying, *Are you kidding me? Three interviews. I am only here for the job in your lawn and garden center, not your frigging district manager position. Fuck!*

For that brief moment my mind went blank and if I was asked about anything she said during that span of time, I would not have been able to reiterated it because of the conscious thoughts her last words had provoked. I quickly snapped out of that funk, however, and grasped her next line of questioning when she asked me if I had any questions thus far. To which I conscientiously replied, "No ma'am – Ms. Susan."

This drew a little smile from her, and then she continued to speak. "Everyone we hire has to go through at least three interviews before such a determination is made. I give the first interview, your zone manager or assistant store manager does the second, and Bill, the store manager, does the third. You will be asked a series of questions and given a score for each one. Based on how your final score stacks up against those I have already interviewed for the same position, I will be able to determine whether or not you get to interview with Danny and then Bill."

Right there and then, what Bill had said earlier became clear: "Hopefully, I'll see you later." It also made me realize that if I wanted to win this job, I would have to knock their socks off (kick ass and take no prisoners). Plus I might have to lie a little to impress them, even though I did not like to lie. Still, I immediately started to search through my mind for a real or made-up military story I could flaunt in response to questions she and the others were about to ask, without even knowing what the questions were. However, thank God I did not have to.

My interview with the resource manager lasted about twenty minutes. I was sure I had not impressed her enough to move on. It wasn't that the questions were hard—they were easy, customer-friendly-based, commonsense questions. However, instead of giving the politically correct answers on some of the questions, I let the truth slip out of my mouth and then tried to redo my answer. So I walked out of her office feeling pretty down.

Moments after I sat back down across the table from the other guys, Ms. Susan summoned me back to her office. I was sure that my chance of getting the job was over, but to my surprise, she said, "I will page Danny to come and give you your second interview, so hang tight."

I do not remember if I leaped to the table or walked, but the next thing I knew, I was sitting there thinking to myself, *Are you kidding? For as bad as I think I did, it is not mathematically possible for me to move on. Plus, how could she have made that determination so quickly? It took less than two minutes. The only way this is possible is if she had the other interviewees' scores right at hand or if I was the only one being interviewed for the position. If I had to pick one, however, I would bet on the latter.*

I made it through the interview with my zone manager and scored high enough to move on to the store manager that afternoon. I completed my interview with him by about 4:45 p.m. He regurgitated that the store used first names and that I should call him Bill. Well, I thought that was disrespectful because of the way I had been brought up, reinforced by twenty-five years in the air force where I had had to address those who outranked me with sir or ma'am. So I just could not get away from doing so that easily.

Calling the boss Bill was not appropriate in my mind. Mr. Bill did not sound right. Mr. Bill Mosaic was too long and cumbersome to pronounce. Therefore, I used Mr. Mosaic, the title I called him several more times before our conversation ended. The final thing he told me was that the resource manager would contact me in the days ahead with a result. Then I got ready to depart. Before I left, I stuck my head back in the conference room to chitchat with Ms. Susan and to wish the other two guys good luck.

On Monday, April 18, 2011, at 10:00 a.m., I received a call from the resource manager. She told me that they had chosen me for the position. She said that with my permission she would like to initiate a background check. I agreed and in turn asked her, "Do you know how long it will take to get the results back?"

"Not that long," she replied. Then she added, "Usually, anywhere from two days to a week."

"Oh," I uttered.

"I will contact you as soon as I get the results back," the human resources manager said.

"Sure. I'll wait to hear from you," I replied before hanging up the phone.

My family was very excited to hear that I had made the phase where I would be investigated. They were even more excited when I told them about the call that came later. At around 8:30 a.m. on Wednesday, the resource manager again called and told me that their investigation had turned up nothing to disqualify me.

I immediately thought, *No shit. I could have told you that. I just spent the last twenty-five years of my life in the air force. Do you think I didn't commit an offense in the last twenty days since retired because I was just biding my time while waiting to venture into lawbreaking? I would have spent another twenty-five years in the air force if they had let me and am still holding out the faintest hope that they will recall me, mind you.*

While I was still trying to get the ringing of the words, "Nothing to disqualify you," out of my head, I heard her ask, "Would you mind coming down sometime today to do a drug-screening test so that we can complete the last aspect of the hiring phase?"

"Ms. Susan, I sure can," I replied. Then I asked, "When is a good time for you?"

"Any time today is fine. If I am not in the office when you get here, the young lady from customer service who sometimes works with me will be around to assist with the process," Susan explained.

I was there in the conference/training room shortly before eleven o'clock. Shortly after I sat down, another individual arrived. He was dressed casually and sat down at the table across from but to the right of me. He did not say a word or made direct eye contact with me, which I thought was rude. However, after another minute or two had passed, I made sure his glancing eyes looked directly into mine. At that moment I nodded and asked, "How are you doing?"

He told me that he was fine. From there, we struck up a conversation, and my mind did not linger on his first behavioral impression. Moreover, I couldn't be too damn mad at him or his parents for not teaching him better. I'm pretty sure that they had.

Let's take my kids for example. All of their lives, I've been teaching them that they should say, "Good morning," to the people they see when they wake up. They should say, "Excuse me," if they have to walk in front of someone, whether it is in the grocery store or in a situation where they have to walk between two people who are in a conversation because there's no other way to avoid it.

Along with saying, "Good afternoon," and "Good night," and greeting people at every opportunity, they should always remember that it is their responsibility to speak first if they walk into an open area and find someone else there. It could be an open field, a ballpark, an office, a public restroom, or their bedrooms, etc., etc. As a little boy, my grandmother, Delmathia "Delseita" Stibble, told me it was a common courtesy to speak first.

Forty-plus years later, I still use it to govern my life. As I said, I have also tried to implant this same knowledge in my kids' psyche. However, they have thus far refused to accept it, do it in front of me, or show me that they have attained any inkling of my teachings. They would even come home from school and step over a person lying dead across the entry to our home, as if he or she was just part of entryway. Therefore, to be mad at this individual I did not know would have been totally wrong when I couldn't even change the same behavior in my household.

Anyhow, during our little chat while I was waiting to be summoned to have my drug test administered, the guy imparted some information that further confirmed my previous thinking. After I told him that I was there for the job in lawn and garden, he told me that he was there to do his fourth and fifth interviews. Then he stared at me with a puzzled look on his face. After a few seconds, he said, "Oh, so you are the one who took the job I wanted."

"What do you mean?" I asked out of curiosity.

"I wanted the job in lawn and garden, but when I came in to interview on Monday, they told me it was already filled. So they offered me this other position."

"Oh, I'm sorry. I did not know that they had other jobs available. The lawn and garden one was the only opening I saw when I searched online," I apologetically said to him. Then we sat in silence for a while. Well, not really. A few vender workers, three or four department managers, two assistant store managers, a head cashier with Mona Lisa smile, who was built like an Amazon brick house, and one six-foot-three-inch blond woman, who was tattooed from head to toe, paid a visit to the training room during that time.

During the silence between the individual whose job I supposedly stole and me, I thought about making the cut. It kind of confirmed the feeling I had that I had been the only person who had interviewed for the position.

After the swab drug test was administered, I was asked if I would be available to start training the following morning. I had no other work planned, therefore, I jumped at the opportunity, especially when I found out that I would be paid for it. However, when I signed the paper informing me that I would only be making eight dollars and fifty-four cents an hour, I became a little distraught. It is all I could think about on the drive home.

I realized how good I had had it in the military. I still could not believe the meager hourly salaries people were being forced to survive on in the United States of America (the greatest and richest country on earth). I recalled Bochepus singing that "pride is not too hard to swallow, once you've chewed it long enough," and I swallowed mine and attended the training. I figured that on a good month, I could make around $1,200 per month, and in these hard economic times, not many people would give me that much money for nothing on a monthly basis.

Still, I must admit, throughout the entire training class and beyond, I kept on wondering how the employees survived on these types of wages. Even if they were making twice what I will be making, it still would not equal what I had received while on active duty, not to mention my housing and food money and uncounted free medical benefits. Damn, I had it good.

Training continued each day until midday on the following Thursday. Every morning at eight o'clock, our gang of five (including one guy I had not seen at all throughout my interviewing process) reported to the training room. We picked a computer and sat at it all day. Besides lunch, a fifteen-minute break, and the occasional bathroom break, we read and took tests out the yin-yang.

I really did not know or believe that a person had that much to learn in any particular area of a home improvement store. I took thirty-three tests for the outside lawn and garden department, and that was not counting the seven I failed and had to retake. Plus, retaking a test did not only involve retaking the test. I had to go through the whole shebang again. Then once I satisfied those requirements

(I'm speaking only for my area of responsibility), I needed hands-on training for forklifts, Gators, Cherry pickers, lift trucks, and pallet jacks before they turned me over to my department manager. Luckily, the air force had provided me with some of that training already, so I did not have to spend an exhaustive amount of time with hands-on equipment training.

On Thursday afternoon when I returned from the bull pen where I had spent all day getting my hands-on training for different types of utility equipment, the resource manager summoned my department manager. She informed him that she would be bringing me out to him upon my return from lunch, which she did, but before that, she gave me a guided tour of the store.

That tour consisted of us talking about our common likes and dislikes and the fact that I was glad she had mentioned something about what I should wear on the prior day. I also touched on the subject of going to school and needing to get off work by 4:30 p.m. on Mondays, Wednesdays, and Fridays in order to make it to school by 5:00 p.m. It was an idea they totally supported at that time, and had no problem working around.

At that moment in time, even though I was only going to be with my new boss for about ninety minutes before my workday came to an end, I was very nervous. The pressure of his expectations, not knowing my fellow coworkers, and the helping new customers had me sweating like a dog before I went out into the hot afternoon April 22nd sun. .

My new boss was very busy and did not have much time for me. I spent most of the ninety minutes running behind or after him, grasping bits and pieces of unexplained job functions here and there. d My boss apologized to me at the end of my shift and promised that the following day would be better.

However, the next day was a mad house and was basically more of the same for me. By lunch, I had logged a few miles on my legs and had accomplished nothing for the eight dollars and fifty-four cents I was making per hour.

Upon my return from lunch, Donovan, who was one of my fellow coworkers, sensed my frustration and decided to take me under his wing. He showed me how things were done: pulling supplies, pulling carts, putting busted items in recovery bags and labeling them, requesting supplies for the front of the store, and looking up the price of an item in the computer.

I vocally expressed my thanks to Donavan many times for taking me under his wing. Once I expressed it in an action. Later on, however, I became displeased with him due to the fact that he would drop everything as soon as the store closed each night. From the moment I first noticed this (on our first Sunday night closing together), I started to hope and pray that we would not be schedule too close together.

I have never and will never believe that a person's workday is finished just because the that person has ended his or her duty hours according to the clock. But he abided to that regiment, and it upset me. When I found out about his situation, I sympathized with him but did not believe that it gave him the excuse to abandon his duty.

A month and a half into my customer service associate training, my boss and I became cool in the sense of mutual respect for each other. I enjoyed being around some of my fellow coworkers. Some of the cashiers had developed a mutual respect and admiration for each other.

I would always get giddy whenever the brick-house head cashier was out there supervising them. The first and only time I ever got within inches of her (we actually touched hands) was on a fairly busy Saturday afternoon when she introduced herself to me upon finding out that I was new. Her touch, her aroma, her looks, and the rock on her finger told me that I needed to stay far, far away from her. This is something I have been doing successfully.

Although the same can't be said for others, especially after word got out that she was not married but only engaged. Guys from all over the store gravitated to her, clamor around her, and talked about her and what they would like to do to her. Of course, it was mostly macho guy talk. Only one out of every thousands of us could actually do the things we professed. But who am I to shit on someone else's wishful thinking about a woman that magnificently built. One close look at her eyes, one touch of her hand, and one whiff of her aroma, and I felt like flubber for an entire afternoon.

Somewhere between working with these intriguing people and fully grasping all aspects of my job, I began to take serious notice of some of the customers' faults. Some of these faults were annoying and some were intriguing, to say the least. However, when they were compounded with the stories and the people behind them and with some of the relationships I had developed, it was mind-boggling.

This dichotomy of events has led me to share what I experienced at the store, as well as events from when I worked part-time in Germany back in the 1990s. Although this will not be in any particular order as far as dates are concerned (except for the first story). The more I think about these experiences, and how much I've learned since I thought I knew it all, the more I have to ask myself, "Are you kidding me?"

CHAPTER 3

INSPIRED REFLECTIONS

A S CUSTOMERS, WE have done some head-scratching things. Well, other customers have done some head-scratching things that will never cease to amaze me and some really screwed up things that led me many times to ask, "Have we really progressed that far, or are we just holding true to Jessie Jackson's motto of keeping hope alive?" What I mean is, have we gone from carrying a club and building a fire in a cave to where we are today?

I don't think we have. Well, to be truthful and in terms of time, we probably have, but in terms of common sense, heck no. Far too many from our two-legged bloodline are still stuck in la-la land. Here are some reasons why I think a whole slew of us are still caged in nincompoop land. Mind you, I digress a lot, so bear with me because it will be worth it when I get to the point.

Earlier today, I was acting as a shopping cart retriever, which is not my official duty but a task I'm obligated to do. Why? I'll digress and tell you because as I have stated before, I digress. My paper name tag had my name on it (surprising), and right below it these words are printed, "Customer Service Associate in Training." The words "in Training" are particularly important. We will get to them at a later date and time.

For now, we will deal with "Customer Service Associate" because that's what I was hired to be. I have learned thus far that whenever an individual works in the outside lawn and garden department, regardless of what the name tag reads ("Department Manager," "Floral Specialist," "Customer Service Associate," "Head Cashier," "Cashier," "Loader"), one has to be somewhat competent on all its aspects. This includes pitching in to bring shopping carts back from the parking lot, which I find myself doing more and more of lately. This is self-imposed, I might add to be fair. Still, although it is a partially self-imposed duty, it's the second of four indications to me that after the seasonal hire cuts come in June–July, I will no longer be gainfully employed there. Customer service associates do not usually spend as much time as I have on cart duty unless termination is not far off.

The job of a loader is to retrieve carts. Their duty day is basically broken down this way: 30 percent of their time is spent on cart duty, 30 percent on helping customers load their vehicles, 30 percent policing the front end, and 10 percent being idle. Of all four, employees only do two of these exceptionally well—being idle and helping customers load their vehicles.

Being idle consists of taking many breaks. The ones I have seen thus far are breaks taken in between customers, water breaks, socializing breaks, restroom breaks, and an exceptionally large amount of unauthorized fifteen-minute breaks.

Policing the front end consists of consolidating stock, sweeping, and watering plants. But these are rarely ever done willingly. Things are different when the store manager or one of the two hated assistant managers appears. There are six assistant managers who have one zone (a few departments) of the store that he or she is responsible for, and of course there is the big guy.

Occasionally, all of them come to the garden center but mostly when they are paged. When the store manager or the two hated assistants come, regardless of whether they are paged or not, they put the chill in everyone's bones. The instant they disappear, it was back to business as usual. While they are around, their chill factor, ranging from deep freeze (the female assistant manager), to cold (the assistant over the garden center), to lukewarm (the store manager), makes people work. As far as I know, they aren't bad leaders.

It's a rare thing when a store manager is not the most-hated person in leadership, but I can see the reason why that was not the case in this instance. As for myself, I have to honestly say I don't like it much when he comes around, mostly because of the tone of his voice. Otherwise, I admire him, especially when I see him walk the old folks out to the parking lot and load their vehicles for them. He also buys drinks for the folks working outside in the lawn and garden department because it gets extremely hot out there in the summertime. I don't care if the money is actually from him or from the store's petty cash, when I watch him pull it out of his wallet, it shows that he cares. A leader who takes care of his people is okay with me.

The assistant manager over the garden center is disliked because people think he's a micromanager. No one is willing to say it to his face, but it's always said in front of mem, as if someone expects me to speak on his or behalf. After all, I was the last to be hired and will probably be the next to be fired. In fact, I am sensing that I won't be employed there much longer.

As for the female assistant manager, who is hated most of all, she is mighty good looking. She just gives off an aura that says, "Hate me even though you don't know me," which I don't particularly like. When you are employed in customer service and are mingling with the customers daily, your outward expression needs to show joy, even when you do not feel that way inside. However, one can never tell if the sun is up or down when that person looks at her. Therefore, I can see why she is disliked by many, even though it might not be justified. I have even heard it said that she is a closet racist, but I'll explain how that came about at another time.

Now back to the loaders. When it comes to helping customers load their vehicles, all employees want to do this. Unfortunately for me, I did not understood the reason during my first month and a half working there.

The situation and the employees actions used to bug me a lot because of the way I was. If I started a process, I liked to see it through to the end. But now, I was fighting with others to even get halfway through the jobs I had initiated. I would help a customer put goods in his or her cart. Sometimes, I would push the cart through the store and up to the registers. However, as soon as I got there, one of the loaders would come up to me and say, "I'll take it from here, John Leslie."

Well, they mostly used the name John because we all were on a first-name basis. However, there were times when the loader would say, "John Men," like he was trying to patronize me. An employee would use the name he or she had settled on and then would cunningly march up to me and wrestle the cart out of my hands.

As disappointed as I was, it was the loaders' job to load the customers' vehicles. Therefore, I would let go begrudgingly and then go in search of another customer to help. As this began to happen, time and time again, I accidentally discovered why they were so quick to volunteer to take over. It was also the same reason they would not leave the front of the store, other than to walk a customer to his or her vehicle. The customers were tipping them for the great customer service (loading of vehicles) that was being provided by the loaders.

So heaven forbid they would venture into the parking lot and retrieve some shopping carts. There was no extra money to be made that way. That is why the parking lot had carts scattered all over it and there were hardly any inside the store for customer use. Therefore, since I was tired of the imbalance and customers asking me to find them a cart—I had to run to the parking lot for each request—I took it upon myself to change that dynamic. One of my first acts on each duty day, regardless of what time I had to report to work, was to make sure we had more carts inside than outside. This is why I imposed this duty on myself. Now we are back to where I made my detour.

While carrying out my shopping cart retrieval duty, I stopped in the shade beneath one of the parking lot's trees to rest my weary self. While I was there, a lady pulled up in a white car close to where I was resting. This part wasn't unusual for a store parking lot is where customers stop in order to go shopping and to do other strange things. Believe me, I have personally witnessed some strange things over the years. Still, what this lady did was high up on the mind-boggling totem pole.

The lady parked her nice car between two shopping carts. The carts, especially the one on the front passenger's side, were so close to her car, it was a good thing she did not have a passenger. One could not have taken an eyelash and have passed it between the car's right side and the shopping cart. There was not that much of a difference on the driver's side either. All I could say quietly to myself was, "How the hell is she planning on getting out without hitting the cart? Maybe, she's planning to climb into the back seat and get out that way."

However, by the grace of God and some long relaxed breathing, she squeezed out through the cracked door and onto the asphalt. Then she looked at the cart like it had offended her as if it had been placed there by some other idiot and not her. I guess if it could have talked back, it might have had a few choice words for her. Then again, from the way she was staring at it, she might have been carrying on that conversation secretly with it.

Apart from the fact she had put her nice or borrowed car in such a predicament, she was not a small lady by any sense of the word, and the parking lot was not overly full, but first things first. The lady was about five feet, eight inches tall and weighed roughly between 180 to 200 pounds. Therefore, getting out of the car was no small feat as far as she was concerned. At those dimensions, she had no business parking her car so close to anything else. She needed open space all around her, which was readily available. Like I said before, the parking lot was not overly full. We could have given her some props because she could obviously perform magic and have become extremely well versed in it.

It was a fairly hot day, and no one wanted to walk a long distance from a car. In fact, take me for example. I was supposed to be working but and instead was standing under a tree resting. Still, I'm glad I did when I did, or else, I might not have witness such first-class stupidity and laziness.

If she had looked to her right or even in the section behind her, she would have noticed many more parking spots. But no, she just wanted to be lazy (a point I will back up soon) and to park as close to the store as she could. If the place she had parked in was a spot for the handicapped, she probably would have found some way to park there. For all I knew, she probably had stick-on handicapped decals, which she carried in her glove compartment, and stuck one on whenever the need arose. I would also bet good money that she was one of those types of people who would park her car inches away from the front door of the store if she could get away with it. Thank goodness there were boundaries for vagabonds like her.

The hypocrisy of this lady's laziness spoke volumes. Shortly after she rumbled her way into the store, I came in with the lined-up carts I was bringing in. However, before I could even enter the store properly and to my surprise, who was standing there asking for one of those carts? Yes, the very same dang lady, of course. Nevertheless, I handed her one because I'm in customer service, and regardless of how I felt about a customer, I would not let it show or express it.

But damn, the rules did not say I could not cuss her out in my mind, and that was where I let her have it.

First of all, I thought, *Are you kidding me?* Then I lashed her with my mind's tongue: *You sorry sack of potatoes. You just left two carts outside welded to the front doors of your car. Couldn't you take one off and bring it inside with, you lazy bastard? How hard would that have been? One was attached to your ass when you got of the car. It was so close, I couldn't tell if you were sitting on it while you drove here or you had a magnet under your dress, pulling metal objects close your ass. I hope that you do not find the things you are looking for and it becomes just a wasted trip and use of gas for you, you lazy vagabond. Where the heck did you grow up, behind a barn?*

This is one of the many customer quirks that have me scratching my head. I will highlight quite a few more, but before I do, I must jump into the one that concerns my biggest pet peeves—manners. I touched on it earlier with my kids and some of the people who are now my coworkers. I also touched on uniforms and the respect they bring, but now I will look at them through the lens the customer.

Due to the way I was raised, I am quick to extend some form of greeting to each person I meet, and it does not have to be a formal meeting. It could take place on some of the occasions I mentioned earlier. The problem I have encountered is that if I am not in some form of dress attire (because the outfit represents authority), 70 percent of the time, I do not get a response back from my greeting. One out of the three people that do respond will only give me a smile (which is usually fake) or just move the muscles in his or her face to project an expression. Out of the other two people, one will completely ignore the question I asked and reply, "Hi," even though my question might have been, "Hi, how are you doing today?"

Such a question should invoke an answer such as, "Hi! I am doing fine," or, "Hi! Fine, thank you." I would even have settled for, "Hi! Fuck off," letting me know the individual preferred not to be bothered. Yes, it would be kind of rude, abrasive, off guard, and in the eyes of some, disrespectful. But I should be prepared for anything and be willing to accept the response because it was an unsolicited question. After all, the customer was calmly minding his or her own business when I decided to stick my nose into his or her honeycomb. So if that person turned into a bee (hopefully not an African one) and stung me, then by golly, I should be man enough to suck it up and to carry on. This is life, and things don't always work out like we expect them to, despite the exhaustingly hard effort we put into it. The same can be said for questions. We don't always get the answers we would expect to hear or that are packaged the way we would like to hear them.

Here is a case in point. Last semester, my Religion 201 class's professor told us a story about a question he had to ask when he was in seminary. He told us when he was in his junior year, his college decided to dig up all the highly respected theologians it could muster and bring them in for a question and answer seminar. Students were told to think of as many questions as they could and then to choose the ones they thought were best. All were required to come to the seminar with one question and that they would be part of their semester grades.

Well, he and his two roommates decided to have a brainstorming session. They came up with a list of nine good questions. The list was pared down to three questions. One of those questions happened to be, is masturbation a sin in God's eyes? Of course, they all thought it was an excellent question that needed clarification, but none of them wanted to be the one to ask it. Therefore, they decided to draw straws, and like his height, my professor came out on the short end.

On the day of the seminar, he was called on just after others students had asked their brilliant religious questions. He momentarily changed his mind. When the effect of what would happen if he didn't ask the question popped into his mind, he nervously got up. He looked around the auditorium, swallowed a few times, and looked down at his roommates, who were sitting beside him and giving him the go ahead to ask the question by signaling with their hands. He looked straight ahead at the theologians on the stage and asked, "Is masturbation a sin in God's eyes?" In an instant, all eyes were upon him, and you could have heard a pin drop anywhere in the auditorium. One of the theologians without skipping a beat replied, "If God had wanted you not to, he would not have made your hands long enough to reach it. Next!"

The response that has me pissing rocks is the non-response that comes from the 70 percent who just walk by like I do not exist. My store has a ten-meter policy. This means that once you are on the clock (wearing your vest) and see a customer within ten feet of you, you must engage him or her ("Hi, how are you doing?" "Hi, may I help you with something?" "Hi, would you like some assistance?").

Do I like that approach? Yes. Is it only at work that I engage someone near me? No because that's the way I was raised and will live that way until my last seconds on this earth. Furthermore, when I get to the other side, wherever that might be (hopefully on the inside of heaven looking out), I will take that same attitude with me, if I can. My grandmother taught me well. My grandfather, mom, aunts, uncles, and a few of my older cousins never let me forget to do this. Therefore, I look for it in others, and when I can't find it, it disappoints me.

One of the things that distinguished us from the four-legged creatures that roam the wild is the common courtesy we display to each other. If a person takes the time to recognize and acknowledge you, the least you can do is extend the same courtesy. Even if they don't, there is no reason why you can't take the first step.

It takes nothing away to say hello to another person. It does not make you more or less to extend a greeting to a stranger or even to someone you've known your whole life. Sometimes you will get dumped on, but you will never know how much a kind word might lift someone up unless you sow the seed. Yes, I get pissed off when my kids walk around with their heads up their asses. Of course, I get pissed off when I greet a customer and that individual walks by me like his or her head is stuck in his or her rear end.

A change comes when people are in uniform. Just about everyone respects a military person when he or she is in uniform. The same can be said for doctors, nurses, paramedics (people tend to change their stripes when their lives are in someone else's hands), fire fighters, and police officers—well, not totally 100 percent for police officers. Drunk people still cuss them out like it is going out of style, but you get the picture.

I have proof that this is true. Like I said before, when I am dressed like a fellow customer and extend greetings to customers, seven out of ten people do not greet me back. The moment I put on my vest, the percentage goes up to nine out of 10 customers, or 95 percent on the positive-response side. Yes, every ninth customer will answer me if I am wearing my vest. It is a crying shame that it takes a position of authority to get someone to speak to you or to extend a friendly greeting.

Here's a case in point. A few days ago, I was coming back from lunch with about ten minutes left before I had to punch back in. I decided to waste those minutes in the reduced plants section. On my way over there, I spotted some legs following a shopping cart off to my right and out of curiosity, decided to make a detour. I said legs because when I got close to her, I realized that she was about six feet tall and also wore high heels, which added about three inches to her height. As for the shorts she was wearing, I had seen more people in Virginia Beach wearing bathing suits that were made with more cloth. She did not even have to bend to expose anything. All she had to do was cough.

Anyway, I walked up to her and said, "Hi, may I help you find something?" Well, if it had been an answer I had been looking for to save my life, my mom would not have her eldest son around today. So I tucked my tail between my legs and walked away saying, "Be sure to let one of us know if you need some help or if you change your mind," to implant in her that I indeed worked there.

Upon signing back in from lunch, my boss tasked me to water the houseplants inside the store. While I was doing so, I had my vest on along with the straw hat I usually wear when I work outside. When I wear these, the hat makes me look different, and the vest adds a little store-authority mystique over my regular appearance.

Oddly enough, the lady with the giraffe legs, who was too high class to speak to me earlier, was now strolling down to where the houseplants were. The closer and closer she drifted to me, the less and less mind I paid her, except in my peripheral vision.

Yes, let's face it. The lady had some gorgeous legs and a stunning body from what I could see. Obviously, I could tell from the provocative way she was dressed, she wanted people to notice her, or else she would not have dressed like she was on her way to a nudist camp. So yes, I was looking, and looking hard. I feel that window-shopping does no harm, as long as you buy at home. Even though my eyes were glued to her backside (until later), it did not mean that I totally supported her clothing choice. I believe there is a time and a place for everything, However, just because the timing is right, it doesn't mean the place is also.

Anyhow, I watched her through my peripheral vision and kept watering the plants. Soon, however, she was a few feet behind me. I turned around with my head slightly down and said, "Hi, may I help you with something?"

It was no surprise when she smiled and said, "When are you guys going to mark these plants down? You guys need to put these on sale. Why don't you mark one down so that I can have it?"

I returned the smile and said, "I wish I could, ma'am. There is one here that I've been eyeing myself, but I don't have the authority to do so. However, if it's a good value you are interested in for a great price, the reduced-price items are located in the back of the garden center."

"Where at?" she asked immediately.

In turn, I directed her to the reduced plants and products location, and she joyfully strolled away. However, in less than two minutes, she was back, which told me that she did not go where I had directed her to go. Still, I did not let her know this while I was listening to her explanation of her supposedly wasted trip.

First, she told me that all the reduced plants were gone, which I knew was a flat-out lie because we had had over a dozen three-staged-high, eight-foot-long carts back there a little over an hour earlier. Secondly, she said she had looked all over on her way back inside and had not seen any like the ones we were standing in the midst of. I knew that was not completely true. Earlier in the morning, the plant specialists had combed through all the ones we had inside and had marked down nearly half of what was there. Then I had lent a hand to take them out to the reduced area. So if she had actually gone back there, she would have found some. They might not have been as pretty as the ones we had inside at that very moment, but that's why they were being sold at a reduced price. You cannot beat purchasing a thirty-nine-dollar-and-ninety-five cent plant for eight dollars and ninety-nine cents with a one-year guarantee.

There was a cart on aisle twenty-four that the specialists had placed some additional plants on before they had gone to lunch. They were due to be marked down first thing the next morning. Therefore, since she seemed so desperate to leave with a plant or two at a reduced price, I told her to go over and to take a look. If she saw any that she liked, I would take it to one of the specialists and have it marked down for her.

Once again, she excitedly walked away, and yes, I took a few steps (maybe six or seven) to follow her progression with my eyes. Then while I was checking out the view, I noticed a gentleman approaching through the sliding glass door about thirty feet to the left of me. He was holding the hands of two small kids and he couldn't stop looking at the lady's backside. When the gentleman was about four or five feet away from me, I saw the little girl shout with laughter, "Mammy," and the glow on my face dissipated.

The lady immediately let go of the shopping cart and spun around into a catcher's crouch to scoop up her running daughter, exposing the lighted side of her moon. I had never seen the moon shine so bright before, and it was not the only view I would receive in the next two minutes or so. After giving her daughter a big bear hug, the lady stood up and said to her smiling husband, "Come over here, honey. Come tell me what do you think about these plants," and then turned to look at them again.

The little girl started to run back to her father, who was drawing nearer and nearer to the mom with the little boy by his side. So far, the little boy had been the only one who was indifferent to the situation. Maybe, he had been pissed off at the way his mother had been dressed. Anyway, when the husband was about ten feet away from the wife, she bent over to pick up a plant off the cart's bottom level, and I and everyone else could see all the way to the roof of her mouth, and no, she was not yawning.

Now if I had been her concerned husband, I would have let my wife know that the moon did not shine inside a store in the middle of the afternoon. Better yet, I would have moved in closer to shield her exposed area while she examined the plant in her hands. But no, he basically stopped and stared at her too, as if he hadn't seen a close-up and personal view of it either.

His reaction puzzled me to no end, and I thought that unless those kids were concocted through artificial insemination, he ought to have seen her moon up close and personal at least a time or two. The kids did not look like twins. The boy was about four, and the little girl was at least two. So why did he react that way to the outfit she wore in public with two young innocent children?

I believe in women's liberation but also believe there is a time and place for everything. A mother should not go in public with two young kids dressed that way. You can dress like that if you are a stripper; in your bedroom or home with no kids around, or on the way to the airport to pick up your husband who has been away for months, just to name a few. Heck, she could even dress like that if she was running to the neighborhood adult store to pick up some entertainment because once she got back home, she would not be clothed for long.

Let's get back to the point of the story. She spoke to and even carried on a small conversation with me when I had my vest on. Thirty minutes earlier when I had showed no mystique of authority, she would not have spit on me to put out a fire.

The wearing of my work vest can also be very pulverizing. It implants in customers the need to ask stupid questions and the audacity to get mad at me when I cannot provide an answer instantaneously. Customers have come up to me and asked for the whereabouts of a certain plant, and toward the tail end of the question, they have informed me that they do not know what the plant looks like.

At times like that, I have had to scream in my mind, *Jesus, Savior, pilot me. If you don't know what the heck you are looking for, lady, how the heck do you expect me to know? Just because I'm out here working in the lawn and garden center does not mean that I am aware of or know what every plant, flower, tree, and shrub, the good Lord ever graced this earth with, looks like.*

On another occasion, a customer asked me to look up the price of an item for her, and when I got back to her, the first thing out of her mouth was, "Why? Why is it so expensive? Shouldn't it be selling for two dollars and ninety-nine cents or something? Isn't nine dollars and ninety-nine cents a bit too expensive for this?"

At moments like that, I think, *Listen to me, you cheap bastard. The least you could have said was, 'Thank you, sir, for looking up the price.' But since you did not extend some common courtesy to me, let me extend some choice words in my mind to you.*

First of all, yes, there are other items selling for two dollars, but this is not one of them. You can find those in the back of the store among the reduced-price plants. Secondly, look at this item. Does it look like it's worth less than nine dollars? It is a fourteen-inch hanging pot with a protective ring on the bottom. It has dirt with some partially dissolved Miracle-Gro plant food, not to mention the beautiful Mexican heather, inside the pot. So search deep in your miserly bucket of a heart and tell me if that is worth less than nine dollars to you.

These days, it is genuinely hard to tell those who can afford something from those who cannot because the ones who have money are trying to get away with it, and ones who do not are also trying to get away with it. Then there are those who try to get away with anything regardless of how minute, trivial, or dishonest it seems. Yes, it is great that people are becoming bargain hunters. They even have highly rated shows on television, which highlight anything from coupon clippers to house hunters. Heck, I will even add storm chasers because I believe that they are bargaining that the storm they are chasing will not take their lives from them.

The ones that enter a store looking for a bargain, however, should come with an open mind and stop getting mad at the store employees because the things they want are not marked down to a dollar, the employee cannot find an item, or the store is just completely out of something. Customers, go and find management. They make enough to take the abuse. The lowly paid hourly employees do not.

On another occasion, a customer walked up to me and asked, "Where are your pool supplies?"

Being the wiseass that I can be at times, the first answer that popped into my mind was, *Where the pool supplies are, dumb ass.* However, because we were in a customer-service environment, I could not say that, although I was tempted to. So I gathered my wits and said, "All the pool supplies are on aisle one toward the far end under the canopy."

The customer left, and I went to take down a water fountain for a lady. However, I had barely gotten to the top of the twenty-foot ladder before customer who had inquired about the pool supplies was waiting at the base of it for me.

I could tell that he was a little bit steamed, so I hurried up and grabbed the heavy water fountain off the shelf and held it in a dropping position in front of me. I was not about to take any chances with Mr. I-don't-know-the-right-way-to-ask-a-question. Although he had come back huffing and puffing, I did not drop the fountain on him like I wanted to. I had given him the correct answer and direction based on what he had asked for. If he was mad enough to try to tip the ladder over with me on it, he was going to have the worst headache the world had ever known.

He allowed me to get down the ladder peacefully and thankfully for his head. However, the very moment I loaded the water fountain into the lady's cart, the gentleman said to me, "You didn't tell me you guys were out of pool salt."

For a moment I was dumbfounded and just stood there with a look of wonder on my face before my mind started to understand. I said to myself, *He must be kidding. He can't be mad at me for an answer he never asked me about, can he? I'm a mind reader who is good but not that damn good.*

Next I heard the gentleman say, "All I saw was the empty space. Do you guys carry it anywhere else in the store?"

I knew right there and then that he was not kidding, and the wiseass portion of my brain kicked into gear again and said to me, *Tell him yes. It was moved to the part of the store called the ocean floor.* I overruled that thought because there was a strong possibility that my mouth could be writing checks my butt couldn't cash. So in other words, I said, "Wow! Sorry about that, sir. From my understanding, we've been out of pool salt for over a month now."

"Do you know when it is expected to come in?" he asked

"From my understanding, it's any day now, sir, but the exact day is hard to tell because I am not privy to that information."

"Is there anyone else around who would have that information?" he asked.

"My boss, the department manager, but he's on his lunch break right now. However, he closes tonight, so you can wait until this evening for him," I said to him.

"No, no, that's okay. I'll just check back another time," he said. Then he walked away saying, "I hope from your understanding, you realize that providing good customer service is the key to having a successful business."

"Thanks for handing me the lost key I've been searching for all my life, jackass. Until now, I never knew what the key to success was. I only know that the key to failure is trying to please everyone," I spoke aloud until another couple that was walking by thought I was talking to them.

"Pardon us," the husband said.

I quickly gathered myself and dealt with them by saying, "No, no, not you guys. Just thanking my last customer. Can I help you guys with anything?"

They both told me no and continued into the main part of the store. I reminded myself to keep my thoughts to myself, which forced me to start arguing with myself again, which is never a good thing. At that point, however, I kept it simple. I said in my mind, *There is an idiot born every day of the year, and I just met the one was born on 8 December 1988.* Then I called him a jackass one more time and moved on to the next adventurous customer.

A few days later, I was sweeping the path between the plant stands and racks when a lady stopped me to ask a question. She asked if we carried an item in the lawn and garden center. I told her that I didn't think so because I had never seen it out there before. To be honest though, I might have been lying because I did not know what the item was or what it looked like. I knew it did not sound like something we would carry in the garden center, hence my answer.

Naturally, based on my answer, she asked if I knew where it was located. Even I did not know what the name of the item was or what it looked like, it sounded like something we would have in kitchen supply. I found out later that I was wrong from the guy that had taken me under his wing and had trained me. He told me that the item was in the bath and tub area on aisle forty-two.

I had already sent the lady to look on aisle nine, where I was sure she would find it. However, about seven minutes or so later, the lady was back standing in front of my push broom. Another minute later, and I would have been done and gone because I had school that day, but she had caught me. "You sent me to the wrong location," she said.

"Sorry about that ma'am," I said apologetically. However, in my head I was thinking, *And you came back out here to tell me this, after being gone that long. You didn't even ask someone else inside. I'm not the only employee you see here.*

While those thoughts were swirling around in my head, she said, "How can you work here and not know where things are located?"

I became livid at that moment and said to her, "Ma'am, do you see what's written on my name tag? It says, 'Customer Service Associate in Training.' Now if you will please excuse me, I'll go find an answer for you." Then I walked away, hotter than a blowtorch.

That was when I found out that the item was on aisle forty-two. In the course of finding that out, I thought, *The nerve of her to think that just because I work here I should know where every single item is located. It is impossible to know every detail about a store as big as this. I bet if I ask her how many nails the builders used to hold the roof of her house down, she couldn't tell me, yet it's her house. She probably could not tell me the exact mileage on the car she is driving without looking at the speedometer, yet she will claim she owns the car if it gets stolen. No one ever pays attention to my whole name tag but just the portion with the name and nowhere else.*

Plus, customers never stop to think that just because an individual wears the vest of a certain organization, it doesn't necessarily make that individual an all-access subject-matter expert. Moreover, if the person is in training as I am, that person will not have complete knowledge of where most things are. That's why it's called training. My name tag says, 'Customer Service Associate in Training' and not 'Customer Service Associate since 2001, 2004, 2009, or 2010', just to highlight a few I've seen on other employees name tags. Mine does not have a date. It just says, 'Customer Service Associate in Training,' meaning I do not know damn much about the store.

I hope she was happy when I sent her to the second location. If I had to guess, I would say she was because she never returned to argue with me about being sent to the wrong location a second time. I'm sure glad she didn't because an unsatisfied customer might not be a return customer. The goal was to keep them coming back, again and again. Although if you knew their full intent, you might wish some of them would not come at all, like the person I had dealt with.

Not long ago while I was with my boss and another individual who thinks his shit does not stink, a lady walked up to me and asked if we carried CD holders. The expression on the other guy's face changed to a look of what a ridiculous question that is, but nothing came from his lips. I, on the other hand, told the lady that I did not think so, but if we did, it would be inside on aisles twenty-eight to thirty-one. Then I proceeded with directions. I told her to go through the sliding glass doors and to turn left immediately. The aisles could be found about fifty feet on her right.

After the lady had left, as if both my boss and the other guy were thinking the same thing, they looked at me and asked, "CD holder? Why didn't you tell her, 'No, this is not Walmart'?"

"Hey, you both knew the correct answer and you just stood there with silly looks on your faces like you wanted to laugh at her," I said to them.

"We did," they said simultaneously before my boss was paged away and the other guy followed him like a little puppy dog as always.

A few customers later, I was asked if I knew where the canopies were located. This lady was much older (probably early fifties) than the one who asked for the CD rack, but she had some gorgeous legs. They were all tanned up, shiny, firm, and as smooth as a baby's ass. Therefore, I decided to walk her to where they were located (aisle twenty-eight) instead of telling her. This gave me an opportunity to make good with the CD-holder lady if she was still in that part of the store.

The CD-holder lady was not in the aisle when we got there, however, in the process of helping the older lady pick out a canopy, the CD-holder lady came down the aisle with one blue box and one white box in her cart. So I took that opportunity to smile at her and then asked, "Did you find what you were looking for?"

"No. You guys do not carry CD holders, but I found something that I can make do with," the lady replied. Then she added before walking by us, "It is a little bit more than I intended to spend, but at least I can put it on you guys' card."

I thought nothing of the CD-holder lady after that and could not even if I wanted to do so. The canopy-purchasing lady kept on sticking her legs in my face as if she wanted me to kiss them. I spent the better part of the next twenty minutes trying to help her pick one out but not by choice. They were located on the bottom two shelves, and she would pick any or them up. She would point to the one she wanted to look at next, and as soon as I stooped down to get it, her legs would somehow move closer to my face.

During this time, she pointed to three items that were in one row, which kept me on my knees and so close to her that I could have looked up under her blue jeans skirt if I had so desired. Yes, it had crossed my mind because I had come to the conclusion that she was doing it on purpose. Although her suggested purpose at the store was to purchase a good-quality canopy that would preserve a room of family belongings from inclement weather, it did not seem that way in the end.

She settled on one for $129, which I had gotten on my knees for. Then she asked me for the strings, which were nowhere to be found. However, someone from the seasonal department (which we were in) told us that the strings were on aisle sixteen. To my surprise, she asked me to take her there. I was happy to oblige because it allotted me a few more working minutes to admire her gorgeous legs.

After I finished helping her, I decided to head back to my department before Jerry, the fat lazy-ass cashier, who mostly worked at the registers in the lawn and garden center paged me. He was so lazy and hateful that it pained me to even be on the same shift with him. He was the only person there who did the bare minimum and got away with it. He checked customers out, and that was it—nothing more and nothing less. When he had no customers, he would just watch others, who were doing extra stuff to keep busy. Instead of lending a helping hand, he would plop his fat ass down on top of the counter and expand the dent he had already put in it.

Maybe, it was because he had been with the company for over fifteen years that he thought he was beyond anyone's reach. He liked to page loaders over the intercom so it sounded like they were not around, even if they were standing right outside the door, which was twenty-five feet away from the registers. You never told him you were going to the bathroom because as soon as you walked away, he would find a reason to page you. But enough about this jerk.

When I made it back to the garden center, I saw a crowd standing by one of the registers, so I decided to see what was going on. When I got up close, I saw my zone manager jotting down notes on a pad. Beside him were two cashiers and the CD-holder lady.

Apparently, the blue and white boxes in her cart had stickers that read "$7.99," but the actual barcode on the box came up as $49.99. So she was there arguing with them that she had not been the one who had switched the price tags and that they should let her have it for the sticker price. The zone manager in return told her no but he that he could let her have it at a 10 percent discount off the barcode price. However, that was not good enough for her. It had to be $7.99 or bust.

Needless to say, she did not get her wish and left rather upset. It also left the cashier who had stopped her claiming another stoppage on his watch. According to him, it was the twentieth customer he had caught trying to steal, that year alone, in the three years he had been working there. Thank goodness for his keen eyes because he was probably making up for the areas where I and others were failing.

The closet I've come to catching someone stealing ended up in a disagreement with my manager, and I did not get my way. However, this is what went down. It was during a week when I had worked Saturday, Sunday, Monday, Tuesday, Wednesday (I don't know why, but the work week starts on Saturday). I was off work that Thursday and then came to work at seven o'clock Friday morning. At about eleven o'clock however, a gentleman pulled up in front of the store and brought a propane tank up to Jerry's register.

About thirty seconds later, Jerry paged me, even though I was no more than fifty feet away watering plants. Anyway, I bit my lip and marched up to the register to see what he wanted.

"John, what do you want to do about this?" Jerry asked. "Apparently, this guy bought two tanks of gas yesterday, and when he got home, he realized the tanks were empty. I guess whoever gave them to him handed him two empty ones instead of full ones."

I am no fool. I know that people make mistakes. Sometimes it is hard to tell a full propane tank from an empty one. However, one would have to be a real dumb-ass not to realize that the two full tanks he or she is leaving with feels more like the two empty ones he or she just turned in. Therefore in this case, I would have to see some documentation.

"May I please see your receipt?" I said to the gentleman.

"I did know I had to have the receipt," he replied.

"Unfortunately, you do, sir, because without it, I can't prove that you purchased the gas here yesterday," I told him.

"Well, to tell you the truth, I can't find it. I thought that I had it in my pocket, but I could not find it when I got home," he stated.

"May I see the credit card that you put it on? We can pull up the info that way," I suggested, before realizing that I had blown that one.

"Actually, I paid with cash," he quickly replied.

"Well, I am sorry, sir. Without any proof of purchase, I'm afraid there isn't much I can do for you," I countered, to gain the upper hand.

"Are you saying I will end up on the short end of the stick due to your mistakes?" he questioned.

"Sir, it's not my mistake. I wasn't here yesterday. Besides, you still haven't proven it was our mistake," I stated.

"But I am the customer," he replied.

"That you are indeed, sir, and this store is big on customer service. So let me go and find my department manager and see what he says," I suggested.

I walked away thinking that once I explained the situation to my boss and gave him my unsolicited advice, he would side with me. Unfortunately, once I found him and explain what was going on, he just looked down at me from his seat, which was high up on the forklift, and said, "Just go ahead and exchange them."

At first, I thought he had said something else, so I left saying to myself, *Yes*, until it actually hit me. Instantly I lost all energy and appetite to work that day and walked back to the customer, deeply resenting him.

By then, he had already gone to his truck to retrieve the other so-called empty tank and was now standing there with both. Needless to say, It did not make me happy to give him the two full tanks, but it was my boss's decision, and I had to carry it out. For them, customer service was job one, and I did believe in that. However, I did not and will not believe that the customer is always right or that as an owner, you should not take a stand when you could prove that the customer was wrong.

I will forever remember in my heart that this guy squeezed two tanks of propane out of the store and laughed his ass all the way home—or wherever he was on his way to that morning. I am also damn sure he wasn't the first to do this and won't be the last.

CHAPTER 4

MULCH FOR NOTHING

LESS THAN A month after I started the job, I was sent outside to sub for one of the loaders so he could go to lunch. This was long before I found out that they were getting tips, and just my luck, no offered me a tip to me while I worked the front during that hour. However, I serviced about twelve customers. If anyone asked me today to identify those customers, I would be unable to do so. The same can be said of the things I loaded during that hour—well, all but one.

A lady bought ten bags of rustic-red mulch and brought the receipt to me, which is what a customer is supposed to do. I took it for verification purposes. Then I instructed her to bring her vehicle up and to back it in. I also asked her if she needed me to place some plastic in the vehicle before putting the mulch inside. "Yes. It would be greatly appreciated," she replied before strolling off toward the parking lot.

I ran back into the garden center and behind one of the cashiers' stations to grab a sheet of the four-by-six-foot clear plastic covering. My intension was to do so and to make it outside before the lady backed her vehicle in. However, that was not to be because she had already returned and had backed her vehicle into place like I had instructed. She also had opened the trunk of her red Durango and stood beside it with a big grin on her face.

A few minutes earlier, I had not known her from Jane Doe; therefore, I gave little thought to her smile. The only thing that crossed my mind was that she was probably thinking, *I saw you run and try to make it back before I did. You didn't think I was parked that close, did you?* I didn't really know if the smile she was wearing was brought on by such thought, but I sure would have been thinking it if our roles had been reversed. No doubt my galloping goal was to make it back before she did, but she beat me to it. So I just carried on with business as usual.

I neatly spread the plastic out in the trunk of the vehicle, including her folded down back seats. Then I walked over to the pallet of rustic-red mulch and grabbed the first bag. This began my counting up to ten, adding a bag every ten to fifteen seconds.

Upon loading number six, I started back for number seven when I heard the lady say, "Wow! I really didn't need to fold my seats down, did I?"

"Not for ten bags, you didn't. With them down, you have room for at least a dozen more," I replied as I laid number seven down.

"A dozen more," she echoed with laughter.

"At least," I reaffirmed with a little chuckle of my own.

"Well, I don't need that many. I probably need about twelve total," she suggested.

"If you are sure about that, you are two short," I quickly informed her upon picking up number eight from the store's stack.

"I am only guessing. Hopefully, ten bags will be sufficient, and I won't need the extra two," she commented.

"Well, I hope you are good at guessing," I immediately said. Then I quickly added, "Gas is too expensive these days to be doing unnecessary running around," before placing the ninth bag into the vehicle.

"You are right. It is expensive. Almost four dollars a gallon everywhere," she said with a grin. Then without a pause and with an even broader grin she added, "I guess you should just go ahead and give me the other two bags, ah!"

I will be the first to tell you, I am not tremendously quick-witted as I used to be, but I still catch on to certain things at the drop of a dime, and this was one such instance. So I thought, *Oh, my gosh! At long last, I understand the true meaning behind her cunning grin*. Still, I paid the comment no mind. I just kept on moving as if I had not heard anything.

Upon placing the tenth bag into the Durango, I signed off on the receipt and handed it back to her. Then I reached up for the trunk to close it. However, at that moment, she said to me, "You are not going to give me the other two bags?"

"Ah! Oh, I thought that you were kidding," I immediately said.

"You know that I wasn't," she countered quickly. Then she just as quickly added, "Come on, it's just two bags. Throw them inside and forget about it."

"Ma'am, I can't," I replied while closing the vehicle trunk.

"Sure you can," she countered.

"No, I can't," I reiterated.

"Why not?" she questioned.

"Cause I'll get in trouble," I replied.

"It's only two. No one is going to know," she suggested.

"I will," I quickly countered in the hope that she might get the hint, but she didn't and persisted.

"Oh, come on. It's only two bags. No harm, no foul," she said. Then she added, "Besides, I won't tell anyone."

"Ma'am, I believe you, but I just signed off on your receipt, pledging that you purchased ten bags of rustic-red mulch and that I have loaded only ten bags into your vehicle," I explained to her.

"Yes, but if you give me two extra, who else is going to know?" she asked. Then she added, "Look around, there's no one else out here except us. I promise I won't tell a soul."

Well, like I stated before, I'm not always outrageously quick-witted, and like a person falling in love at hello, she had me at that moment. She had made what had been a very valid point, "No one else was around." I needed something heavy to counter it with.

I stood there for a moment with a smile on my face, looking into the I-got-you smile on hers, while hoping like heck that something brilliant would pop into my mind quickly. Then something clicked. I remembered that on one particular day during my initial seven days of training, I had overheard the resource manager telling an individual that he should stop parking his vehicle in the customer area. According to her, she had been noticing that he no longer parked his vehicle in the employee-designated zone and that that was against the store policy.

I also remembered that I had been warned (well, told because I wasn't doing anything wrong) that on occasions the store manager entered the store through one of the side gates. Although all employees were required to enter and exit the store through the main entryway, he did not abide by that policy. He mostly used another entrance on his way back from lunch so that he could catch people off guard or goofing off.

Along with those two facts, my memory bank kicked in another gear and added the fact that I had seen a car parked in a suspicious place on more than one occasion. Then one day, I had seen my zone manager get out of the vehicle after the car had been parked in that area for about twenty minutes. I must add that my zone manager had not been wearing work clothes but blue silk shorts, a white T-shirt, and white sneakers. He had entered the store through the main front door. Anyhow, after those three things had popped into my mind in succession, my mind said, *Throw them at her, dumb-ass*, and I obliged.

"Ma'am, I can't because there's a strong possibility we are being watched. Our manager has been known to show up here in his spouse's vehicle in order watch what's going on outside," I stated.

"Oh, come on. You're just saying that because you don't want to. You could have loaded them by now and sent me on my way," she said with that same crooked smile.

Now I was thinking, *Damn, this woman just won't give up. She came here with the intension of leaving with some mulch for nothing, and by golly, even if it's only two bags, she's going to give it her best effort.*

Luckily for me, I did not have to say another word to her because the store's lead floral specialist walked out the garden center's door. Someone who had been upset with her had once told me that she was a lady who was not color blind. I must add that I did not spend any time trying to substantiate the individual's story because it was not in my lane, I had no cause to, and I know how people can get once they've fallen out of grace. Besides, even if it was true, who was going to believe a customer service associate in training over a career employee?

The only problem I ever had with the floral specialist was the way she would boss me around sometimes. I could never tell if she liked me by the tone in her voice. She had more years of seniority than me and others who worked there, and she used it effectively. That's what a leader is supposed to do.

Anyway, despite my feelings due to the way she had treated me to that point, when she stepped out the garden center door that afternoon, I did not give a damn how she had talked to me. I just wanted her to say something that would pull me away from the small-time criminal who was standing in front of me.

The floral specialist, who was on her way to Sonic for lunch as usual, sent joy to my heart when she stopped, had a smile on her face, and said, "John, once you are finished with this customer, I want you to start watering the plants on the outside tables." After she said this to me, she shook her head, smirked at me, and walked on. She must have thought I was trying to pick the lady up. If she only knew.

The lady was the one trying to do the picking—trying to pick the store's pocket.

I said, "Yes, ma'am," to the floral specialist and took off running like my ass was on fire. The whole time I was there watering plants, however, I thought, *What on God's green earth is wrong with people these days? Has everyone gone mad? Is stealing the only thing on their minds? Why steal something as petty as two bags of three-dollar mulch? Why would she think that I would go along with her? I don't know her from Jane Doe.*

She didn't even offer me a tip, although that was before I knew tips were being offered. But she could have been the first or at least have done something to let me know that I would not be stealing in vain. There was no, "I'll take you to lunch if you do it for me." She could have at least offered to give me a ride in the Durango.

Hell, if it meant that much to her to have those two free bags of mulch, she could have offered me a kiss or to sleep with me in exchange. If she had, she would not have even had to carry it out once she received the mulch, if I had been crazy enough to give it to her. Still, she could have at least said it to try and get me excited about giving her the mulch. But she gave nothing and expected me to put my job on the line. Worst of all, she expected me to rip off the people who trusted me enough to hire me just because she wanted two bags of free mulch free.

Maybe it was a setup the store had planned. Stores have been known to send individuals, which they call mystery shoppers, to check out other stores' operations. So if that was the case, my store could just as easily have called in mystery shoppers too to see if their employees were looking out for the best interest of the company. They might have been trying to test me because I was new.

Well if that was the case, I hate to tell you, but you failed miserably. You will have to come at me with something more impressive. If you really wanted to test me, then you should have nonchalantly taken me by the cash room, had all the money lying out on tables, had no one inside tending to it, left the entry door wide open, and had disco lights flashing to attract my attention. Then you would just need to indulge me in a meaningless conversation as you eased me passed the entrance. Oh, and please don't do it on any ordinary day either. It must on a day when the store is number one in sales throughout the whole district.

There is nothing in my past, that I'm aware of, that would preclude me from being a criminal, now or in the future, period! Yes, I could go against everything that everyone from my grandmother onward has taught me, but I just choose not to. This is mainly out of fear of disappointing them. I would be indirectly saying to the world, "What they instilled in me was all for nothing and in vain." Still, if I choose to go astray, it's going to be worth it.

When I was in the military, one of the things that used to drive me up the wall were the young folks who would join but neglect to let go of the destructive behaviors from their lives before the military. A year or two after they had joined (some within months), they were put out of the military with a bad-conduct discharges and were given a prison sentences for things that were mostly avoidable: shoplifting in the base exchange, doing illegal or banned substances, watching pornography on government computers, stealing from their roommates, possessing stolen goods, writing bad checks, and so on.

When asked, "Why did you join the military and then waste the government's time and mess up your life?"

"I was stupid. I wasn't thinking," most of them said. Undoubtedly, they were damn right when they said that.

If you screw up in the military, the rest of the world takes it as an indication that you will be a screw up everywhere. Still, young people are not the only ones who do dumb things. There are seasoned veterans who are just as destructive to their bottom line.

A few years ago, after twenty-two years in the military, a buddy of mine came up hot on his urine test. Let me remind you that he had been in the military twenty-two years. That's two years past the official date he could have retired. Moreover, it wasn't like he was hanging around to make the next rank. He wasn't. He had not been doing necessary things like going to school or working on other required military courses—far from it.

If smoking pot was that important to me and my well-being, I would have retired and then sat on my front porch and smoked all the pot in the world my body could stand. There is very little the military can do to you once you have retired. My biggest concern would be in remembering that I could not do any illegal substances while I was on terminal leave because I could still be recalled by the military. But once I actually entered the official retirement date, the world would become my playground. There would be problems between the local authorities and me, but regardless of what happened (anything short of death), I would still receive a monthly check from Uncle Sam. It makes no sense to me, as is the way people get in trouble for minor avoidable actions due to temptation.

If I'm going to be tempted, my actions have to be worth the temptation. If I'm going to be charged with robbing a bank, it will not be because I knocked off a teller. It will be because I took the whole damn vault. Therefore, the same would be apply to my work. If I was going to steal from my employer or the store where I currently work, it would not be two bags of mulch. I would hit the store so hard that it would have to go out of business the next day. Therefore, others should think about cause and effect before soliciting my involvement.

Honestly, I do not think that was something the lady had considered. I guess she figured that since she was the same color as me, if she smiled and asked me to do something, I would do it, even though I did not know her from Jane Doe.

All the watering I did that afternoon could not get that crooked customer out of my mind. Even when I left work at 4:30 p.m. and was on my way to school, the sound of her voice was still ringing in my head.

CHAPTER 5

SIXTY-FIVE CENTS

NOT TOO LONG ago, another cheap-ass customer got mad at me over dirt—yes, dirt. Moreover, it was not even the most expensive kind of dirt that we carry but the one-dollar-and-twenty-nine-cent brand, the cheap-ass variety, and the generic brand of dirt, as far as dirt is concerned. It was also linked to a fact that I must admit. Dirt and pine needles are two of the last things in this world I thought anyone one would sell for a living or would be the root cause of a business.

How can anyone seriously push the business of selling dirt, wheat straw, and pine needles or expect to be taken seriously when the subject is brought up? However, it is being done. Dirt is being sold for one dollar and twenty-nine cents and upper, for a forty-pound bag. and Wheat straw and pine needles are being sold for four dollars and ninety-seven cents per bale without any public outrage. Yet if a woman tries to sell the pleasure of her pussycat to earn a living, it is frowned upon and could possibly land her in prison. Where is the justice? Anyhow, bear with me as I take you through a brief synopsis and then into this dirt-cheap lady's malfunction.

She came to the store at about eight o'clock in the morning every two days in her beat-up pickup truck (I mean literarily beaten up). She called it her work truck, which led me to believe she had a lawn-care business, although I never confirmed this. Still, her shopping habits lent credence to it because she would always go back to where the reduced dirt was staged first. It was a great place to shop. She made sure that no one beat her to it.

Usually when she left, all the Miracle-Gro products, decorative stones, lava rocks, pea gravel, paver sand, mulches, dirt, and a whole lot of plants were gone, providing we had any of these items in the reduced area. Then she would say, "See you in two days," right before pulling away.

Anyhow, a few weeks back she came in on a Wednesday morning and got mad at the fact that we had no dirt. She claimed then that she was not angry at me but at the fact that we had none. Yes, we had dirt—plenty of it—but none in damaged bags for her to scoop up at half price. So upon hoarding away everything else that she wanted, she asked, "Are you going to have any half-priced dirt on Friday?"

"I don't know, ma'am. It's hard to say," I replied.

"What is so hard about that?" she inquired immediately. Then just as quickly she added, "You're either going to have or you're not. I just don't want to drive over here for nothing."

"Well you don't have to. We have dirt now," I countered.

"You know what I mean," she said quickly.

"Well, that where it gets tricky, ma'am. I can't stand here and accurately tell you if we are or are not going to have reduced-price dirt by Friday because unless we find some damaged bags, I won't any have to be mark down. If I don't mark any down, there won't be any to put in the recovery bags. Even if I get some between now and then, they probably won't be here on your next visit," I explained.

"I'll be back on Friday," she quickly informed me. Then she added, "Will you save what you get for me?"

"That's kind of hard to do. It's a first-come, first-serve basis," I said.

"Well, I am coming to see you Friday, first thing in the morning," she informed me.

I walked away thinking, *Don't be too disappointed if you get here and there isn't any.* I was off that Thursday, but sure enough, bright and early Friday morning the lady strolled into the store like she was part owner. She did not see me, however, and I immediately reached for one of the hoses under the canopy and proceeded to help the older lady, whom I had dubbed the female water lily, water the plants.

Seeing that there was no reduced-price dirt available, it did not take long for the lady to go on her search and encounter mission. As she was approaching me from one end, my boss, the department manager, was approaching me from another. But my boss, who always moves at lightning speed, made it to me a few steps before her and instantly asked me for some forklift support.

To my embarrassment, however, the lady walked up and said, "You were supposed to save me some dirt. There is no dirt back there. What happened to the dirt you were going to hold for me?"

My boss did not say anything, but I could tell from the curious look on his face that he was thinking something.

So I tried to play it off by saying, "Dirt? What dirt?" and emphasized it with shrug of my shoulders.

The lady did not pick up on my drift and continued on as if it was her intention to get me fired that morning. "Don't play games. The dirt we talked about Wednesday. You were supposed to have some ready for me today," she added.

At that moment, I started to sweat a little. My mind yelled, *Are you fucking crazy, woman,* and at the same time tried to think of something to explain away the little misunderstanding. "No, no, you got it wrong. It wasn't a promise. I believe I said we might find some more damaged bags by then, but there were no guarantee they would be here on your next visit. In fact, we had some, but they were all purchased yesterday," I said politely to her with a touch of anger added.

My boss sensed the added tone and instantly chimed in, "We apologize for the confusion, ma'am. Normally the stocks at the reduced-staging area do not stay there for long, and we cannot hold stuff for more than twenty-four hours for a customer, unless it's been paid for. Again, I apologize. Please let me know if there's anything else we can do for you."

"No," the lady said to my boss. Then she added, "I brought my pickup, hoping I would get some dirt today." She said this as if it was the first time she had ever done it. Still, nothing else was said to her, and my boss and I walked away.

He eventually said while strolling toward the forklift, "Don't worry about her. You know how customers are. They always hear what they want to hear." I do not know if he believed it or not or if he was just saying this to make me feel assured. Whatever his motives were, I was still steaming under my collar and wanted to go and give the lady a piece of my mind. I was so angry that I was overly glad when we got to the forklift and my boss hopped up on it instead of telling me to get on.

Before my boss could start up the forklift, he was paged over the intercom by the store manager and immediately flicked open his store-issued phone and called the manager's extension. Then he said a few, "Yes, Bill. No, Bill. I'll get on it, Bill. I had that as part of my to-do list, Bill. Okay, sir, I'll be right there," and then he was gone in his fast moving pace.

Instantly we were separate entities again. My boss headed toward an entrance leading to inside the store, and I headed to the main garden center gate leading to the parking lot. I tossed my vest to one of the cashiers as I blew by him to chase down the lady. It was perfect timing because I found her one parking spot away from her car and not far from where the dumb-ass (in a previous chapter) had parked her car between the two shopping carts.

I ran up to her and yelled, "Hey, what the heck is your major malfunction today, lady? Didn't you see me going like this, telling you to knock it off? That was my boss, the department manager, you were saying all that crap in front of, in case you didn't know."

"Oh," she echoed like an innocent but unsympathetic child.

"Oh," I shouted. Then I added, "Oh! All you can say for yourself is oh after standing there and acting like you and I had some cozy, unscrupulous, stealing-of-store-goods relationship going on? I really don't know you from Jane Doe.

"Do you know that so far this summer, the store has shown 123 bags of its Nature Scape red mulch unaccounted for? In other words, it's missing and now under investigation by loss prevention personnel. Yes, I know that that is the real expensive mulch, and you would not dream of spending five dollars and ninety-seven cents on a bag of shredded tree. But can you imagine how your display made me look?

"It was all over a bag of dirt that cost sixty-five cents. Yes, sixty-five cents. The undamaged ones' regular price is one dollar and twenty-nine cents, and you come in here and scoop up the damaged ones for half that price—sixty-five cents. That's what you put my job on the line for or at least doubts in people's about me—sixty-five cents!"

I went back inside feeling a sense of relief after my parking-lot outburst but still hoping that I would not ever have to see that woman in the store again. However, on Saturday of the following week, faith would say to me, "Not so fast," or maybe I just did not send up the right prayer. I tend to do that quite often, and it's the main reason why I have not won the lottery.

Anyway, that particular Saturday was a hot enough day to make the devil sigh, and I was sitting on the forklift with a load of landscaping timber. I was waiting there with my spotter for the hated female assistant manager to come and let us through the garden center's side gate. However, about two minutes into the wait, which was not long as far as waiting time is concerned out there (It normally takes them an average of five minutes to come and open the secure loading/unloading gate), my spotter said someone was trying to get my attention and pointed in the direction of my left shoulder. I pivoted my upper body immediately in that direction, and to my surprise, the lady stood there with a bottle of water in her outstretched right hand.

"Here," she said. "I know that it is pretty hot, so I brought you a bottle of water."

I said, "Thank you," to her and then reached out and took the ice-cold bottle from her hand. Then all kinds of thoughts started to flow through my mind, including what my oldest cousin would do.

During the short time I was thinking, the lady spoke again. "Now you can't say I've never done anything nice for you," she said and walked off in the direction of the reduced-plant-and-product staging area.

Then the ribbing started from the girl who was spotting me. "John's got an admirer. John's got an admirer. John's got an admirer," she said and was going to say again when I jumped in.

"Be quiet, child. You won't believe half of this story when it's explained to you," I said to my spotter. Upon getting the full spectrum of the story, the spotter told me that I was crazy for chasing the lady down in the parking lot and that I should think twice about drinking the water she had brought me. But what she hadn't been told was the that I was already two thoughts ahead of her.

The spotter might have thought I was crazy, but I didn't think I was. The lady might have thought the same thing too or her intentions might have been good. However, I am very, very, very particular about who I accept food and drinks from. I imitate my oldest cousin in these matters, and it has served me well over the years. Some of the reasons for this can be found in my book *The Bathroom Comedian* as well as the story that I am about to tell about my distrust when others ask me to digest something.

A few years ago, I dated a lady that I cared very much for. One night after we finished our business, we were lying in bed trading life stories—the good, the bad, and the ugly. I don't know if she forgot to whom she was talking or how I felt about certain things. Whatever the case might have been, she let following story slip out of her mouth after my simple question, "What is the meanest thing you have ever done to someone else?"

She told me that it had been something that had happened a little over a year before. She also said the incident had taken place at a location where she was currently employed. She said that a customer once entered her work establishment and ordered a particular sandwich. She took the gentleman's request and passed it along to her coworker, who was working the grill. According to my friend, she took the sandwich basket out to the table where the gentleman was sitting.

Shortly after she had returned behind the counter, the gentleman was standing there with the whole sandwich basket (sandwich, fries, and the nuggets for his little son). He told her that the meat on his sandwich had not been cooked the way he had ordered it and that it was missing some of the condiments. She said that she took the sandwich from the customer, apologized to him, and then passed it to her coworker to fix. When the sandwich was remade, she once again took it out to the customer's table. However, just as before, the customer had a complaint, but this time, he complained before she had even walked away.

Apparently on the second go-round, they neglected to put the lettuce and tomato back on the sandwich, which I thought was a legitimate complaint. However at the time, my friend and her coworker did not think so. So when she took the sandwich back the next time to remake it, both she and the coworker remade it, and not in the way you would imagine or with the behavior you would expect from someone working in a food-service establishment.

She said, and I quote, "My co-worker and I were pissed at him because he complained too much. So we took it [the customer's sandwich] to the deepest part of the back where no one could see us. Then we opened up the sandwich and silently cough up the biggest chunk of spit and gunk we could mustered. Then we both took turn spitting it on the guy's sandwich, placed the missing tomato and lettuce over it, and then I delivered it to him and walked back to the counter. From there, my coworker and I watched he eat it all. Then we high-five each other and went back to work ... Served him right for coming so close to closing time and pissing us off with his changing demands."

Although I did not know who the individual was, I did not think they had served him right. I can say to you with all honesty that that was the moment my balloon started to lose air her, and within a week, we stopped hanging out. I took that incident personally on three accounts.

First, it happened on a military instillation, and you don't fuck with anyone who has served or is currently serving this country of ours. Like I said before, I have no idea who the customer was. I never asked for his name. I am quite sure that they did not ask for his name so that they could match it up with the food they had spat on.

I will be even more candid with you. I am not sure if the individual was in the military, but he was on a military instillation eating in a military establishment, and that is good enough for me. Only military civilian employees, military personnel, their dependents, and their guests can purchase food in such an establishment. Therefore, this person had some military connection. Plus he had his young son with him, and that's more of an indication of a someone who would serve in the military. So you do not mess with our past and present defenders. It's because of their service and sacrifice that we have the freedom we enjoy today. Because of this, you cannot earn the right to spit on their food under any circumstances, period!

Secondly, when you work in a customer service industry, the customer is trusting that you will treat him or her the way you would like to be treated and not the way you believe that person should be treated, regardless of what you are going through. Customers put their faith in you, especially when it comes to handling their food, and that is not something you should take lightly. No individual should spit on another person's food because you wouldn't like it if the shoe was on the other foot. Most people won't even swallow their own gunk, so how on God's green earth, could you stand by and watch someone else eat what you spat on their food?

Thirdly, my grandmother told me, a long, long time ago, that cleanliness was next to godliness, so I started to imitate my oldest cousin. My mom, on the other hand, often teased me about how nasty I was before I became a teenager, but I don't believe that because I met my oldest cousin long before then. His influence on my life caused me not to eat food from just anyone.

I am in my forties, and besides going to restaurants, I have only eaten food fixed by a handful of people outside of my immediate family. In fact, I am so picky that I have family members that I will take food or accept a glass of water from, even if I was dying of thirst. A person has to have high food scruples if he or she wants me to indulge in anything that is prepared. If I can't trust you with my food, you and I can't date. There is no point in me being with you if I can't or won't eat the food that you give me. I do not have the time to go around and keep tabs on the environment or the conditions under which someone is preparing something for me to eat on a regular basis. Therefore, I have to be able to trust you unconditionally.

I will, however, find the time to inspect something that a first-time food offeror gives me, just like the bottle of water the lady handed me when I was on the forklift. Even though it was a very hot day and my bottle of Gatorade was gone. I was not going to drink a bottle of water that some woman I had cussed out in the parking lot a week earlier had handed me. No way!

I might be a fool for love, my kids, thinking that I'm going to hit the lottery before I'm fifty, fast cars, and hot women, but I'm not one for the things that go down my digestive tract. Therefore, I inspected the bottle of water that the lady had given me. Mind you, I said earlier that her intention might have been genuine. Moreover, it looked like she had just bought it for me. In fact, I could see the truth in it because we carry that very same size and type in the coolers by the checkout registers.

The bottle that she gave me was 23.7 fluid ounces. It had a blue flip-top cap and a white screw on top. Although my thirst was asking to be quenched, I noticed that the seal around the blue cap had been broken, yet the water inside was ice cold. In fact, you could still see a chunk of ice inside it. That spelled home refrigeration to me.

I am not aware of any stores that sell frozen bottles of water. Moreover, I don't believe a person genuinely wants to make up with someone else by bringing him or her a bottle of water that looks like it has been tampered with. Still, I didn't know if that was the case. I did not drink the water or have it tested to find out. However, someone once told me that the first impression is always a lasting impression. The first and lasting impressions I got from that bottle of water were not a good ones.

Firstly, she had supposedly bought it in a store just for me. Secondly, it had cost one dollar and twenty-five cents before taxes. Thirdly, she had gotten highly upset at me for not saving her a bag of dirt that cost sixty-five cents, Therefore, I did not buy the generosity act. Nope, I didn't buy it!

CHAPTER 6

DIRT

O N A DIFFERENT occasion, another lady pushed me to the brink of reprising the last scene of the movie, *Dr. No*, when 007 used the helicopter to drop Dr. No down the astronomically long chimney. I must say, however, I have no explanation for the way I felt that day, but somehow or another, the lady touched my last good nerve and irritated me to the highest level. How I react depends on the day because sometimes it is hard to irritate me and sometimes it is easy. Regardless of how I feel, I usually never let it show, but that lady somehow touched my set-me-off nerve that day.

She was a heavyset person riding around on a motorized shopping scooter. It appeared to be a personal one and not one from the store because it was fancier than ours were. Plus ours always run out of battery power either when the customers are in the store or after they've paid and are trying to make it to their vehicles.

Because of this fact, someone getting run over has been one of my two main concerns since I started working there. The amount of time it takes a manager to respond when requested to unlock the customer-servicing garden center gate is the other. I mostly worry about one of the store scooters running out of power in traffic, which is entirely possible. They always seem to start losing power the moment they get outside. Specifically, it is the second they begin to cross the long straightaway between the store and the parking lot.

In the short time I have been working there, I have seen enough near misses to boggle the mind. Drivers seem to use the little straightaway as their own Daytona International Speedway. They approach it starting at the fast-food restaurant next door at fifteen miles per hour and then floor the pedal. Some are going so fast, I can hardly see the vehicles. I can tell something has gone by because of the sound—engines spitting out horsepower or music blasting through open windows. So when the low-battery-life scooters are added, it becomes a disaster waiting to happen.

The things die so much that I've seen more many elderly people dismount them and use their badly needed energy to walk to their vehicles than I care to remember. There are also numerous times when I've seen employees go to the parking lot with intentions of riding one back, only to call for help to carry it back.

Unfortunately, if there was ever a day I wanted one of those battery-operated carts to die, it was the day the fat-ass rode it across the street. She had rubbed me the wrong way so bad that when she was skittering across the garden center's floor, I wanted to jump on the forklift and use its fork to toss her and her riding cart over the fence. She was one of the most stuck-up, bitchy-assed people I have ever come across.

While the lady was in the store, I asked her on four separate occasions (Three of them were deliberate) if I could help her, and not on one occasion did she answer me. Now, I'm not going to say race had anything to do with it. After all, she seemed to be somewhat wheelchair bound and not in any position to harbor ill feelings toward anyone. Still, I'll just provide you with the factual scenarios and leave the judging up to you.

The first time I tried to get a response out of her, it was not deliberate. She was within the ten-meter policy; therefore, I took it upon myself to ask, "How are you doing, ma'am? May I help you find something?"

She did not blink however, but just scooted on by. I thought nothing much of it except that she was a little bit rude. Still, I wasn't going to let that get to me. I would tackle her on the next go round, which I sure did.

I reached out to her again close to where the reduced plants were located. As before, I asked her how she was doing and if there was anything I could help her with. Once again, she did not make any sound of life in my direction. She scooted away like the wind.

Discouraged, I was not. I told myself that the third time would be the charm and pressed on. I watched her enter the canopy area of the garden center and travel past the rubber mulch and play sand. At that point, I decided to work my way toward the registers. I then would veer left to possibly meet her head on.

I saw her on aisle three looking up at the wire fencing. I walked up to her, directly approaching her from the left in the path of her vision, and tried once again to induce some sign of life.

"How are you doing today, ma'am? Would you like some assistance with one of those?" I politely asked.

So much for the third time being the charm because the lady immediately rolled her eyes to the right, hit the forward button on the motor scooter, and was off to the races. It was as if I didn't exist. She paid me as much attention as she would a pile of dirt.

At that moment, I softly said to myself, "Fuck it. She obviously has something up her fat ass, and I can't do anything to unplug it." However, even after telling myself that in my little outburst, I decided to give it one last shot. My name tag says, "John, Customer Service Associate in Training," and when you're learning, not all the nuts are easy to crack. It was up to me to pound them until they cracked. This one might be three times as hard, but I would pound it a fourth time and see what came out.

While helping two other customers, I kept close tabs on the scooter lady. When I decided to approach her again, twelve minutes had elapsed since my last try. Now I had to hurry because she was close to the registers. I had no idea if she was done shopping or was just there admiring the eye-catching knickknacks the store had on display there.

Before I made it up to the registers, she had scooted over to the right front corner of the store where most of the Miracle-Gro garden products were located. So I made a beeline in that direction while thinking to myself, *If she wants one of those, she will have to talk to me because there is not enough room in her scooter basket for any of those items.* With such thoughts at the forefront of my mind, I stopped by the Knockout rose aisle and grabbed a green two-staged shopping cart before heading off to face my toughest customer.

"Good afternoon, ma'am. How are you today? May I provide you with some assistance?" I politely said—at least I thought it was politely, but I guess she didn't think so. Once again, she scooted off without even uttering a grunt. She went by me so fast, it was hard to imagine the wheels of the scooter touching the ground.

Her action tugged on my heart, and I became livid. I pushed the green cart up against the wire fence between the birdbaths and the sixty-four-quart Miracle-Gro moisture-control sacks. I had never wanted to run anyone over that bad until that moment, but since I couldn't do it without getting in trouble, I pushed it out of my mind.

Screw it. Screw her. I hope the wheels of her scooter get tangled up with one of our watering hoses, and the scooter flips her fat ass on her fat-ass face and put a dent in it. Who gives you the right to treat me like dirt—like I've done something unforgivable to you or made you fat and need something motorized to take you from place to place, you fat fuck! I cursed to myself.

Still, that was not the tipped my boiling pot. It overflowed onto the stove about five minutes later when I saw her with my white boss over by the patio blocks. He was loading cobblestoned patio blocks onto a blue flatbed cart for her.

I was so hot, I needed something like Niagara Falls to cool me down. However, the closest thing I could find at the time was a watering hose. So I grabbed it and turned my attention to the plants that close by.

If those plants could talk, however, they would tell anyone willing to listen that I did more damage by overwatering them than the dry, dry dirt they were sitting in would have in a whole month. I had the water pressure so high, it was flowing through the water wand like nothing was there. Half the soil was out of the pot, roots were exposed, and leaves and flower buds were all over the place. The area was literary looking like a category-five hurricane had passed through that part of the garden center.

The most comical thing was that when the lady got ready to leave, there were two cashier stations open on the garden center side of the store. The one on the right was manned by a black male who was entering his third year at the University of Hampton. Of course, no one would have known that or anything else about him other than his obvious color. The register on the left was manned by a while female whose only claim to fame was her seven years as an employee with low self-esteem and a mouth that never stopped running. All anyone needed to do was come within twenty-five feet of her to get the full details of her ongoing life.

Not to labor my factual scenarios to death, but when the lady got ready to pay, she chose the white female cashier, and believe me, that only added to my suspicions about her. However, they were mine and mine alone.

After she paid, my boss looked over in my direction and gave me the come-and-help-me-load-this-vehicle head nod, but I pretended like I did not see it. Because we were quite a distance apart from each other, I knew he would not yell my name because company policy told us not to yell after any customer for any reason, and the same was true for employees. Plus, if I had had to move from where I was at that time on account of that woman, the hose would have had to come along with me. However, it would not have been so that I could continue to spray water on other plants. It would have been so that I could wrap it around her fat-assed neck, providing it would make it around once.

When my boss reentered the store, he came to find me, which I totally expected. After all, I had been looking directly at him when he had nodded at me and had turned away like I hadn't even seen him.

"Why didn't you come and help me? Didn't you see me nodding to you? I know you did," my boss said to me.

Being the opportunist that I am, I used that moment to levy two complaints. One was about the resource manager's attitude toward me (what I called my third of fourth indication that I would not be around after the summer cuts were made). Of course the other one was about the lady in the motor scooter he had wanted my help with.

First, I said, "Two reasons. One is that the resource manager has not been real nice to me lately. In fact, the attitude I've been getting from her says I am no longer wanted as an employee here."

"Why would you say that? I like you and hope that you will get one of those open positions, especially the one over here," my boss said in a genuine tone, and I believed him.

"You may, but that's not the vibe I've been getting. Did you know that two days ago, I was standing in the break room with a few of the store's longtime employees when Bill walked in, and one of them asked him question. He looked in my direction and said, 'I don't. I'm still trying to decide which one of the summer hire employees I should let go next week.'"

"Yes, that's Bill. He's got to make cuts," my boss said. Then he quickly added, "What does that have to do with Susan?"

"That is true. The whole store knows that cuts coming. We know that twelve positions need to be filled after those cuts are made. However, just because he is the store manager and has all the power in his hands, it does not give him the right to make any of the employees feel uneasy or unwelcome in the workplace," I stated before he could interrupt.

"True, true," my boss agreed.

"Now as for Susan, we used to laugh and talk all the time, but lately, she has been acting like she would only spit on me if I was on fire," I said before he interrupted me again.

"Well, it's better than being pissed on," he said quickly. Then he just as quickly added, "Then again, some people like that. Didn't that R & B singer what's his name make a video about that?"

"Something to that effect. Yes, people indulge in some crazy off-the-wall shit. In my lifetime, I've gotten requests to give a girl a pearl necklace, to cum on another girl's face, and to pea in one girl's hair so it could run down her body," I said.

"Wow! All three. Did you?" he excitedly asked.

"No, I did not pea in anyone's hair. And yes, I did fulfill one of the other two requests. It was more of a fantasy—a strange one I admit. But when you are dating someone, if you do not take care of business at home, someone else will gladly do it for you. If or when you do something like that, it's not something you capture on tape. It should be vividly implanted in your mind for all times. It shouldn't be easily forgotten, not for the giver or the recipient.

"Anyway, back to Susan. Earlier today when I asked her for some help in applying for one of those twelve pen positions, she gave me a major attitude. She acted like she had the weight of Australia on her back and I was asking her to pick up Europe too," I said.

"So she didn't help you?" my boss asked.

"Yes, after the almighty performed an unforeseen miracle that caused her to move. However, another miracle was needed for her to unwillingly exert a little effort. She came over and stood beside me like I had a sun-lit glare bouncing off of my head and into her face."

"I told you that you should stop shaving your head before coming to work in the mornings," my boss jokingly said. The he seriously added, "Just keep after her. Make sure that you apply for all the available positions. I want you to get one. And don't worry about Susan, she's probably having a bad day."

"Ah, I don't think so. There's more to it than just that. This bad day toward me has been going on for quite a few weeks now. I can't even joke with her about the buying of plants anymore, and that's one of the things we had in common," I said to my boss. Then I sarcastically added, "I get the sense that someone has insider information. Someone knows what's coming down the pipeline and has decided that the best action now, is to sever all human emotional ties—a preemptive action. Bad news is much easier to pass on to someone you have no emotional connection to rather than to someone you do."

"Oh, come on, stop being so negative. Look, once we're done here, I want you to go back over there and finish those applications, and if she gives you a hard time, you let me know right away," my boss stated with vigor before I interrupted.

"Sure, boss man. No wonder the guys in lumber wish they could hang your ass from one of the trees those four-by-four planks are cut from," I Jokingly said.

"Hey, I stand up for my folks whenever they are messed with," my boss stated. Then he asked, "So why is it you did not come and help me with those heavy-ass cobblestones?"

"The lady messed with me. She pissed me off. She was beyond rude. During the time she was here, I asked her four times if I could help her, and she did not say a word. She even turned and looked in a different direction once, as if she was too good to look at me, or I was too terrible to look at for that matter," I said before smartly adding, "Do you think she was having a bad day too?"

"Maybe she did not hear you?" my boss suggested.

"Did she speak to you in sign language when she asked you to get those cobblestone pavers? I asked my boss.

"No," he answered.

"And she did not use sign language to communicate with you and Nicole at the register, did she?" I inquired.

"I must admit, she didn't. But that doesn't say anything. It's quite possible she did not understand what you were asking her," my boss said in her defense.

"Selective hearing, eh? Or was it a case of selective color help?" I asked my boss.

"Selective hearing," my boss replied.

"Are you sure about?" I asked my.

This time my boss did not answer but just looked down at me with a smile on his face as if to say, "I heard you the first time smart-ass," and then he pointed as if to say, "Go take your ass over to the training room and work on those applications."

I walked away saying to myself, *Selective hearing, my ass. You and I both know what it was, but you're just afraid to call it what it was because of political coerciveness. Selective hearing, my backside.*

Here's a case of selective hearing for you or something damn near close to it. A few days ago while discussing the everlasting angry look on the face of our most hated female assistant manager with one of my fellow coworkers, I implied that she might be a 'closet racist' instead of a 'man hater,' which was what I meant to say. The wrong words came out when I tried to give my reason why I believed she had that angry look all the time. I did not say that she was but that she might be.

Still, a few days later when discussing that same assistant manager with another employee, someone told me that the assistant manager was a closet racist and that was not what I had said to the first individual. Again, even though I meant to say man hater, because she occasionally smiles at or speaks with some of the female employees but is often cold toward the males, I did used the words closet racist. However, I never said she was one but that she might be one. Therefore, it should not have come back to me that way two days later. So to me, that's the case of a person having selective hearing or something close to it. That cannot be dumped on the same playing field with a person not answering you, even though the person was spoken to four times.

My mom has always said to me, "John, everyone like a little ass, but nobody like a smart-ass." However, I believed then like I do today that in this crazy-ass world of ours, we need to be smart-asses, once in a while, so we can pull back from the ledge that others sometimes try to push us over. We just have to keep reminding ourselves that if we get our asses whipped for being smart-asses, we have to be willing to take it like grown men and keep on ticking like Big Ben. Because without the humor of some smart-asses, there would be a whole lot of *Dr. No* 007 helicopter and wheelchair-down-the-chimney scenes taking place. Worst of all, there would be a slew of substitutions for this equipment.

Yes, being a smart-ass may very well lead some people to take action against you as well as against the customers. Many people out there do not subscribe to the notion that the customer is always right. By the same token, I do not subscribe to the notion that employees should be rude to the customers.

When one is in a customer-service industry, an employee who treats a customer badly should be terminated with few exceptions: a death in the immediate family or your mouth being wired shut after a broken jaw. On the other hand, I would much rather lose the business of a rude customer than have him or her come into my establishment and treat my employees like dirt.

CHAPTER 7

VANESSA

NOT LONG AGO on a fairly busy Saturday afternoon while I was manning the front of the store, I looked up from the pallets of dirt I was consolidating just in time to see a lady gliding by. I did not get a good look at her face but mainly her backside. I could imagine what her face looked like from the way her light-brown pantsuit fitted her and how she seemed to be gliding more than walking.

Shortly after those happy thoughts had filtered through my mind, doubts about her looks settled in. My thoughts drifted to all the sexy-sounding people that I had spoken to on the phone over the years. When I had seen them in person, they had looked like they had been chasing parked cars. So I shook off the idea of chasing her down and continued with what I had been doing before. Besides, I hadn't seen if anyone was with her. For all I knew, she might have been trailing her husband, and the moment I ran inside to see what she looked like, some guy would come up and knock my lights out.

Well, the burning desire to see what such a creature looked like finally overpowered me. I decided to run to the parking lot and grab the few empty carts that were there. It did not take me very long to bring them back. In a matter of minutes, I approached the garden center door with a line of seven shopping carts in front of me.

I entered the store with the row of carts traveling at about twenty-five miles per hour. I flew by the cash registers so fast, I doubted if the cashiers even saw me go by. I'm pretty sure they could tell that something had gone by because of the wheel tracks the carts left behind. But I did not care because I was racing towards two different "'Wow" situations and was eager to find out which of the two was going to leave my heart feeling content.

When I got to the end of the entrance lane and made the left turn for the shopping-cart-staging area, I saw the lady standing there. She was looking at me like I owed her money or something of that nature, so I immediately applied my brakes. For one thing, I did not want to hit her with the carts. For another, I did not want to get any closer to her and have her smack the heck out of me for reasons that were unknown to me. Thirdly, when you see beauty like that, it is necessary to stop and to admire it. So yes, she was more beautiful than I had imagined, which turned out to be the better of the two wow moments.

I placed the three carts at a time in the staging area without taking my eyes off her, and she stood in the same spot without taking hers off me. So my concern level grew at an alarming rate, which sent my blood pressure through the roof and caused my hands to more tightly grip the seventh and final cart. I had not figured out yet what her staring was all about; therefore, I held on to the last cart to protect myself just in case she decided to bum-rush me. Before I put the cart away, I heard the lady say, "May I have that cart please?" in the sweetest voice ever.

It shocked me immensely, and instead of gently passing the cart to her, I chucked it with both hands. Luckily for both of us, my grip had been so tight around the handle that it had not moved an inch when I had chucked it. I'm not quite sure if I had been nervous or overly surprised when she had spoken, but something made my hands continue to grip the cart when she tried to pull it toward her.

"What, you don't want me to have it?" she softly asked.

"Ah … sure! Sure!" I said without completely letting go.

She tugged it away from my hand, thinking I was playing a joke on her. Then she said, "Can I get some assistance, Mr. Funnyman?"

I wanted to race after her because she was so sophisticated, but my legs would not move. It was as if I was planted in month-old set cement. However, I took off like a bullet when she turned back around and said, "What is this? First you did not want to give me the cart, and now you don't want to help me? I guess I'll just have to find another employee who is more willing to help."

I instantly became as light as a feather and floated like a butterfly over to where she was near the trees in lawn and garden. As I landed beside her, she nonchalantly let go of the cart and glided away as if to say indirectly, "There, you push!" After I followed her for about five seconds, she said, "What kind a name is John?" without even looking back at me.

"My given name," I replied, raising my eyebrows.

"So tell me, John, how much do you know about plants?" she sweetly asked.

"Enough to keep angry customers from running me over with their carts," I said with a chuckle.

"Well, John, let's see if you can keep that streak alive," she said before turning around with a smile as bright as the sun.

I did not know if that was a "good smile" or a "bad smile." One that was saying I'd be happy to carry on a conversation with you, or one that was saying I'm smiling out of politeness, but honestly I don't want a fucking thing to do with you because I don't like your kind. Still, I quickly said, "We do have plant experts available. The people in the brown vests with the words 'vendor' marked on the back are the experts. I can quickly fetch one for you."

"You're not even going to try and help me first?" she casually asked.

"Sure! I meant that if I couldn't help you and you were about to lose your cool, I could fetch one," I said out loud.

"Surely, you did," she said with a chuckle.

"Absolutely! Go ahead and test me," I suggested.

"Okay, John, I have some fruit trees at home that are not growing like they're supposed to. Someone told me that I should replant them in garden soil. What do you think?" she inquired.

"Replant them? I'm not so sure about that," I said. Then I quickly asked, "How long have you had these trees?"

"I bought them last year," she responded/

"You do know that they are guaranteed for one year, so you can bring them back if they are dead," I informed her.

"They are not dead … just not growing like they're supposed to," she replied.

"Well, I wouldn't uproot them since they've been in the ground for so long," I said before she jumped in.

"That's what I was thinking. I wanted to dig deep around each one and then fill the space with garden soil," she stated before walking back to me.

"That's what I would recommend," I added.

"Okay then, which soil do you recommend?" she asked. Then before I responded she added, "Something that is going to help them produce fruits this year."

"Are you going to bring me some?" I asked.

"Sure! If what you recommend works, I'll bring you some," she suggested.

"You bet," I said excitedly. Then I added, "You should try the Miracle-Gro Moisture Control or you can try the store generic bran."

"What's the difference?" she asked with a friendly smile.

"First of all, how many fruit trees are we talking about?" I inquired.

"I have six: two Japanese citrus, two apple, one peach, and one pear," she answered.

"I guess I won't be getting any fruits then—especially pears," I suggested with a smile.

"Why is that?" she quickly asked. Then just as quickly, she added, "I'll bring you some if what you suggest works."

"My suggestion will help your plants grow, all right. More than likely," I commented before she interrupted.

"I detect a but!" she said with a little chuckle.

"Well, as for fruits, I don't know much about the two citrus trees," I said.

"Well, I've had those for two years now, and they are supposed to bear fruit this year," she stated.

"By themselves?" I quickly asked.

"Yes! Of course by themselves," she uttered with a broad smile.

"Well, like I said, I do not know much about those. As for the two apples, they might be able to help each other out, but I'm pretty sure that the peach and pear will need another tree of its kind so that it can pollinate," I explained.

"No, they won't," she said as she slapped my right bicep. She did so with a feeling motion like she was indirectly trying to find out if I really had muscles or if it was my elbow brace giving a false impression. It was really unexpected and thrilling at the same time, but I did not let on. I just casually continued with the conversation.

"Yes, they will," I answered.

"Uh-huh!" she uttered with another slapping grip, as if the first time had been inconclusive.

"I'm not 100 percent sure about the peach, but the pear will definitely need another pear tree," I explained. "I'll get everything that you will need right now, and if the pear does not bare any fruits, you have to take me to lunch," I said to her.

"Deal!" she quickly agreed. Then she asked with a smile, "And what do I get if you're wrong? Are you going to take me to dinner?"

"How come dinner? Why not lunch?" I asked with a smile.

"I live over here but work across the water. Therefore, dinner works best for me," she said followed by the most beautiful laughter. It was like a robin on a window's ledge singing, and it sent chills up and down my spine.

Then I noticed for the first time that she had a ring mark on her wedding finger. This got me wondering, *Why is it off?* Still, I didn't let on and just continued with the conversation. "Right! You just wanted to up the ante, lady. That's all," I stated with a smile.

"Whatever! You just be ready to pay up," she said with a chuckle. Then she added, "And you will need to get us a bigger cart because I need eight bags of the Miracle-Gro product."

Her comment stopped me in my tracks, and I said, "Eight bags? I thought that you only have six trees,"

"I do. I will pour at least one bag around each one," she explained. She followed that up by asking, "Why? Isn't that enough?"

"It's more than enough. I'll go and get you a flatbed cart," I suggested before running off. Then I mumbled to myself while taking the shopping cart that I had given her earlier back, "If you plan on digging a well around each one."

I made no mention that I thought it was overkill. She was the customer, and my job was to sell her what she wanted and to try to talk her into buying more or additional items, which they had taught us during training. It really didn't matter if the individual needed the items or not. Part of my unwritten goal as a customer service associate was to make sure that the customer left with more than they had come to the store to buy. The arithmetic was simple: The more stuff the store sold, the more money it took in.

This fueled the daily competition between the store's department managers because everyone wanted to be number one in sales when the day's figures were released. Not only that, it also fueled the competition for sales within the district. Every store manager wanted his or her store to be on top when the day's figures were released.

It was such a big hype tool. I had had the unfortunate pleasure of having to sit there and listen to a speech that would make the turning of water into vehicle fuel an unworthy accomplishment. I am not saying that we do not need hypes or accomplishments to brag about—far from it. We need them to a certain degree, at certain places and times, for the right amount of time, and under the right circumstances. We did not need them to be overdone like this.

One June afternoon, I was sitting in the conference room at work, studying because it is much quieter there than in the break room. Anyhow, while there, the store manager walked in with his phone, clipboard, and a bunch of paper and sat down at the head of the makeshift conference table.

After he had sat down, he called the manager of another store, which was within our district, to let him know that one of his employee's had screwed up twice while helping an individual. The individual had come to our store to see it could be fixed from there. However, before my store manager tried to explain this, he went into a long bragging spiel of how our store had kicked butts and had taken no prisoners the day before.

I would guess that the total conversation lasted about seven minutes, and the first four minutes were spent on bragging rights. The conversation went something like, "Hey, Fuzz, this is Bill at store [number of store]. I need your help fixing an order that one of your guys screwed up twice. Oh, by the way, we were number one in the district yesterday. Have you heard?" Then blab, blab, blab, blab, then what the problem was, and them what kind of help he needed from that manager's end.

I found the whole thing unpleasurable because even though the screw-up and fixing it were the main reasons for calling, bragging about being number one became the main topic, and resolving the customers problem became second. That was contradictory to what we had been taught during training and what we should be practicing as we dealt with customers. A company should support its employee to the best of its ability, even if it didn't fully support or agree with that person in private.

It was something I took into consideration even while dealing with this customer, whom I happened to think was the most beautiful lady I had ever stood face-to-face with. She wasn't the sexiest lady I had ever seen though. In fact, I have often said that if her head was put on the body of the lady in the story "Bought and Paid for," she would be the world's most perfect woman. Still, she was the most beautiful one I had ever seen.

Even though I was going "gaga--gaga" over her on the inside, I still couldn't tell her that she probably didn't need more than six bags of Miracle-Gro. Doing as I was taught would help me keep my job. So I took the blue flatbed cart over to her and loaded the eight bags onto it.

I stacked the bags in two piles of four each, close to the handle haft of the cart, and then I said, "Lady, you have half the cart left. Would you like to get anything else or is this it?"

"Is this all I will need?" she asked me.

"Well, you could get some topsoil to go along with it and some fertilizing spikes for trees and shrubs," I replied.

"Will those help?" she asked curiously.

"Certainly," I answered sharply.

"How many bags do you think I need," she asked.

"I think you should get two bags for every one bag of Miracle-Gro."

"Sixteen bags?" she shouted.

"They aren't that big. The bags are very small," I replied.

"How small?" she asked.

"They weigh forty pounds each," I answered.

"That's a lot," she said with a smile.

"Not really. The bags are just yay big," I said with the motion of my hands. Then I added, "Its dirt. It's not going to take a lot to weigh forty pounds."

"Yeah, but that's still a lot for me to do myself," she responded.

"Have your husband help you," I said to her.

"Who said I was married?" she asked with a smile.

"The ring mark on your finger," I replied.

"Why couldn't I be a single woman with plans of doing some gardening?" she asked.

"Two reasons: the ring mark on your finger and the fact that women as beautiful as you are never on the market," I replied.

"On the market," she said with laughter. Then with the same laughter she asked, "What am I, a piece of meat now?"

"Oh, no. I didn't mean it like that," I quickly said.

"Don't be silly. I know what you meant. I get it wherever I go. Guys believe girls like me are always married."

"Exactly!" I said aloud while thinking inside, *Lady, you are the filet mignon of women.*

She interrupted my thoughts when she said with a smile, "Thanks, but I'm not that beautiful."

"You're not?" I inquired.

"Not really. I'm not saying that I'm a car chaser either. I think I'm the typical average girl," she stated.

"Average, my butt, lady. You are the most beautiful woman I have ever seen in person," I told her.

"You don't leave home a lot, do you?" she asked. Then she added, "You must really live a sheltered life."

"Sheltered enough to know that you are a Filipino," I responded with certainty.

"Sheltered! I'm from Cambodia," she responded to my surprise.

"No, you're not," I replied.

"Yes, I am," she countered with a smile. Then she added, "Really!"

"Okay. Well, it really doesn't matter. You are still the most beautiful woman I have ever seen in person," I reiterated.

"And again, thank you," she cordially replied. Then she asked, "Where is the topsoil you said I should get?"

"It's out by the front of the store. Just pay for it when you check out, and I will load it in your vehicle for you," I explained.

"What kind of cologne are you wearing?" she asked to my surprise. It caught me off guard so much, I couldn't remember which one I had put on before I had left the house for work. Therefore, I quickly started to search my mind like a bumbling fool until she interrupted the process by asking, "You don't what you're wearing?"

"Actually, I don't. Whenever I put on cologne, I usually don't pay attention to the name. I just reach for the bottle that has the most inside of it and use it until I get to about the same level as the others," I explained.

"I have never heard of anything like that," she said laughingly.

"Strange, isn't it?" I asked.

"You can certainly say that," she said with a chuckle.

"Occasionally, I reach for the one with the least in it, which I think was what happened today, but I'm not quite sure," I added.

"How can you put on something and not know what you're putting on? You're not blind, are you?" she asked with laughter.

"I wouldn't have been able to tell that you were as beautiful as you are if that was the case—which you are," I said with a smile.

"Sure. Sure. That's what you say," she said as she fanned me with her hand. Then she added, "For whatever it's worth, I like the smell of your cologne. You smell real good."

"Oh, thank you. And you are as beautiful as a rose that's been kissed by the morning dew," I responded.

"Wow! You're just a sweet talker, aren't you?" she inquired.

"No, far from it. You are really beautiful. I hate to labor this point, but you are the most beautiful woman I have ever seen in person, bar none," I stated in a convincing way.

"I guess I'll have to believe it," she said and grabbed onto my arm with both hands, as if she once again really wanted to make sure I had some muscles.

I got a little excited and wobbly and had to brace myself against the cart to prevent my knees from buckling. She felt my reaction and thought that she might have physically pushed me when reaching for my arm, even though she couldn't have hurt a fly with her petite little self. Still, she pulled back on my arm and said, "I'm sorry. I didn't mean to push you."

I was smiling to myself at the touch of her warm, soft, tiny hands on my skin and was thinking, *Oh, please don't let go. Ask me to run away with you.* Then my brains sent these words flowing out of my mouth and off the tip of my tongue, "I guess you best be going now before your husband starts missing you."

Those words instantly sent her back to another time and place and for that matter, me to the 1990s where I should have learned a lesson but apparently hadn't, even though I had told myself that it would always be a lesson to me. Some fools never learn. While going through a divorce, over a three-and-a-half year span during that decade, I started to date a young lady who was going through the same thing. We really cared for each other and started to do things we had promised we wouldn't do until both of our divorces had become final. However, the first time passion led us to uncharted territory, words rolled off the tip of my tongue and cast a blanket on top of it, as cold and as deep as a black hole.

Moments after we were in our birthday suits and in the missionary position under the blanket, I heard my mouth say, "What if your husband walks in on us right now?"

All I heard in return was, "Get up! You need to go home. You don't bring up a person's husband at a moment like this, jackass!"

I felt so ashamed and embarrassed that I started dressing quickly. Then when I reached into my closet to get my shoes, it hit me that we were at my place. That led us to another conversation and me back into my bed beside her, but nothing was going to happen. That was one thing she made clear before I got back into the bed. She would stay the night but I should expect nothing, and nothing is what I got.

So I knew there and then, I had blown what was happening between this beautiful customer and me— at least in that moment. I literary felt her grip loosen, and before any spoken words were spoken, I hung my head and started to push the flatbed cart in the direction of the register.

Although my untimely words had disappointed me to no ends, the Cambodian beauty wasn't as upset as I had originally thought, or if she was, she was someone who could easily let things go. Whatever the case, while I was pushing the cart, I heard her said from behind me, "Hey, wait. Let's go look at the for-sale plants."

I quickly pushed the cart to the side and took off running behind her like a death-row inmate who had just been exonerated by DNA evidence. Unfortunately, all the good plants that had been on sale had already been scooped up, and she did not see any that she liked. Therefore, our conversation did not last long, and before I knew it or wanted to, we were on our way to the cash register once again.

After she had paid and we had gone outside, I loaded the sixteen bags of dirt on the flatbed and pushed it over to where she was parked instead of having the Cambodian beauty pull her vehicle up. She tried to help me, but I could hardly tell that she was doing so. Three of the bags of dirt weighed more than she did. She probably weighed about 105 pounds with her clothes soaking wet, but damn, she was beautiful—beau-ti-ful!

When she opened up the back of her vehicle, I could see that it was thoroughly clean, and the aroma flowing out almost made my head turn as much as the stunning beauty of the Cambodian beauty had. It smelled so good, I almost crawled inside and lay down while I was putting the protective plastic inside the car.

While stacking the bags of dirt inside, I said, "Is your hubby going to unload this for you when you get home, or would you like me to come and do it for you?"

"No, I'm gonna do it," she replied.

"Why? He doesn't like gardening?" I asked with a smile.

"No and no," she softly said.

"No and no?" I said with a confused look.

"He doesn't like gardening, and he's not home to help. He's at work," she said with a little smile.

"So leave it here until he comes home," I suggested.

"I can't. He works in Florida," she replied.

"He's in Florida! Why are you here?" I asked.

"I have family here," she answered.

"He's family too, isn't he?" I asked in return.

"Yes, but he works there," she replied.

"What kind of work? Is he in the military?" I asked curiously.

"Uh-huh!" she unconvincingly said.

"So why didn't you move down there with him?" I asked her.

"My family is here," she reiterated.

"Do you have any kids?" I inquired.

"Yes, two," she answered.

"Maybe they can help you unload it," I suggested.

"They are only eight and ten, and they despise being outside," she said with a chuckle.

"What? Every kid likes to be outside," I stated.

"Not mine. They both dislike it very much. It's amazing I can get them to go to school," she said with a smile.

"What do they do at recess? Don't they have to go outside then," I asked.

"I don't think they can get around that," she replied.

"Well, keep them from getting around it when they get home or on Saturdays this way: Go home, call them outside, and then lock the door so that they can't go back in until you say so," I suggested.

"I can't do that, I'll get in trouble. That's cruel and unusual punishment," she suggested.

"No, it's not. It's called tough love. You'll be saving them from themselves and from becoming a coach potato. You'll be forcing them to absorb a little sunshine and to suck up fresh and unfiltered air," I said between chuckles.

"That sounds like boot camp," she said with a little laughter.

"It looks like you're about to overworked yourself when you should make others help you," I said while pointing to the bags of items I had just loaded in her vehicle.

"Oh, I can handle it," she said sweetly.

"Just don't work yourself to death before you deliver my fruit," I said with a smile.

"But once I bring it, it's okay for me to do so, right?" she asked with a smile.

"No, not at all. In fact, if you bringing me some will keep you alive, then by all means, keep it coming," I replied with a chuckle.

"All right, Mr. Sweet-Smelling Funnyman. I will keep that in mind," she suggested.

"How come that doesn't sound too convincing?" I asked. Then I quickly added, "I bet I won't see you here anymore."

"Of course you will. I come here all the time," she said with a smile.

"No, you don't," I stated.

"Yes, I do," she replied. Then she said, "This is where I come to buy most of my flowers and plants."

"I've been working here for almost three full months now, and this is the first time I have ever seen you in here," I stated.

"I do, though. I was even in here last Saturday," she said.

"I was here last Saturday, and I didn't see you," I quickly countered. Then I waved my right index finger at her and said, "Still, I'll take your word for it if you say so."

"Well, thank you, Mr. Sweet-Smelling Funnyman," she said while bowing playfully. Then she looked me in the face and said, "Now please don't hate me, but I must go."

"So what's the deal with lunch?" I asked as she headed for the front of her vehicle.

"We'll talk about that the next time I come," she said while opening her vehicle's door.

"Is that supposed to convince me that you'll be back?" I asked.

"I hope so," she replied while getting into her vehicle.

I stepped back from the vehicle when she started it, and moments later, she had it in a slow reverse. However, when the driver's side was parallel to me, she applied the brakes and said, "Sweet-Smelling Man, it was nice talking to you. Thanks for all your help. I hope you won't get fired for spending so much time with me. I will see you around."

She then extended her right hand, and as we were shaking hands, I said, "Do I at least get to know your name before you leave."

"Vanessa," she replied and continued backing up the car. Then right before she drove away, she gave me one last big smile and shouted, "Sweet-smelling Mr. John, my name is Vanessa!"

CHAPTER 8

SIX WEEKS PAST GLORY

O N JULY 3RD, one of my coworkers, who was like my assistant boss, sent me over to the landscaping area to find out if the young lady who was standing timber posts up needed some help. I almost turned to him and asked, "Why the hell can't you do it, you lazy bastard?" However, because I had only been there a short time (about a month) and I had never been fired before,

I obediently strolled toward the lady. I was still in the phase of trying to figure out if working for a living was my next best career move or if I should be doing something else; starting a business without the necessary resources or publishing another book or books, which would be more soothing to my soul. Besides, the lady, who had on a blue-and-white blouse, blue jeans shorts, and black flip-flop slippers, did not look bad from a distance.

Up close, her moderately sexy legs were even more appealing in the morning sunlight than when I had been walking toward her. By golly, her face was even prettier up close. Additionally, she turned out to be much friendlier than I would have imagined. In the end, I was thrilled that I had obediently approached the lady and said, "Hi, how are you doing? May I help you with something?"

With the biggest smile possible, she said, "Please. I'm not sure what I'm doing."

"I believe you're picking out timber," I jokingly said.

"Well, that's my intention, but I don't want to pick out the wrong ones," she stated.

"How many of the not wrong ones are you planning to get? I jokingly asked.

"Thirty-six," she answered with a chuckle.

"Thirty-six? Major yard work, eh?" I shouted with a chuckle of my own.

"Something like that," she replied.

"Well, first of all, you will definitely need a cart—maybe even two," I suggested before dashing off to the special cart row, which was not far away.

"Should I get one too?" she asked when I returned.

"No, just one will do—hopefully," I replied.

"Will they all fit? Won't it be too hard to push?" she asked.

"No, no, I'll put ten on this side, ten on that side, and sixteen in the middle. You will still be able to stack something else on top if you have additional shopping to do," I suggested.

"Just a few bags of cement," she replied.

"In that case, you'll have to help me push the cart," I jokingly suggested.

"You got it, just as long as you help me pick out the good ones," she said with a smile.

"Sure, but there aren't many so-called bad ones except a few here and there," I told her.

"There aren't?" she surprisingly asked.

"Not really. Basically, what I have gathered from helping other customers is that as long as they are not cracked on both sides, they are considered good. Also, most customers like to pick out the ones that look a reddish color, but normally there are only three or four in each hundred-bundle stack. So they just pick the ones that are not cracked on both sides, and I throw in the reddish ones, if I come across any," I told her.

"So what's the deal with the ones that are cracked on both sides?" she asked.

"Oh, don't get me wrong, customers do purchase them. Some customers have no preference, while others claim they do not last as long or are as stable when they drive large nails into them," I said to her. Then I picked up one and continued, "You see this one here? It's only cracked on one side, basically at the end. Ones like these are fine. So this will be your first one."

"Well, thank you. I am sure glad that you came over to help," she said with a smile.

"That's okay. There's no need to thank me. If I didn't come over, someone else would have. I'm just doing my job. Besides, it's our policy to assist each customer or at least ask if the customer needs assistance," I explained.

"Yes, but I'm sure glad you did when you did because I did not know where to begin," she stated.

"Get out of here. You have picked up this much timber and don't know where to begin?" I said to her.

"No, really, I was told to pick up thirty-six because that's how many my boyfriend estimated," she said with a little less luster in her smile.

"Oh, so your boyfriend sent you to pick these up, eh? That's nice of him," I said.

"Actually, I'm the one being nice. He just told me to stop by the store and pick up thirty-six fencing poles," she responded.

"Fencing poles. Woo … wait a minute. This is going to be number eleven, but its best that I stop here until we get this figured out," I suggested.

"Figured out? What do you mean?" she asked with a look of wonder.

"Well, from the sound of things, you're not sure if this is what you're supposed to get. So I'll break it down for you. The ones here are landscaping timber. They are mostly used for landscaping. Some people, however, occasionally use them for fencing. Now if it's fencing posts you're looking to purchase, they are the ones further down," I said.

"Where? Let me see those," she requested instantly.

I walked her over to where the nicely cut and more expensive ones were and picked up where I had left off with my explanation. "As you can see, these are four by four by eight. They are the same length as those over there—ninety-six inches. However, these are mostly used for privacy fences and not for landscaping. That's one of the reason these are almost seven dollars apiece. The ones on the cart are one dollar and ninety-eight cents each," I explained.

"Those … the seven dollar ones are definitely the ones he wants," she said.

"Are you sure?" I asked.

"Definitely!" she said.

"Well then, let's go back over there and pick out the best ones we can find," I said with a smile.

"Let's do it," she said agreeably.

We walked back over to where the cart was, and I picked up where I had left off: picking up one at a time and showing it to her to get her yea or nay. When I reached thirty, I paused for a second or two and said, "How come your boyfriend did not come and pick these out himself?"

"Who, him?" she inquired. "He never leaves the house unless it's to go to work."

"Never?" I uttered.

"Hardly ever. He spends most of his time in the playroom," she replied.

"You should be a happy woman and good too, if I'm at liberty," I remarked.

Obviously she and I were on the same page. We had the same understanding of what playroom was. However, we were miles apart regarding what the playroom really meant. So she made her best attempt to clarify what she meant, using as few words as possible. "Okay, so I said the playroom, not the bedroom," she said.

"Ah!" I uttered.

"The game room—Xboxes and a slew of other systems you guys like to play," she stated with barely a smile.

"Oh, I see," I said.

"Instead of playing with your woman who is dying for affection," she continued.

"So who is going to put up these poles?" I curiously asked in an attempt to change the topic, not because I wanted to but because she had an angry expression on her face—an understandable one.

"You guys will spend forever and a day massaging the remote to those systems but can't spent ten seconds putting those remote pistol-pointing fingers on your naked woman, who is beside you," she added.

As a man, I could not agree with her more, and little did she know that I was standing there feeling as desperate as she was. All I could think was, *My woman wouldn't have to be naked. I would touch her twenty-four hours a day if she'd let me, but I can't touch mine for ten seconds, naked or dressed, because she said that her body is hers and that only she decides when it gets touched, which is maybe once every three months or twice when the stars line up. We have even gone over a year without having sex, even though we sleep in the same bed and neither one of us has had a major health issue preventing us from performing.*

"I'm sorry. What did you say?" she asked.

"I was just wondering who was going to put up the poles, you or him? I replied.

"He suggested that I go and purchase them. I'll take them home in the truck and then see how long they sit there," she replied.

"Isn't that just a waste of money?" I asked.

"I'm trying to get him to do something without begging him to," she explained.

"Begging him to? A woman as sophisticated as you shouldn't have to beg a man to do anything for you. You don't look that desperate to me," I stated.

What she said next totally blew my mind and at the same time, caused me to feel sympathy for her because

I could totally relate with what she was going through. However, it caught me so much off guard, I accidentally dropped the last plank of timber as I was reaching out to place it on the cart.

"Would you believe I haven't had sex in six weeks?" she asked with a sad-looking smile.

"Six weeks, and you looking the way you do?" I said.

"Yes! Well, almost six weeks," she said. Then she quickly asked and answered her own question, "What's today? Oh, tomorrow is July 4th, so today is the 3rd."

"Certainly is," I added.

"Well, add this up," she said while moving a little closer to me. "The last time my boyfriend and I had sex was the weekend before Memorial Day—that Friday to be exact. We've gone from that day through the whole month of June, and now we are in July, and I haven't been touched."

"That's about five and a half weeks," I said.

"Like I said, six weeks … six weeks past glory," she quickly added while moving her face closer to mine like she wanted to kiss me or threaten me like a mother with her child in a crowded store. While we were in that up close and personal position, she added, "And I was the one who initiated the action, like all the others before."

"Wow!" I uttered nonchalantly.

"Yes, wow," she quickly interjected. Then she suddenly asked, "Where's the cement?"

"Oh, yes, the cement. It's over there in the corner," I said while pointing. Then I added, "It's probably best that we go over there and talk. It's a whole lot quieter over there."

While she walked beside me as I pushed the cart, she surprisingly asked, "Be honest, what do you think of me?"

"I think that you are a very nice lady who shouldn't have to beg for anything to be done for you or even to you, if you get my drift," I replied while looking down at her legs.

"My face is up here. You know that, right?" she asked with a little laughter.

"Yes, but it only tells part of the story—a wonderful part. Don't get me wrong," I suggested while climbing her body with my eyes.

"But my legs add that extra value to it, eh?" she underscored.

"Ma'am, you read my mind," I implied with a smile.

"You are sad," she suggested with a smile and a slap across my left shoulder like we were coworkers in the break room carrying on meaningless macho talk. Then she let another surprising revelation fly. "Do you know that I sleep naked every night?" she asked.

"No, I didn't know that, but—" I said before she interrupted me.

"And I have to beg like hell to get touched once a month if I'm lucky," she added. Then she quickly added, "And no, you can get that thought out of your head. I carry myself pretty clean. Damn clean if you ask me."

"Actually, I wasn't thinking that, but truth be known, I was wondering what was wrong with you," I explained.

"Nothing! I'm just a woman who wants to be touched by the man she's in love with, without begging and pleading. My ex-husband would have lived down there if I had let him," she added.

"Why didn't you?" I asked sarcastically.

"His wish was granted for the most part, but then he started wishing he could share me with this lesbian friend … well, bisexual friend of ours," she said.

"I guess you weren't into that, eh?" I inquired.

"Listen, I have a twelve- and a sixteen-year-old. It's up to them whom they choose to fall in love with. While I'm raising them, they'll only receive my influence my man's and not mine, a man's, and a woman's.

"So why won't your boyfriend pay any attention to you?" I asked out of curiosity.

"He keeps saying he's getting too old for sex," she replied.

"Old! You can never get too old for that," I said.

"That's exactly what I said too," she added quickly.

"The way I look at it, as long as a man can get it up and there is someplace warm and willing to receive it, then by golly, let it be," I added.

"Exactly, but he keeps complaining that he's too old, when I should be the one saying that. He's thirty-eight. I'm three years older than him, yet he's the one who's too old," she explained.

"He's too old at thirty-eight," I said aloud. Then I asked, "What's going to happen when he in his forties or fifties?"

"I hate to think that far in advance. It puts too many things in my head," she responded.

"Have you ever thought about cheating on him?" I asked bluntly.

"As I said before, I don't think too far ahead because it puts too many things in my mind," she commented quickly and shrugged her shoulders.

"Say no more. I will use my better judgment," I calmly said before she surprised me with her follow-up comment.

"I'll say this though, people who get cheated on have no reason to point a finger when they are the ones who drove their partners into other people's beds," she said

"Or arms," I said.

"Yes, there too," she agreed. Then she added, "I guess the arms first and then in their beds, cars, offices, hotels etc., etc., wherever two people can make out when they are still connected to someone else. You get the picture," she said.

"I'm with you, lady. The human body knows what it wants and is missing and tends to go looking for it," I stated.

"I agree," she added before continuing on. "How can you have someone sleeping naked next to you, night after night, and still not get aroused?"

"Well, maybe if he gets aroused, he thinks he will get pushed away like a dog. There are women like that, you know," I suggested.

"Well, I'm not one of them. Women shouldn't be like that. You provide your man with pleasure so he won't seek it elsewhere and vice versa. You sleep naked beside your partner for a reason," she stated.

"What's the reason?" I asked with a smile.

"To turn him on and so you can feel the comfort of his warm body," she answered quickly. Then she just as quickly asked, "What else?"

"Maybe, you sleeping naked beside him won't do the trick," I said in the guy's defense—well, in an attempt to find out more.

"I do other things to him as well, but he just rolls over and goes to sleep, either before or after," she commented.

"He just leaves you hanging after he gets to his glory!" I said.

"Ninety-nine percent of the time," she quickly added.

"Wow! That's not cool," I said out loud.

"Not at all. Not the least bit," she said with a fake grin, which led to a short, silent pause.

"How long have you guys been together?" I asked.

"One year," she answered.

"One year, and he's already tired of having sex with you," I uttered.

"Well, we've known each other for fifteen years, but we've only been dating for one," she explained.

"Still, you don't lose sexual interest in a woman like you that fast—ever!" I said.

"Well, thank you," she said with a big smile.

"What have you not been doing?" I asked.

"Not doing!" she echoed. "I do everything I can to please him. I'm the one who constantly goes down on him, but I can't get him to go down on me. I sleep naked beside him but can't get him to touch me; I do things to arouse him, but he's unresponsive. I feel like saying, 'Look, look, here I am.' He's the one that suggested that we needed thirty-six timber poles, and here I am at the store picking them up so he wouldn't have to worry about it," she explained in a convincing fashion.

"I see your point," I uttered.

After a short pause in the conversation but while we were still standing close to one another and looking into each other's faces with a smile, I heard her said, "I just hate women like that. Well, more like dislike. I really don't hate anybody."

"Like what?" I immediately asked.

"The ones who think that just because they don't want to have sex, their men should go unsatisfied too. The same goes for men too," she stated.

"How about yours?" I curiously asked.

"Oh, I'm getting there. He's going to be the loser if he pushes me that far," she said. Then she added, "They all should be killed and fed to worms."

"Wow! That is kinda drastic, isn't it?" I asked.

"Kinda, but who feasts on their bodies once they are dead and buried? Worms, right," she convincingly applied.

"Right!" I equipped.

"So they might as well be fed to the worms sooner rather than later. They have their bodies and don't want to share them. They don't want others to enjoy them. They can't keep them looking that way forever, and they're no good to anyone once they are old and shriveled up except the worms," she convincingly explained.

"I see your point. I never looked at it that way before," I told her.

"Not a lot of people do, but I'm a pragmatic person. Listen, I'm not a nymphomaniac by any stretch of the imagination, but I believe when you're with someone, it's perfectly fine to expect to have sex at least three or four days a week," she commented.

"I feel your pain. I don't think a minimum of three times a week is asking too much," I interjected.

"No, three days a week, not three times a week," she quickly clarified.

"Oh!" I uttered with an I like this woman kind of smile.

"You can do it three, four, or five times a day, providing you have the time and your body can take it, but at least three days a week. People need a healthy sex life, and for me, that is a healthy one and one that should be enough to keep your partner faithful to you.

"As a woman, I believe sex is not something my partner should only get when I'm in the mood for it. I give physically, mentally, and/or imaginatively to ease his sexual frustration even when I'm not in the mood. Just because I am not sexually frustrated myself or do not have the desire for it that often does not always mean my partner does feel the same way.

"Some people are just too selfish when it comes to sex, but let their other half step out on them and see what happens. They are the first to say their other half cheated on them without taking any responsibility for opening the cheating door. On the other hand, I never say no to sex. It is part of my female duty in the relationship," she commented before a short pause. "Well, you know … I do say no during those female days. But I would be willing to do and have done other things during those times to please my partner, and he has appreciated it."

"Would you like to trade?" I asked her with a big smile.

"Oh, stop it," she uttered with an even bigger smile and a swat of her hand.

"No, I'm serious," I added. "The only difference between you and me is that I luck out about once or twice a year, which will put me at a grand total of about fifty times over a twenty-five-year marriage, if mine lasts that long. However, at this rate, you might get to glory about nine times a year, which means we are both suffering unnecessarily."

"Wow, that's sad, isn't it?" she expressed.

"Exactly!" I said in agreement.

"Nine times in one year. There are people who get it that much in one week," she said with a look of sadness.

"You are absolutely right. I once met a girl who said she tried it twelve times in one day," I stated.

"Twelve times!" she shouted.

"Yep!" I confirmed.

"Oh, my gosh. You're lying," she added.

"Not at all," I added.

"Twelve times!" she reiterated again.

"Yep! She said that she and her boyfriend got up horny like two alley cats one morning after not having sex for a few days. They decided to go at it as many times that day as they could, and so started their quest," I stated.

"Wow! Twelve times. I don't think I could walk after that," the lady said.

"Me neither," I added.

"I could see four or five times, maybe six—maybe—but not twelve times. That's too much in one day," she said.

"Well, as a guy, I'll have to be macho and say 'let's go for twelve.' Still, four or five times in one day is a hell of a lot more than we are currently getting over any six-month span," I said.

"Oh, thanks," she uttered with a smile. Then she added, "But you're absolutely correct. I would give just about anything to decrease my misfortune in that area. After all, I'm not one of those women who say no. I am willing to give even before the question is asked," she stated.

"My kind of woman. So what do you say we do if things don't turn around by the end of the year for both of us?" I said.

"You mean if our partners don't start turning over more for both of us," she said with laughter.

"Exactly! We should consider making a trade then," I said, and we both started to laugh like old friends.

After our laughter subsided, I energetically threw the eight sixty-pound bags of cement on top of the timber. I wanted it to appear that I was working harder than I was shooting the bull with this lady who was six weeks past glory and telling a complete stranger about her sexual debacles.

I presumed that when you are sexually frustrated through no fault of your own, a stranger is as good a psychologist as any paid professional. After all, there more than likely won't be any need for a follow-up visit. You won't have to worry about writing checks to someone on a continual basis. You only have to worry about what he or she will be thinking and smirking at on your next visit.

Anyhow, before I started to push the over-stacked cart, I continued to talk about my trading idea. It was an idea she found amusingly funny in the end, and she said she would think it over and give me a call if her prospect for the playoff didn't improve. Then I egged her on in hopes of finding out where the disconnect lay.

"Do you think your boyfriend is cheating on you?" I asked.

"Highly unlikely, but his sister thinks he's been jerking off in the bathroom," she said.

"His sister," I said. Then I asked, "Why does she suspect that? Does she live in the same house?"

"No, but we are pretty close, and she's aware of what's going on. I put this together with the fact that my boyfriend always locks the bathroom door whenever he's inside," she stated.

"Maybe, he's afraid someone is going to walk in on him," I said in the guy's defense.

"It's the master bathroom attached to our bedroom. The kids are not going to come barging in. They know better than that," she stated.

"Well, in his defense, kids will be kids. They often do the unexpected," I suggested.

"True! I'll give him that, but he has no excuse in our case. I taught my kids to knock on closed doors and to wait for a response before entering," she stated.

"Most parents with common sense do, but kids get in such a hurry that they sometimes forget to do that," I said.

"True!" she replied.

"And ruin good affectionate moments," I added.

"True! Absolutely true. But I sleep with the bedroom door closed, so that's an added buffer. Therefore, the only other inside intruder he has to worry about is me. I don't keep the door locked whenever I'm using it," said when I gave her my go-on-I-have-nothing-further look. However, she took it as a bullshit look and immediately said, "Well, I do when it's that time of the month."

At first, I did not catch on to what she was implying by "that time of the month," even though she had made a reference to it earlier. So I did not change the expression on my face to state so. I was still wearing the go-on-I-have-nothing-further one, which she mistook again (correctly this time) as a look of wonder, even though it wasn't one of my many looks of wonder.

At times my facial expressions lag behind my actual feelings, and this was obviously one of those cases. Anyhow, to set my mind straight she said, "You know—mother nature!"

"Oh!" was my immediate reaction. "Aunt Flow," I added.

"Aunt who?" she asked.

"Aunt Flow," I reiterated. "That's how I refer to a woman's time of the month."

"A little cute but no doubt good," she said. Then she added, "Yes, that's the only time of the month I usually lock the bathroom door. Many men, except a few like the one I'm with, like to go there before and after. Only a few like going there or to see what comes out during that time of the month."

"Ooh, gross but true," I added.

"Therefore, most women usually take care of that in private. Otherwise, they use the bathrooms in their bedrooms and keep the door closed but not locked," she explained. "So, yes, he's worried all right—that someone, namely me, is going to catch him doing his thing."

"I get your drift," I said to her.

"It's freaking unbelievable. It takes a miracle to get him to touch my body, but if I go into our bathroom after him, especially if he's in a rush and unable to cover his tracks, I can find evidence of him touching himself," she said.

"In a rush," I uttered.

"I think he mostly does it when he's getting ready for work in the mornings, which puts him behind the eight ball at times, and limits his ability to completely hide the evidence. Then, I can clearly see it and understand, I may add, why his sister thinks the way she does," she added.

"That's not a very good sister. That's not something you tell your brother's girlfriend," I said.

"Actually, they are very close," she stated.

"With a sister like that, who need an evil stepsister?" I asked with a smile.

"No, come on. It's not like that," she said. "When things like this occur in a relationship, one goes looking for answers, and his sister and I are very close."

"So she tells you that her brother is the king of jerk offs," I cracked.

"I told her what was going on and about the evidence I've found. She said that it is similar to when they were teenagers," she stated before I cracked on her boyfriend once again.

"Oh, so he has a long history of pulling on his stick, eh?" I asked with a giggle.

"Oh, you're bad," she said with a giggle of her own.

After the giggling died down, I prodded, "What evidence have you found?" I should not have asked this because I did not really want to know. However, once the words left my mouth, I could not retrieve them, and she was not about to hold back the detailed list of her evidence.

"There are times when I've found drops of cream-colored stuff stuck to the sides of the toilet bowl, inside and out," she said.

"Yikes!" I exclaimed.

"Or it's flowing in or sinks to the bottom of the toilet. Or I find sticky, folded-up toilet paper left on the counter or thrown in the corner like it was meant for the toilet bowl or trash basket. I can definitely tell from the girly magazines he has. Their pages always stick together like someone accidentally spread glue on them and tried to wipe it off in a hurry," she said.

"Yikes!" I said with a disgustingly look on my face.

"Exactly!" she said and then paused as if she was waiting on a response from me.

"Maybe he wants you to go and please yourself with your hands too," I suggested.

"Oh, hell no," she uttered aloud.

"I've been told on numerous occasions that I should go and do that," I added, thinking that she hadn't heard me.

"That's disgusting for a woman to do," she added. Then she surprisingly said, "So you are feeling my pain too, eh?"

"Like I asked before, would you like to trade?" I replied.

"I'll give it some thought," she said with a friendlier smile. Then she asked, "Have you ever helped yourself out like that … chosen that route for satisfaction?"

"I would much rather find someone to cheat with than to do that," I told her.

"Why so?" she asked with her lovely smile.

"Because in 1998, a female coworker of mine laid it out to me like this: She told me that if she was crippled from the upper body down and was only able to satisfy her husband by way of her mouth, she would gladly do it for the rest of her life. She believed that out of love for her husband, for his satisfaction, and so that he would not look for pleasure elsewhere, it would be her duty to please her husband sexually that way or however possible. She believed in doing her part to keep him from going into another woman's arms," I said.

"How do you know she wasn't pulling your leg?" she asked

"She pulled something all right, but it wasn't my leg," I replied with a chuckle.

"What? What did she do?" she prodded.

After a short hesitation, I said, "She got under my desk at work, unbuttoned my fly, and made me wish that I was her future husband and that she was crippled from the upper body down."

"No, she did not," she uttered with a chuckle.

"Yes, she did, but don't think badly of her. We were both at the same place—single with kids of our own and in undesirable relationships—pretending we were nothing more than friends at work," I explained to her.

"Wow! She did that at work?" the lady asked again with amazement.

"Oh, yes, she did," I said. Then I added, "My long-held belief is that if you take care of your partner's needs at home, he or she should have no reason to do more than window-shop on the streets."

"My sentiments exactly," she added agreeably. Then she stressed, "No man should ever sleep next to a naked woman yet still go into the bathroom to relieve himself sexually … and the same should apply to a woman. I refuse to go into the bathroom and use my fingers to take care of the things. I have a man for that. No! No way. I use these hands to cook for my kids. I can't be digging my fingers into you know where and then use them to make dinner for my kids. No, that's not right."

"Wow! That's another way of adding a twist to not doing it," I said with a smile.

"Like I said, I'm a very pragmatic person," she reemphasized.

"Well, that is cause for concern all right," I said. Then I asked, "So pragmatic lady, have you talked to him about it?"

"Yes, but it always comes down to him getting too old for sex," she said.

"Too old, and the man is thirty-eight," I said.

"Don't tell me. Go tell him," she said with a pointing motion. Then she excitedly said, "Take a look at this." She reached into her handbag, pulled out her phone, turned it on, and walked up close to me while punching in her pin number. She was so close that passersby who did not know us would think that we had something going on. What would have been more intriguing to the average passersby was that when the phone came on, she pushed it up to my face and moved slightly behind me so that she could also view what she was showing me.

"That is my boyfriend," she exclaimed. Then she asked, "Does he look old to you? Does he look like someone who doesn't have any energy for sex?"

To be honest, I was very surprised to see the picture of the individual she called her boyfriend. I expected her to show me someone who looked bone skinny and resembled an someone who was strung out on drugs. However, she showed me someone who looked like he should have been a movie star, at least starring in B movies or just waiting to be discovered. So at that point, I had to give her my honest opinion.

"Lady," I said and then paused before continuing on, "Your boyfriend looks as healthy as a horse that is ready to hit the Kentucky Derby. He doesn't even look thirty-eight like you said he is. He looks like someone who just turned thirty at the very most. I'm not good at speaking, so please excuse my French, but that mofo of yours should be a sex machine!"

"Shouldn't he?" she interjected with sweet kissable breath flowing over my shoulder and into my nostrils.

"You bet he should. Mofo should be putting a hurting on you every day or very chance he gets," I said with emphasis.

"Tell that to him. The opportunity is there for him to take," she said.

"I would. In fact, I would come over and knock some sense into him if I knew where you guys were living," I said.

"Thank you. I appreciate that. At least you, even as a stranger, feel my pain," she said in a romantic tone.

"Not a problem," I said in return.

"Well, at least you understand why I shouldn't be settling for it as little as I do," she replied.

"Absolutely!" I said gutturally. Then I added, "He looks too damn healthy not to want sex every day or at least three or four days a week."

"Hell, I would even settle for it once a week, given the fact that he had let so many opportunities slide by," she said.

"I absolutely understand. Sometimes one has to settle with hopes of things changing for the better," I said with regret in my tone.

"Thank you for agreeing with me even though I just met you," she said and banged her forehead against my shoulder blade twice while still holding the phone in front of me.

"Well, just so that we are clear, it's once a week with another warm-blooded human being and not the hand-job shit you guys suspect him of, right?" I said.

"Amen, brother," she softly uttered while chuckling.

"And with that said, lady, you're just too dang sexy for a man not to want your body every day," I said while smiling over my shoulder at her.

"Oh, thank you. You are just too kind," she replied with a smile of her own.

"No, honestly, you are very sexy, and it boggles my mind why your boyfriend pays more attention to video games and his girly magazines than he does to you," I added.

"I keep wondering the same thing too. No one sex drive can be that low," she stated with a sound of despair.

"Not if the individual can get it up for a picture in a girly magazine, it's not," I added.

"Exactly!" she amplified.

"Lady, you might have to take some nude pictures of yourself and tape them over the pictures of the women in those magazines so that he can get a better glimpse of what he's actually missing," I suggested with a smile.

She returned the smile and said, "I don't even think that would work at this point. Remember, I sleep naked next to him every night, and he won't even come close to me. We might as well be sleeping miles apart because that's the way it feels at times."

"Sorry to hear that," I said in a consoling way. Then with a smile, I added, "If you would like to pull off that trade sooner rather than later, you just let me know right now."

She returned the smile (well, it was more like a laughter) and said, "You're just too funny. I needed it this morning."

"Along with someone to rip your clothes off," I added jokingly.

"He's there. I just can't get him to set off my fireworks," she said.

"Oh, look at you cracking your sly jokes," I said with a smile.

"What?" she said with a surprised look.

"Fourth of July … fireworks … tomorrow," I explained.

"Oh, you're right about that. I guess I better go home and see if I can get my world lit up before the sky gets lit up tomorrow," she replied.

"You should. It is long overdue," I said.

"It certainly is," she said. Then she added, "I should get laid tonight, don't you think?"

"Why wait until then? Try to get some today and again tonight if you can," I interjected.

"That might be pushing it, but I'll try. Nothing ventured, nothing gained, right?" she exclaimed. Then she quickly added, "After all, it's the Fourth of July weekend. The sky shouldn't be the only thing that gets lit up."

I walked her up to the register without saying another word, and after the transaction was completed, I asked her to pull her vehicle up. She came back in a nice fire-engine red truck, and I loaded the eight-foot-long landscaping timber poles and sixty-pound bags of cement inside.

She thanked me with a hug, jumped into her red truck with the most wonderful smile, started it, threw it into drive, and slowly eased forward before quickly hitting the brakes. She threw it into park, hung her head out the window, looked back at me, and asked, "Do you like to kiss?"

The question was totally unexpected. To say it caught me off guard would be the day's understatement. All I could muster in response was, "Ah!"

"Do you like to kiss, mister?" she inquired again.

"Do I? I haven't had a decent one since October of 2008!" I responded while walking back up to the truck.

"I haven't had a decent one in a long time either, but that doesn't answer my question," she stated in response and pressed the issue again. "Do you like to kiss or not? You have nice kissable lips."

"Well, thank you. Sure!" I responded. Then I quickly uttered, "Why?"

"Oh, nothing!" she said with a smile that was a mile wide.

"Nothing? It can't be nothing," I said with a wide grin of my face and moved closer to hers at the open window.

"You asked me for a trade," she stated with the same big smile.

"Why? You're not still thinking about that, are you?" I asked with a curious grin. Then I quickly added a false disclaimer, "Oh, that was just for conversation's sake."

"We are having one now, aren't we?" she countered.

"You're absolutely correct," I responded.

"Well then, I need supporting conversational facts for my options' consideration," she said with a slightly serious look.

"Hey! I miss romance. I know that much," I replied with a more serious note.

"It still doesn't answer my question," she commented and revved the engine while the vehicle was still in park.

"Since you asked, it's one of the things I miss most in my current relationship," I stated.

"Me, too! I am just tired of butterfly kisses," she interjected. Then she quickly added in a much more serious tone, "I hate when a man has to beg for sex or a woman for that matter. Yes, we each own our own bodies, but when we're in a committed relationship, our bodies are there for the pleasure of each other. Each person knows what wanting to touch and make out feels like. It is undeniable. Certainly, there are going to be times when one is not in the mood, but just because you're not in the mood, does not mean your partner doesn't want or need to get pleased.

"Some women think that even though they are in a relationship, their bodies are exclusively theirs and that they should only give it up when they deem it necessary or when they feel the need to be pleased and not at the request of their significant others. I think that is just wrong because they are the first ones to cry foul whenever their significant others go out on the street and find the things they are lacking at home.

"On the other hand, I hate the fact that I leave myself open for sex, with certain things being limited on the three to five days each month when Mother Nature comes calling. Still, I am there to provide relief during those times if the opportunity comes and on any other time during it. I'm there for whatever he desires but only get touched less than twelve days per year. What is a girl supposed to do with the other 353 when he doesn't even hug me, touch me romantically, or engage in heavy petting?"

"Consider this," I said. "I miss being with a woman who is not afraid of being held or afraid of falling asleep in my arms because she thinks it might lead to sex. I also miss leaning up against a wall, a car (or any vehicle for that matter), something solid, or anything you can touch—even the wind—and being kissed like nothing else exists but us. I miss lying on the couch and playing the kissing game until our hearts content. I miss both of us falling off the couch and onto the floor without breaking a part, or hanging on hopelessly before falling over the edge of it. I miss kissing in a parked vehicle while listening to the birds chirp and the wind whistling through the trees.

Most of all, I miss lying in bed or on the bedroom floor with the lights out and just having good old-fashioned, tongue-watering, lip-smacking, everlastingly long kisses while rolling from side to side, on top and over each other while doing everything to make sure our mouth's stayed connected!"

"Wow! I think that you just got me extremely hot. I have to go now," she abruptly said with glittering eyes.

She threw the truck into drive and drove away without us ever exchanging phone numbers. I had pushed the envelope, but there was no dice. Now she was pulling away and then yielding the right of way to the vehicle behind her. However, before she had driven away, she had said, "If I ever decide to trade, I know where to find you."

Moments later, she was gone. After spending a good forty-five minutes or more with her, it was time to turn my customer service attention toward another customer. But as I walked back into the store, the conversation I had had a few day ago with the lesbian chic, who also worked in lawn and garden, popped into my mind.

I knew of her (not the lesbian part but that she was a hard worker) before I had even met her because the resource manager always raved to me about how good the recently hired young lady in lawn and garden was. I had been unable to put a face to the person until after I had been hired. The first time I saw her, I said to myself, "She's a lesbian," but that was never positively confirmed until our most recent conversation.

Yes, over my short few months of employment there, we had spoken many times, especially about who we believed was going to make the summer-season cut and the work ethics and attitudes of some of our fellow employees. However, not once had I ever dug for proof of my suspicion or cared to because it didn't much matter much who she loved. Anyhow, as we were talking a few days earlier, I said to her, "What wrong? You don't seem too happy today."

After a few beating around the bushes, she finally said, "If I am not kept on or get one of the other open positions, I'm going to move to Florida."

"Florida! That's kind of drastic, isn't it? Why don't you just find another job around here?" I inquired.

"Well, there's a little more to it than that," she said and then paused.

"Why? Not getting along with your family?" I asked out of curiosity.

"No! I am here by myself. All of my family is in North Carolina," she replied.

"So what's the added pressure? Is it significant other trouble?" I asked. I was so glad I had used significant other and not boyfriend because right there and then she confirmed what I had originally thought.

"Well, things are not going too well between my roommate and I. She does not save any money and always depends on me, which I don't mind. But she does not help out around the apartment and does not have time to socialize with me anymore," she stated. Then she contradicted herself, "I left my family in North Carolina to come up here and be with her, and now it's as if we were still living apart. We … well, she doesn't have time for romance anymore. We don't kiss. I can't get her to go out—not to the movies and not to the mall—even though we live a stone's throw away from them.

"She definitely does not look at me with those wanting-you eyes anymore. All she wants to do is sit at home, play video games, and watch TV. She won't look at me even if I take a shower, put on the most alluring perfume I own, and walk naked back and forth in front of the TV. She'll just try to look around me. I can't even get her to want to touch my body anymore, and I miss it so much. I really do."

At that point, I started to feel a little sympathetic for her, but more for myself and for a different reason. You see, I have the same problem at home. My significant other is very sexy. She's undoubtedly the sexiest woman I have ever seen naked. She loves to pose in her birthday suit in front of mirrors, the TV, and me, but only as a tease.

She does not want to be touched and usually screams like crazy for the kids (calling their names like she needs them) whenever I reach for her. Therefore, I do not pay her any attention when she starts her modeling games or any other sexually-arousing fakeness. I think she thinks her body is a priceless trophy that is only there to be dusted (undressed), polished (body showered, face made up, hair done, enticing perfume put on), admired (looked at from a distance with zealous imagination), and then put back on the shelf (dressed up) until it's time to be dusted again.

Anyhow, that day I asked my lesbian coworker if she thought her girlfriend was cheating on her, but it was a suggestion she quickly rejected as she somewhat stood up for her significant other. "No! Not at all. I am positive she would not do that to me. She just lost interest in me, and I can't find a way to inspire it in her. Nothing I do works anymore. When we do fool around, which is once a month if I am lucky, it's one time and only for a short while and then we are done. There is no romance afterward and hardly any before. There's no feelings or emotions during it but just to the point like she's doing me a favor and that's it."

She did ask my opinion about what she should do, but I will not divulge that here because she is not the basis of this chapter. I only mention the situation because it fits in well with what this other lady and I were going through. It made me realize that like me and the six-weeks-past-glory lady, there are millions of people in this world whose outside appearance does not tell the personal, professional, or sexually-frustrated hell they are living through. It is something others will never know about, unless the one who is suffering is willing to open up to a trusted confidant or a stranger who is willing to give them the opportunity to vent.

CHAPTER 9

DEEP POCKETS

ONE SATURDAY IN the middle of June, three amazing things happened to me. It was about a week after I had received my first two dollars in tips (one dollar from an old black lady and one dollar from an old white Vietnam veteran) and the missing link that clued me in on what the loaders had been keeping me away from.

First, shortly after eleven o'clock that morning and as it began to feel like we were sitting on the equator, a tall white gentleman in his early fifties walked up to the fat lazy cashier who I disliked. The gentleman asked him about pine needles, and of course, instead of just ringing it up, the lazy-ass cashier sent me to go and check. He already knew that we had pine needles, and if he wasn't sure, he could have easily gone into the Genesis screen on his register and checked. But no, he wouldn't do that. He had to exert some type of authority over me like it was my fault he had been working there for over fifteen years and was still only a lousy cashier.

Although it was part of my job, I hated the fact that I had to go and check the pine needle truck. On a normal windy day, it usually felt like it was one hundred degrees inside the trailer. On hot days, nobody wanted to go near it, much less go inside it because it felt twice as hot as the temperature outside.

The bastard knew that was the case. However, he did not care because his newfound purpose in life was to be antagonistic to others without cause. So since it seemed like he was beyond being fired, I might as well shut up and march whenever he called, which was what we all did but with a frown, of course.

When I came back with the answer, the gentleman bought eight bales at four dollars and ninety-seven cents each. Then he walked away from the register toward me, shoving the change into his right pocket and then stuffing the remaining three dollars from his forty-five dollars into my left vest pocket. It caught me off guard because I wasn't expecting anything, and before then, I could have sworn that he had stuffed all his change into his pocket.

The tip was unsolicited, and even the jerk off at the register could see it. However, as soon as I came back from helping the gentleman with the pine needles, sorry ass said to me, "You know that we're not supposed to accept tips from customers, right?"

"No, I did not, and as you can see, I did not ask him for or anticipate it. Moreover, if that's the case, why doesn't someone from management let it be known? No one ever told me that until you mentioned it just now. If what you are saying is true, it must be an unwritten rule. I know ignorance is not an excuse, but this is setting someone up for failure," I said to him.

"Well, I guess it's an unwritten company policy," he stated.

"Unwritten company policy. What the hell kind of policy is that?"

"Hey, don't get mad at me. I'm just telling you what I know," he said sarcastically.

"Who's getting mad?" I asked gutturally. "Hey, I just spent twenty-five years in the air force, and we had a few rules I didn't agree with. If it is a policy, it needs to be in writing, where there's no if, ands, or buts about it. Life is hard as it is. People do not need to add the worries of unwritten policies on top of it—those that just exist for got-you games.

"I understand where you are coming from. I'm just telling you the way things are around here," he echoed out of his flytrap again.

At that moment, I decided to show him that collecting tips was not my main reason for working there. After all, I had only found out about it a little over a week earlier, and I had been there for almost two months now. So I called Donavan, who had just checked in, over and said to him loud and clear, "Hey, since you were so nice to take me under your wing and train me, how about I buy you a drink to quench your thirst?"

"Sure," Donavan said.

"I'm having a red Gatorade," I said to Donavan. Then I asked, "How about you?"

"Yeah, I'll take a red one too," Donavan suggested.

So I purchased two twenty-ounce, red Gatorades at the lazy-ass cashier's register with the three dollars the gentleman had given me. After the cashier gave me the change back, I stuffed it and the receipt into my pocket while thinking, *Now you can go and report that, for all the hell I care.*

The second amazing thing that happened was the amount of tips I ended the day with. I ended up with twenty-one dollars, not including the three dollars I had spent earlier on Gatorade for Donavan and me. It might not be a lot to a person who is used to collecting tips, but I'm working at a home improvement store, and there were four of us covering the outside area on and off throughout the day.

It was my best day to date for tip collecting, and it brought out the ire in me when I thought about how those loaders had cheated me out of my first couple of weeks because I had been wet behind the ears. Still, neither of these two amazing events can top number three.

Somewhere around 6:45 p.m. as the bright evening sun was creating shadows in the garden center, a ghostly pale gentleman lumbered across the store toward the garden center gate.

"Good evening, sir. How are you today?" I inquired, once he had reached me. However, he was barely able to mumble between his feeble steps. If it had been a few weeks later, after I had encountered the motor-scooter lady, I would have had a bigger attitude. However, this was before, and I just told myself that he was rude and that I should not pursue helping him any further. Still, my customer service attitude overruled my mind and sent me a few minutes later to go and search out the old man.

When I walked through the garden center gate and a little past the registers, I saw the old man lumbering toward me. He looked even worse than when I had first seen him outside, and this time, he initiated the conversation. "Sir, may I get some assistance from you?" the old man asked.

"Certainly," I replied as I briskly approached him. "What can I assist you with this evening?"

"I would like to get some mulch, but I don't know which one to get," the old man said like he was gasping for air.

Not knowing what was going on inside of him, I copped an unseen attitude. *Why the heck would you come to the store to buy something and not know what you wanted?* I thought before deciding to take a step back and to treat him the way I would like to be treated. Yes, my attitude could not be seen, but if I felt it, then it wasn't right. Therefore, it was up to me to take the necessary action to prevent me from blowing up at the old man's next perceived and mixed signal. So with a calm mind and soul, I said to him, "Come with me. Let's see what I can do for you."

As the old man stood in front of me, I forgot how slow he had been moving. He was still visibly pale and looked like sneezing would cause him to tip over and possibly die. However, how slow his legs had been moving had slipped my mind momentarily. So after I told him to come with me, I took a few quick giant steps, expecting the old man to follow. Before I knew it, I was almost twenty-five paces ahead, and the poor gentleman was still in the windup of his 180 degree turn.

Seeing how far I had traveled away from him, I practically had to sprint back to get him, He said to me, "That's okay, young man. I'm not that nimble anymore.

139

These bones, they move slowly, and most times, I'm not sure of my footsteps, but I was going to get there somehow. If I go home without the mulch, my wife will kill me."

"Well, that won't happen if I have anything to do with it," I commented.

"Thank you. I'm not ready to die yet," he said in a fading tone.

"Not a problem. You will leave here with something, but I can only guarantee your lease on life from here to your car. What happens between leaving the parking lot and home is all up to you," I told him.

"Will you put it in my car for me?" he softly asked.

"Yes, sir. It's all part of making sure you leave here with something. You just have to get it home," I told him as we baby-stepped toward the back of the store.

"Good, because I don't know if I can pick up one of those bags, but when I get it home, I won't have to worry about that. I'll just back the car up, open up the mulch bag, and scrape it out where it will be used," he stated.

"That's very smart," I said. Then I quickly asked, "How many bags of mulch are you planning to get?"

"I don't really know. I guess maybe two or three should take care of it," the old man replied.

At that moment, I thought, *Now we're getting somewhere*, and that's when the old man first shocked me. "I just need enough to bury my wife's cat under it. I accidentally backed the car over him last night, and now my wife is home crying herself to death and making funeral arrangements."

At that moment, the old man stopped to catch his breath because he was breathing extremely hard even though we had only walked about thirty-five feet. The mulch was still another twenty to twenty-five feet away. Still, I stopped alongside him, and while we were standing there, he pulled a blue-and-white handkerchief from his breast pocket and wiped his eyes.

A minute or so later, he started to move again, and I followed his baby steps with my baby steps. I also restarted the conversation because I wanted to know what was so special about this cat and why they couldn't just dig a hole and throw him in the ground.

"How long has your wife had the cat?" I asked.

"Close to fifteen years now," the old man answered.

"Wow! That's a long time. I can see why she's so attached to it," I commented. "Do you know what kind of mulch you would like to use?"

"She wants me to get something pine or cedar," the old man replied.

"Okay, I'll take you to those first," I said.

"She prefers cedar though," the old man added.

"Okay, I'll show them all to you and let you make up your mind. We have two of each kind. We have the pine-bark nuggets and the pine-bark mulch. We also have a brand called Canadian cedar, which is in a green bag, and another kind of cedar in a purple bag. I guess that's the American one," I explained.

I took him to each bag's location, starting with the pine-bark mulch and ending up at the Canadian cedar. However, that was not his choice. He settled on the cedar in the purple bag because he liked the aroma coming from it and was sure his wife would too.

I had forgotten one thing: a cart. So after he made his decision, I sprinted back to the front of the store and grabbed one of the two-staged green carts. Then I hurried back to make sure he did not fall down.

After I picked up the first two bags and laid them on the cart, I was about to pick up the third bag when the old man apologized for his inability to help me, which really touched me. Whatever he was going through, his condition really showed on his face. Plus I wouldn't hold it against him for not trying because I had seen so many healthy, big, strong, weight-lifting jackasses come into the store and suddenly develop the I'm-sorry-I-can't-help-you-because syndrome. As soon as lifting time came, they instantly had back and shoulder problems or messed up disks. They either had just had surgery, were scheduled for surgery, were in physical therapy, or the whole nine yards.

However, when I looked at someone as sickly as that man, I had to give him the benefit of the doubt and assume his sentiment was genuine. Still, regardless of how touched I was by his comment and about his wife and her dead cat, nothing came close to what he said after I had put the last bag the cart. "I have no strength because I just got out of the hospital two days ago. I had heart surgery," he said.

"Oh, I'm very sorry. I hope all is well," I abruptly interjected.

"They had to give me a new heart. It cost me $55,000," he continued.

Although, he was talking slowly, I knew that he had said other things after $55,000, but I became woozy at his saying, "new heart," and had drifted off into la-la land shortly thereafter. If I had not had a tight grip on the cart, I probably would have fallen forward flat on my face as if I was a baby learning to walk.

A few short steps later, the old man said, "Last night was the first time I got behind the wheel to drive, and I accidentally put the car in reverse and ran over my wife's cat. She hasn't been able to stop crying."

I became teary-eyed at that moment, turned my eyes to the sky, and sent up a little prayer for him. Shortly thereafter, the old man stopped in his tracks, pulled the handkerchief from his pocket once again, and stroked his forehead with it a few times. Then he brought it to his chest, but instead of returning it to his breast pocket, he held it in his clutched fist and said, "Sometimes I feel it pounding away like it doesn't want to stay in there."

I felt the tears in my eyes then, but I just couldn't let them fall—not at that moment. The old man's wife was already at home crying, therefore, if anyone else needed to cry too, it was him. However, from the sound of things, I think he had been doing more praying than crying.

For once, I was very glad the old man was moving slowly. It gave me time to reflect on things before we got to the register. I thought about the organ donor program I was part of. It also made me instantly critical of those who refused to join. I burrowed through ideas in my head of how I might prevent those people from getting another person's organ.

I also reflected on a recent argument at my house with the woman I lived with. It had been about the organ donor program. This had occurred several times over the years and then a few weeks earlier. To put it mildly, she did not believe in being a donor and usually got upset at me for signifying that I was one on my driver's license without consulting her first, even though I had become one long before I had ever met her.

She still disagrees with the decision, and because of this, the last time we argued about it, I took it to a whole different level. I called her a hypocrite, and she did not speak to me for two weeks. I called her that for a reason. She had two kids from a previous marriage plus the one we had together, and I had some kids from my previous marriage. However, unlike her, I had no problem if any of my kids signed up to be an organ donor and had never tried to persuade my kids either way.

She, on the other hand, had forbid her kids from even thinking about or even discussing it. She ruled herself out of ever becoming one and said that if something should happen to one of her kids, she would decide then if she wanted someone else to have their organs.

I tried on numerous occasions to explain to her that during that time of grief, it would be an added burden to have to think about donating one of your loved one's organs, especially if it was her child's. So, if she really intended to do so, she should let it be known, otherwise, it was a bullshit excuse.

Additionally, I had said to her that an organ had to be harvested within a certain amount of time or it did no good for someone who was on a waiting list. I told her she couldn't wait until they were about to lay the body in the ground to decide that she wanted to donate the organs. At that point, the organs would only be good for research purposes. They wouldn't help any of the needy. Still, it seemed that the more I argued in favor of it, the more her mind became dead set against it. So the other day, I tried to put it in laymen's terms.

"Tell me," I said to her. "If one of your kids was on life support waiting on a donor's organ and one became available, would you take it?"

I hardly finished the question when, "Yes! Of course I would," flew out of her mouth.

"How could you? Why would accept the organ of another person's deceased child when you refuse to allow any of your children to become organ donors themselves?" I asked her.

"Why not? My child would need it to stay alive," she responded.

"Are you listening to yourself?" I asked her. "You're being a fucking hypocrite!"

"No, I'm not," she responded. "Don't call me that!"

"Yes, you are. You are being nothing but a damn hypocrite. It's all right for someone else's child to die and to donate his or her organs to save your child's life, but you can't have one of your children indicate the same goodwill," I stated.

"That's not the reason. You know why," she yelled at me.

"Okay ... what's the bullshit reason you are dead-set against one of your kids becoming an organ donor?" I asked.

"I know my reason," she said with a shake of her head.

"Yeah, I know your reason too. It's none other than how you are cold at heart about other people's needs and suffering. It's the same way you are about sex." I stated.

"What?" she yelled.

"Yes, I said it. You heard me. It's the same way you are with sex. You don't want to have sex or your body touched except when you feel in the mood once a month. It's the same way you are being with your organs. Much like your body, you would much rather take your organs to the grave with you rather than have someone else make good use of them. You are downright despicable," I said to her.

"Oh, I see. That's what I am now—a despicable hypocrite!" she exclaimed.

"You certainly are. Your excuse is that your oldest has a very rare blood type and that you don't want something bad to happen to him. You think that instead of trying to save his life, they let him die so that they can harvest his organs and sell them on the black market. That is just as lame as can be," I added.

"Well, it's true," she countered. "Do you want me to go on the Internet and show you how often it happens?"

"No thanks," I replied. Then I added, "I bet you wouldn't think about stuff like that if it came to your child receiving an organ, would you?"

It left her speechless for a moment, and I added, "You allow him to leave the house and to go to school. You are not concerned about him being kidnapped for his organs. You allow him to drive a car down the road, and you are not concerned about others crashing into him so that they can have his organs. He could be walking down the street and be hit by a stray bullet, but I don't see you protesting against gun manufacturers. You allow him to go to the grocery store alone, but I don't see you worrying about him ending up on someone's dinner table while his organs get shipped off to some foreign land."

"I don't see the point you are trying to make," she said.

To be honest, some of these things probably didn't make sense at all. I was just using whatever kind of analogy I could come up with at the time to prove a point, and none of them probably did. But I do know one thing that probably contributed to her not speaking to me for weeks. I told her that she always acted like her kids were better than anyone else's kids. In fact, I know that was the reason because when I said it in front of the kids, she immediately left the living room.

Still, I wasn't lying, and she knew it. She was like most people. She didn't want to hear the truth. I'm not saying it's wrong to love your kids because every parent should. I am saying this: If she and her kids were kidnapped along with a neighbor and his or her kids, and the kidnapper asked the adults to pick one kid to die so everyone else could go free, I believe that rather than picking none of the kids at all, she would pick one of the neighbor's kids.

If you are unwilling to give or make a donor pledge on your driver's license, you should not receive any organs, even if bad luck should befall you. Let's be fair here. I should be held to the same standards as others are. Yes, as I said before, it is duly noted on my driver's license that I am an organ donor, but when it comes to the American Red Cross and giving blood, I have never given because I am afraid of needles. However, the two are not the same.

People willingly donate or sell their blood on a daily basis, so the crisis for blood is not as great as it is for organ donations. I have given blood but not as a donation needed by the American Red Cross or any other agency designated to collect it for other humans' usages.

I gave a vile or two—I think the max was three—when I was in the military for testing purposes. Still, regardless of the minimum or maximum number, each time I had to give, they practically had to hold me down to take it. The same would be true if I had to donate blood to the Red Cross, which I haven't totally ruled out, but they would have to put me under first. Under no circumstances can I just sit idly by and watch the blood ooze from my veins. Even if I do not see the needle, just knowing that they have to stick me with one to extract my blood is just as bad.

I still remember my most terrifying experience ever, even though it happened over twenty-two years ago. When I joined the military, I was twenty-two years old and weighed 122 pounds (It wasn't until my mid-thirties that I started to gain some weight). Anyhow, about eighteen months after arriving at my first duty station, at Carswell Air Force Base in Texas, I had to get some blood work done. So I showed up promptly at the clinic inside the newly renovated Carswell AFB Medical Center while trying to keep my mind occupied with other things and away from blood extraction. After I sat down in the blood-extraction chair, the nurse must have known what I was trying to avoid, so she made it a day I would never forget.

In her attempt to extract one vile of blood, she stuck me in my right arm nine times and in various places. On each new attempt, she claimed she had not been able to find a vein the time before. However, her words were no comfort for my bruised emotions and aching arm. All I wanted to do was strangle her with my left arm. I still despise her to this day, even though I couldn't pick her out from a can of tomatoes.

Anyhow, I have no issues with being an organ donor. I am one because I am pretty sure I won't need my organs in the final analysis, just as long as they make sure I am gone before they take them. Well, not make sure but be sure that I am gone by an act of God first.

I personally believe all human beings should be organ donors. Maybe it would help drive the price down so that more people wouldn't have to worry about paying for them. People like my woman would stop coming up with their communist bullshit reasons why they are not on any donor list. All individuals should pay for life, unless it's the debt the Holy Bible says we owe to the Father, the Son, and the Holy Ghost.

Too many organs go to waste these days (like food) when someone needy could benefit from them. Think about it, if half of the food that supermarkets waste on a daily basis was donated to food banks, imagine how many more people in America would go to bed less hungry each night. If more people donated their organs, imagine how many more people would have second chances at life tomorrow.

The old man said his out-of-pocket expenses were $55,000. It was because of someone else's generosity that he is still alive. It makes no difference how deep your pocket is if an organ is not available. The money will do little good, other than putting your name higher up on the waiting list.

This is what bugs me the most about organ donation. How it is that a poor person can be on a waiting list forever and a day, without a match ever finding him or her. By the same token, a rich person, someone famous, or a celebrity can have a match found for him or her within mere weeks of it being known that the individual needs one. Why is that so? Does a poor person no longer bleed red when it's time to receive an organ? Maybe their blood type instantly becomes rarer than rare as soon as one of their organs decides to go bad. Anyhow, that was too much digression on my part.

The old man also mentioned how he sometimes felt his new heart pounding in his chest, and it made me wonder how I would feel if I was in his place. How does the family the organ was donated from feel? I also wonder if the receiver or anyone in his family ever reached out to thank or pray for the giving family and the deceased loved one.

While being a member of Carswell AFB's honor guard, I represented the base, Strategic Air Command (SAC), and the air force at hundreds of funerals and received many thank-you letters in return. However, the most gratifying thank-you letter was one that was read at a funeral. It came from the family whose loved one had received one of the deceased person's organs.

After the letter was read, everyone was emotionally drained. It is still amazing to me that the members of the honor guard had enough strength left to properly fold the flag without dropping it a time or two. Even more amazing was the fact that we fired our weapons without killing anyone at the burial scene. I guess that's why we were voted the best in SAC.

Gestures like that these cause me to reflect on things I might be able to do to help make this world a better place for my fellow human beings. I also know that most of the good things I've thought about doing, I will never accomplish because I'm not and will probably never be in the position to do so. However, the ones I have direct control of or am in a position to influence like organ donation, I will set in motion so that I can help someone … like someone help this old man.

Personally, I don't believe it's too much to ask of every human being. Think about it. Are you going to need your organs when you're no longer breathing? It's like the six-weeks-past-glory lady told me. She couldn't see the reason why her boyfriend didn't want to have sex, like he was saving his body for when he was dead. What for? The older he gets, the less likely he will want to use it. When he's dead and buried, he'll just donate it to the earthworms. So why not use and enjoy it or at least allow someone else to enjoy it before it's too late. I look at organ donation or the lack thereof the same way.

After the old man paid, I walked him to his car. It was a slow walk to the car, but it was one I would take again if he returned to the store. Anyway, as the old man and I were leaving the store, I walked slightly ahead of him. I saw one of my fellow customer service associates in training, Charlie. He was outside loading some sod into the back of a pickup truck.

"Hey John, how about giving me a hand," he said with that conniving smirk on his face that always traveled up to his receding hairline.

"I can't, dude. I have a customer," I replied.

"What, you don't believe in teamwork?" he asked in return.

"Of course, I do. I'll help you once I'm done with my customer," I responded. Then I stopped and waited for the old man to catch up.

While I waited for the old man, who was once again wiping his face with his handkerchief, I started to think,

What kind a sorry-assed bastard is going to ask me if I don't believe in teamwork. I just spent twenty-five years in the military, dickwad, and you just got out of high school, have a frigging receding hairline, and no future plans. In fact, your head looks like an erosion has taken place up there rather than a receding hairline. You are barely nineteen, and at forty-eight, I have more hair around my dick than you have on top of your damn head. Isn't it about time to make an investment in Rogaine. jerk-off!

On the way to the old man's car, he told me that the plan was to dig a hole in the backyard under one of trees and to bury the cat in it. Then they would cover the spot about three to four inches high with the mulch. He also said that he hoped that his wife's tears would have subsided by then.

I thought of asking if they had invited a lot of people to the funeral since they were going through such great lengths to give the cat a cool burial, but it was inconsequential at the time. Looking at a human being who had someone else's heart beating inside him was more amazing to me.

The old man shook my hand after I closed his trunk. After that, I wished him best of luck. He thanked me for my time and my patience and used the side of his car to walk to the front.

I stood off to the side until he drove away before I headed back over to the garden center entrance. When I made it back, Charlie was still outside. However, he had finished loading the sod and was leaning beside one of the blue lumber carts with his left hand in the pocket of his black shorts.

When I got within a few feet of him, he said to me, "Hey John, since you believe in teamwork so much, how about splitting the tip the old man just gave you with me?"

"What tip?" I asked.

"The tip he just gave you. I saw him handing something to you," he said. Then he obnoxiously asked, "How much was it?"

I looked at his receding hairline and thought, *Listen, you less-than-one-year-out-of-high-school advanced-receding-hairline bastard, I did not get any mofo tips.* However, I just softly said, "I didn't get any tip, fool. The man just shook my hand."

"Oh, I thought he gave you something," he replied.

"Oh, so a customer can't shake someone's hand in gratitude anymore without it being considered a 'he-handed-you-something … a tip'?" I commented. Then after a short pause I added, "Is that what it has come down to now?"

"That's not what I'm saying. Oh, you know what, just forget it," he said and walked away while looking back at me with his usual conniving, backstabbing look. Not that I'm saying he's conniving backstabbing person or anything. As far as I know, he's never done anything evil to me, although I've heard others make charges against him. Plus the way he reacts and the looks and attitude he gives whenever he does not get his way, makes one pause to ponder.

Charlie and I closed that evening without exchanging twelve words, but I did not let it bother me. I have not liked him much since the first time I had a conversation with him and developed a negative vibe from him. Yes, his latest stunt did not do anything to dispel my negative vibes toward him.

The vibes are so bad that I can honestly say that they are at a contempt level for him.

Still, he was the least of my concerns at that moment. I could not stop thinking about the fragility of the heart-transplant customer. I have to admit, even though we don't know when our day will arrive, I wondered several times how much longer he had to live.

CHAPTER 10

BOUGHT AND PAID FOR

IN THE GARDEN center, we have two individuals whose main jobs are watering plants. I have dubbed them as the Water Lilies, even though one is a female and the other is a male. I just love the sound of the words *water lily* because it reminds me of a scene from my all-time favorite movie, *The Ten Commandments*. In the garden center the people I dubbed the *water lilies* were responsible for keeping the plants alive in the hot summer sun, and in the movie, one of the ladies' bringing water to the men in the mud-pit to keep them alive in the hot summer sun was referred to as *water lily*.

Anyhow, about two Saturdays ago at around 1:40 p.m., I was walking around to burn off the last ten minutes of my lunch hour when the male water lily called out to me. He was over by table seven watering the Knock Out roses, so I walked toward him. With a country-wide grin, he tossed a question across my barn. However, before I jump into it, hook, line, and sinker, allow me to digress here for a short while.

Although some of the things people wear are bought and paid for, many others are not. People usually use their hard-earned money to buy the things they want to wear and wear them whenever they see fit. It doesn't matter if it's the time or the place for it, they have to get their money's worth. Furthermore, they will gladly point out what is and isn't your business and how there is nothing illegal about the things they are wearing.

We have to suck it up even though their appearance annoys us because the majority of the time, we have no control over the situation. We can't just tell them to go and change their clothes like we would our kids. Plus many parents out there can't even do that, at times, because their kids are allowed to run roughshod over them. It just doesn't work.

Still, I often wonder why people go out and buy clothes that they constantly have to adjust. If it looked good in the store's dressing room and you took the time to spend your hard-earned money on it, then it should look good wherever it is worn. There should be no reasons for dumb-ass juvenile delinquents to spend every waking second pulling up their pants. Young girls should not spend half their waking day pulling down the back or the front of their shirts to cover up their exposed backs or overhanging bellies. Grown women should not spent so much time adjusting the collars or buttons on your blouses and shirts every time a male patron approaches you.

People, you knew damn well what was going to happen before you left the store with the item, so live with it and stop all these games. You did not do that when you were in the store looking into the mirror at yourself. In fact, you probably went and got a smaller size, one with a wider neck, or one with more of an area so you could expose your cleavage. So do not act as if the buttons just decided to pop open or your T-shirt suddenly grew smaller the moment it saw me approaching. This is hypocrisy at the highest level.

It happens everywhere too, even at my workplace, by employees and customers alike. However, they end up giving you that why-are-you-looking-at-me stare, as if they've been offended and weren't wearing something that says, "Hey you, look what I'd like to show you—peekaboo!"

Even today while I was used the teller line in the bank, it happened to me. For the five minutes or so I was standing there hoping for her to take care of my transaction, the teller spent the better part of two minutes adjusting her top. It was like every stroke she made on the keypad caused her to reach up and try to conceal her cleavage area a little more.

So I was standing there thinking, *Jesus H. Christ, lady, you work in a bank as a teller spending the better part of your day sitting on a stool or chair lower than the standing customers in front of you. So why this charade? Why are you acting like I came here specifically to look down your shirt? Do you think this money that I'm trying to deposit is just a front for seeing your boobs? You knew dang well where you'd be working today and what would happen if you wore it. Why did you wear it if it bothers you so much? Why didn't you wear a turtleneck? If you did, I'm pretty sure my eyes would have been staring up at the overhead camera because you're not that pretty. In fact, you're downright scary to be working as a bank teller.*

Yes, I know that I am only picking on women here, but it's not really picking. I am saying, a woman's body is a whole lot sexier and a billion times more appealing than that of a man. So if a woman finds it necessary to show certain parts that do not equate to nudity in public, then by all means, do so and stop the games. Furthermore, to male children, teenagers, adolescents, and grownups, I have one thing to say to you. I think the congress of the United States should pass a blanket law giving all police officers nationwide the authority to shoot anyone in the butt when they find your pants below your hips.

As a man, I have no interest in seeing another man's ass or his dirty underwear, but any part of a woman, now I'm all for it, as long as you take the time and the place into consideration. However, I do get upset whenever I am given nasty looks because my vision travels to where a woman's provocativeness indirectly led it.

You knew dang well that what you bought would attract attentive eyes when you wore it. Therefore, do not give me any nasty looks when it attracts my attention because that was your intention all along. All should be as bold as the lady who came into the store. She was basically saying that if she had a figure that was eye-popping, mouthwatering, finger-licking, and making everyone wish they could possess it for ten seconds, she would flaunt it.

Believe it or not, most people usually tell themselves that is what they are going to do. It is their main aim when purchasing those tight, short-short, cleavage-exposing shirts and blouses. However, once you've entered public with such things on, it becomes time to play the false impression game.

Anyhow, the male water lily said to me, "Have you checked out the lady in the black dress yet?"

"What lady in black dress?" I asked curiously.

"I guess you haven't seen her," the male water lily said.

"Seen who?" I asked.

"Oh, dude, you have to see this lady. My, my, my," the male water lily emphasized.

"She was fine?" I asked with a smile.

"Dude! She was beyond fine. She puts the K in Special K," the male water lily said with the broadest of smiles.

"Damn, she must really be something else. Look at you smiling from ear to ear," I said with a smile of my own.

"Dude, she is really something else," the male water lily affirmed. He suggested that I should go and see for myself and then come back and tell him what I thought.

I asked him where she was, and he told me that she had gone in the direction of the patio blocks about five minutes earlier. I took off in that direction with an excited look on my face, but after a few steps, I came to the realization that I only had a few minutes left on my lunch break. It was just enough time to make it to my locker to retrieve my work vest and to the closest clock-in machine. I hardly had a second to spare. If someone was using the machine. I would not have enough time to make it to another one without being late. I hate being late, so with that and the other facts in mind, I made a beeline in the opposite direction jogging quickly.

"Hey, that's the wrong direction. The other way," the male water lily shouted.

I did not answer him in words. I only raised my hand in the air as if to say, "I know," and kept on running. I slow jogged all the way to my locker, coming close to knocking over several customers and three employees along the way, which invoked me to issue, "Sorry about that," "Pardon me," and, "Excuse me."

Although I had never seen this woman, it was the fastest I had ever opened my locker to retrieve anything. It was all because in my two plus months of working there, I had never seen the male water lily so excited about anything. His excitement implored my adrenalin to quick in, which drove me to the time clock and back to the lawn and garden sales' floor magically. Then I was off in search of this super human woman.

I spotted the lady on the side of the store across from the peat moss. Her back was turned to me, and she was leaning against a shopping cart near a gentleman off to her right. I did not know what their connection was, so I approached with working caution because Water Lily had not mentioned anything about a husband. He had only asked, "Have you checked out the lady in the black dress yet?" with enough excitement for everyone in Connecticut.

As I approached the lady, I couldn't help from thinking how gorgeous her backside was. It was so scrumptiously beautiful, she should have been starring in a video called *White Babe Got Back*. I walked by and could barely get out the word, "Hi," without biting my tongue. I also never looked back, nor did I remember if she ever responded. I also forgot the store protocol of what one should do when one was within ten feet of a customer.

Yes, I could barely get out, "Hi," and didn't say, "Welcome to [such and such]. May I help you, or are you finding everything? Would you like some assistance?" The assistance part was important because based on what I found out later. If there had been any customer I should have been eager to help, she should have been it.

I went back to the water lily and gave him my report on what I had observed. However, I did not have a chance to speak my conclusion because he blindsided me with questions. He excitedly asked, "So, have you seen her? What do you think? She's something else, isn't she?"

All I could do in return was give two thumbs up, which meant "great" to all of his questions. I figured that would end his fascination with her and that I would be now free to move around the store at will. I would even be able to check this lady out fully for myself. But he was not finished.

Upon smiling and giving my two thumbs up, he asked, "Does she look better from the front or the back?"

I never saw that coming and surely wasn't prepared to answer that question. After all, I did not pay any particular attention to her front end due to how she was crouched over the shopping cart handle. As far as the backend went, I saw enough to know she was packing but did not concentrate on it out of my fear of looking perverted. However, now that the water lily had posed the question, it raised my curiosity. I was eager to go back for a second and more in-depth observation.

The male water lily was wiser than I had thought. He had sensed, right away, that I had not paid attention to some of the lady's features and said to me, "I can't believe you did not check out her front side. You have to see that, man."

Without saying a word, I motioned that I would go and do that. However, after one step, the water lily stopped me. He turned off the water hose, stepped closer to me, and to my surprise, said, "I don't think she's wearing any panties either."

Again, out of fear of seeming perverted, I had paid particular attention to it, or maybe I saw it but did not recognize it. Now that the male water lily had brought it up, it was going to be one of the things I focused on during my second go-round, which I would do at a slower pace.

Upon leaving the male water lily's side, I decided to approach the lady from the front this time. However, somewhere along the journey, I reshuffled my thoughts and decided to take the same approach as I had the first time. In my mind, it provided me with the best flexibility. It's never nice to turn around and stare at a woman's behind after you've walked by. Then even the blind can figure what your motives are.

I found the lady in virtually the same spot I had left her in earlier, except the gentleman beside her was now loading cobblestones on a flatbed cart. It also seemed that she was either comfortable or excited to be crouching over the shopping cart handle because she was still at it while conversing with the gentleman.

Upon passing her gorgeous backside, which was in a silky black dress, I had to agree with the water lily. It appeared she was not wearing any panties. I did not even see the "outprint" of a thong line, and it raised more than just my curiosity. I now had to see her face and more of her front side. More importantly, I needed to see the man who was with this gorgeous (if only from behind) creature.

After I walking by her a second time, I recalled my store-training protocol (It was a little late, but better late than never) and stopped, pivoted, and said, "Would you guys like some help?"

As if the last thing he wanted to hear was the voice of another male offering to help, the gentleman immediately stopped halfway into picking the next cobblestone and said, "No thanks. We are doing fine."

From the lady's reaction, I assumed it was something she had grown used to. She stepped in to play the good cop. She smoothly rose up from the shopping cart handle and said smilingly, "Thanks for asking, but he's here to earn his keeps. I'm putting him to work this weekend."

Very few things have been touched more or have carried more germs than money and the handles of shopping carts. Still, for a brief moment in my life and at that instant, I wanted to be a shopping cart handle. I heard the calming words she was using to smooth out her husband's jealous hedges, but her looks and cleavage were what captured my attention.

In terms of pure looks, she was an eleven on a scale from one to ten. Normally, I'm not a "tongue-wagging" man except on few occasions. And this was one of such said occasions. Because upon seeing her eye-popping cleavage, I knew that my tongue flopped out of my mouth right there and then. In front of my witnessing eyes, her boobs were saying to whatever she had holding them up, "Please release us and set us free."

I cannot say for certain that it was intentional, but she knew that she had captured my attention—in more ways than one. She was indirectly telling me that what I was looking at had been bought and paid for. She made this subtle statement by fully exposing the shiny mountain on her left hand and pretending to place it properly in her left hand.

I walked away saying, "We are here to make shopping a pleasure for the customer, so either I or another employee will probably offer our assistance again before you leave."

"Thank you," the lady said sweetly, but her husband's look said something completely different. His look said, "If anyone offers to help again, it would be in that person's best interest to be a female employee. If another male asks, I will beat him to death with one of these cobblestone bricks."

If only to antagonize her jealous husband, I walked away fully intending to go back to make small talk with them later. So after rushing back to the male water lily to wholeheartedly agree with him, I slipped away from him again under the pretense of the lady's husband needing my help.

It was far from the truth, but it got the male water lily to shower me with a smiling, disingenuous, "You lucky bastard." I shuttled away in search of trouble, actually hoping that trouble would not find me yet wanting to find out why the lady was with this man, other than my assumption that the guy had money.

This time I decided to approach from the last position I had departed from—head on. A few quick steps, and I was twenty-five to thirty feet away from the lady, looking into her expecting smile. It was as if she knew that I wouldn't be gone for long. She seemed eager to see someone could get her husband riled up once more.

Two thoughts ran concurrently through my mind as I drew closer to the extremely gorgeous, earth-walking goddess and the shanty-looking, somewhat-jealous man beside her. One, the only thing that kept her from being the perfect woman was the double row of teeth she had in the lower front area of her mouth. Two, oh what a woman she would be if they could transfer the teeth from Vanessa's mouth into hers. Come to think of it, if they could transfer Vanessa's whole head onto her body, the new person would have replaced the real Miss America 1983 as the most gorgeous woman ever to walk the face of the earth.

Upon reaching them, I said, "Hi, I'm back. Still don't need any help?" while turning my head like I was talking more to the husband but using my peripheral vision to look at the lady's rack. I think she caught wind of what I was doing and apparently didn't mind because she produced an outright laughable grin.

The husband, on the other hand, wasn't so welcoming. He just threw the current cobblestone he had in his hand on top of the others (which were neatly stacked) and tried to move the flatbed with brute force while saying, "Come on, dear. I've got lots of work to do before the day is done."

"Slow down, dear, the worker is here to give you a hand," the lady said.

"That's okay. I can manage," the husband quickly countered.

"Besides, we still need to get that other thing," the lady said.

"What thing?" the husband asked after a pushing grunt.

"The thing for the grass. You know, the mesh thing to keep it from coming back," she explained.

"Oh, right," the husband said in agreement but then quickly asked, "Do we really need that now?"

"Babe, don't be silly. Of course we do. Why else would we be getting the rest of these things?" she inquired.

"No, no, you're right," the husband agreed while continuing to push the flatbed.

At that moment, a little part of me drifted off to one of those man-card beer commercials, and I truly expected to hear the lady says something like, "That's strike two. One more today and you lose access to this body for a whole month," but she never indulged my fantasy. She simply turned to me with this smile that was saying, "I know why you're really here," and asked, "Where can we find the things you lay on the ground to keep the grass from coming back?"

Being the opportunist I was at that time, I looked at her with the broadest of smiles and said, "I certainly do know where they are, and I can take you there."

The lady returned my smile, and with an added bonus, she slightly parted her lips and exposed her tongue in a twisted shape between her teeth. It was as if she wanted to say to me in a playful way, "I bet you certainly do, you little fucker. But you don't have what it takes to get near this body."

Still, what I thought she was thinking did not deter me, and I quickly added, "It's just your luck that I am heading that way next to front the racks over them. Good thing I decided to come and check on you guys one last time before I went there."

"And we greatly appreciate it, but as I stated before, I think I can manage," the husband added.

"I understand what you are saying, sir, but part of my job is to offer each customer as many helping opportunities as possible. That also includes trying to sell you additional items that will aide you in accomplishing your project—items I think you might have forgotten or hadn't thought about," I said.

"Oh, that's nice of you guys," the lady said.

"We try. Customer service is our number one priority. Fortunately for me, unlike most customers, you guys know exactly what you need like the weed suppressor we're on our way to get. Because of that, I don't have to name off a bunch of things you might or might not have already," I told them.

"That's great. That's how you guys add to your bottom line, right?" the husband said in a condescending way.

"In a way, but it's mostly about helping the customer. The goal is to keep each individual from having to make several trips to the store for the same project," I explained.

"I can see where that's helpful," the husband agreeably said. Then he added, "Still, selling someone something they don't really need goes beyond customer service and straight to your bottom line."

"True, true, but a customer has up to thirty days to bring back any unused item, providing a receipt can be produced. Plus, if it is a plant, the individual has up to one year to bring it back, whether it's dead or alive. If the individual paid with a credit card, there is no need to worry if a receipt can't be found. Then the individual, upon returning the item, only has to give us the last four digits of the credit card that was used, and we can look up the receipt in our system," I explained in detail.

"Wow, you guys are really customer friendly, eh?" the lady said.

"Yes, ma'am," I said in agreement.

"I suppose," the husband added while struggling to push the flatbed slightly behind us.

"I presume that with all the help they provide, they still have customers who refuse it and end up making several unnecessary trips here. Right, honey?" the lady asked her husband.

I don't know for certain if her comment had been a shot at her husband or just at customers in general. However, I will go out on a limb and say that her husband took it personally because of the tone in his voice when he added, "I suppose."

I also chimed in with my two-cents worth of expertise, "You would not believe how many people in the past have thought we were just aiming to add to our bottom line and brushed us off, only to find themselves coming here two, three, and even four times before they got everything they needed for the project they were working on." Then right before we stopped in front of the grass suppression meshes, I added, "But fortunately for you guys, you won't be one of those customers because you came prepared with a list of things you need to make your project a success, and here we are."

After going through an array of options such as one was too long and not wide enough, too wide and not long enough, nylon versus plastic, the best mesh for suppressing grass, the average life span, and so on and so forth, a choice was made. The husband settled on four rolls, which made me very happy.

I was getting tired of him changing his mind and on my last nerve when he asked if we had a specific color. At that point and for the first time in a long, long while, I really wanted to choke a customer—well, not since the fat lady in the wheelchair or the one who wanted me to put a few extra bags of mulch in her vehicle.

I looked at him and thought, *What difference does the color make? It will be buried under dirt, mulch, lava rocks, the flatbed full of cobblestones you are struggling to push, and hopefully, some flowers to boot. Mofo, no one is going to see it and say, "Look at that dumb-ass, the color of his grass-suppression rolls does not match the ground he laid it on."*

He pushed further with the comment, "It would be nice if you guys carried it in red like the mulch over there," like he planned on hanging it from the side of his house or using it for curtains. But as ridiculous as he sounded, I could not say a word because I was in a customer service business and should not think of any question as being stupid, even when I begged to differ. Moreover, if I had acted up, his wife might not be inclined to carry on her small chitchat with me anymore, even though she must have believed he was going overboard about the whole situation.

Maybe it was how he made himself sound intellectual or his way of telling me, "I know you are only going above and beyond because you think my wife looks good, but you can't have her because you work in a home improvement store, are not intelligent enough, and can't afford what it takes to buy such a gorgeous creature." If that's what was going through his mind, he was probably correct.

Most definitely, I was working in a home improvement store. For sure, if it took money to have a woman as gorgeous as his, well, they could draw a line through my name because I was one missed paycheck away from being in the poorhouse. It hadn't always been this way and hopefully, would change for the better when the Veterans Administration (VA) got around to processing my claim, which was way past the three months I had been told it would take to render a decision.

By the way, as far as intelligence goes, her husband might have been more educated than I was (Then again, he might not have been, but let's give him the benefit of the doubt), even though I was currently enrolled in college earning my degree in business administration and management. Furthermore, so far to date, I had identified at least five things at my current home improvement store employment that I would change, if I was in charge. I had told management three of these things, but since then, I had stopped going to them because it seemed like I was getting more on their nerves than anything else. It had only offered solutions to some overlooked problems, which would have benefitted the company's bottom line or the very least, the store's.

Another thing the guy did not know was that I could trump his intelligence with common sense on any given day of the week and twice on Sundays, if need be. When it comes to common sense, I think I was blessed for a whole nation. Furthermore, I just spent the last twenty-five years of my life defending this country from the desert sands of Saudi Arabia to some forgotten place I didn't want to remember, such as on an old run-down base in Oklahoma, which was closed in 1969. Arriving there in the summer of 1987 turned out to be the scariest flight and approach landing I've ever been on.

I say all of this because of many things, not excluding the way the young pilot landed the KC-135 refueling airplane on the tarmac and turned the sunshine filled Oklahoma morning into a frightful adventure. My point is that my defending this great country that I love probably enabled him to acquire his intelligence worry free. Due to the price I had paid, he was taking that intelligence and looking down on me because he knew one thing about me: My eyes had found his wife appealing.

Was it true? Of course it was. However, I didn't know who they were and still don't. It is 100 percent accurate to say that I did not ask him to bring her to the store, or to allow her to leave the house dressed the way she was. He directly or indirectly gave his blessing for her to leave the house dressed as provocatively as she had so that even a blind man could tell that she had it going on. This is one case where Ray Charles wouldn't even have to make his decision from measuring her wrist. As gorgeous as she was and still is today, if she had not left the house without her panties while wearing a virtually see-through, silky, long black dress with an unbuttoned cleavage area where her boobs jiggled and tried to jump out of her screaming bra at every step, no one, including myself, would have paid that much attention to her.

What I do not get is why would anyone get mad over something he or she asked for, whether directly or indirectly? This reminds me of the typical customer who goes to dollar stores, grocery stores, home improvement stores, Walmart's, Kmart's, or even fast-food restaurants to purchase goods and services yet looks down on the people who work there. I believe this is hypocrisy at its highest degree. But I will get into this more at a later date and time.

Anyhow, after the choices were made, we slowly and surely made our way up to one of the register's lines. We did share some small talk along the way. It was mostly about the kind of work that would be done around the yard before the summer ended. Most of it took place between the wife and me, with an occasional butting in by the husband.

I strongly believed there was a hidden story to be told. I believed, at the time, I could have gotten the wife to divulge more, if she weren't there with her husband. Mostly, I was hoping I would be able to escort them to their vehicle where she might slip me her phone number. Even better yet, she had said that she came to my store to shop all of the time and that she would see me the next time she came. Vanessa had also said this to me, but I had never seen her there before our first encounter and have not seen her since.

It's like one of my favorite singers (Janie Fricke) sang, "Tell me a lie." Yes, a lie sometimes sounds good to a heart that needs a justifiable reason. Still, none of my wishes came true.

While standing in the back of the line (the only one that remained open because the blob at the other register was about to head to lunch) and two customers away from the front, I asked again if they would like some help loading the vehicle. Without hesitation, the husband replied, "No, thank you. I got it. Thanks for all your help."

It was as if he wanted to say, "I bought and paid for this woman. No phantom of a man will come between her and I at night, so back off, bitch!" Therefore, I did. Well, I was tasked away shortly thereafter by the floral specialist. She told me to get a broom and to sweep up the wet flower petals and leaves that were under the stands. They had fallen there because of the male water lily's heavy watering.

I must admit, there was a whole lot of petals and leaves on the ground. It was as if the water lily had turned the water on full blast. He must have found a way to release some of the frustrations he had developed after seeing the extremely gorgeous lady. Still, who could have blamed him because of the way she was seductively dressed.

I briskly walked outside to the mulches that were displayed in the front where I knew I had the best push broom hidden. Close by, I had my half-frozen, red Gatorade bottle wrapped in plastic and stuffed into one of the concrete blocks, which were being used for an outdoor flower display. I retrieved my drink and took a big gulp before quickly stuffing it back in the hole. I was afraid someone would clue in on my secret and therefore, tamper with my drink.

After doing so, I retrieved the broom from behind the plastic trash bin and started on my journey back into the store. By then, the couple was at the front of the line. The wife was ahead of her husband and appeared to be talking to a cashier named Mark while he rang up their items. From my distance, it was somewhat hard to tell who was doing most of the talking or what the conversation was about.

I knew Mark was a smooth one from the many times he had caught would-be shoplifters (at least seven in the short time I had been working there, including the lady who asked me about DVD holders) to the way he talked in general. Therefore, from the grin on the lady's face, I could tell he had dropped something on her.

I could not say for sure if the conversation was getting too personal, but the lady seemed to be enjoying it to the dislike of her husband, and Mark didn't seem to mind. However, I believed it had rubbed the husband the wrong way because after a few steps closer, I could hear the husband say, "I am right here. You know that? That is my wife you are talking to. How about showing a little respect?"

The lady smilingly looked back at her husband and said, "Honey, stop it. The cahier is just being friendly. They're supposed to make the customers feel welcome."

I know that the husband mumbled something, even though I could not tell what he said. Whatever it was, it did not bother Mark. Without wiping the grin off his face (which I would have at least done), he just asked how many cobblestones they had. Then upon being told the number by the husband, no less, Mark grabbed his handheld scanner and walked over to the barcode log on the wall behind him.

Mark scanned the item number in and then entered the quantity on the scanner keypad while walking back to his register. I am not quite sure if he asked them if they were connected to the military in order to give them the 10 percent discount, but I could tell payment options were being discussed.

The lady reached into her purse and pulled out a credit or debit card and ran it through the machine twice. It did not go through either time, but that was not an indication that they had no money. Many times in the past, the card reader on that particular register has not worked, and the cashier has had to manually type in the card numbers. This time was no different … to a certain extent.

Mark asked the lady for the card. I am not suggesting this was a deliberate act, but what should have been the smoothest hand off because of their close proximity to each other became a bumbling baton pass of major track-and-field disaster. The card eventually fell into the shopping cart, and both Mark and the lady apologized to each other. Then the lady decided to retrieve the card and to hand it to Mark.

However, instead of walking around to the side of the shopping cart where she could easily reach the card without any fanfare, the lady decided to bend over the cart handle and to reach it from there. Needless to say, it took longer than it should have but was very rewarding for Mark and I, and no doubt also for the scruffy old man in the line behind her husband.

I must admit, the further down her bosom I got to look, the more joyous the exposure was for me. I am sure the same could be said for Mark. In fact, his eyes lit up a lot brighter than mine did, even though I got to see a whole lot more of her than I had ever envisioned.

When her husband realized what was going on, he first looked back at the gentleman in line behind him to see if the man's eyes were fixated on his wife's behind, which it was, and no one could have blamed him. I saw what she looked like when she was standing and only bending slightly, so I'm sure it must have been even more gorgeous for him.

Anyhow, after looking back at the gentleman as if to say, "Hey, buster, watch it," the husband raced around to block off our vision of her. By then however, his wife had the card in her hand and was slowly easing up with a devilish grin on her face. It was as if she was indirectly saying, "I hope you two horny bastards have your fill."

Moments after Mark took the card and entered its number, the transaction began to process. The lady had changed it from a debit to a charge and within seconds was signing the touch screen.

Upon Mark handing the receipt to the lady, she stuffed it and the payment card into her purse. She then smiled and gave Mark and me the wave of a female movie star gliding down the red carpet. Then off she went, leading her husband out the door.

I asked the husband if he would like me to push the flatbed of cobblestones outside so that he could go and bring their vehicle, but just as the times before, he once again refused any assistance from me. All he said while struggling to move the flatbed of cobblestones was, "Someone ought to talk to a manager about that cashier. He has no business being in that position."

Our zone manager (assistant store manager) came around shortly after the couple went out the door, and I am glad he did not go outside. If he had, he would have most likely seen the guy outside struggling with the flatbed or loading his vehicle by himself. This would have made both Mark and I look bad but more so me. Mark was assigned to the register, and I was assigned to lend as much support to the shopping customers as necessary: from entering the store to making sure their vehicles were fully and properly loaded.

Moreover, the man might have seen the zone manager and taken the opportunity to complain about Mark, which could have spilled over on me. revealing the initial part I played in the whole scenario. I guess luck was on our side … in more ways than one.

Mark and I never talked at length about what had transpired either. All he did was look at me with a broad grin on his face. He shook his head no, which when combined with the grin meant "Wow!" Then he asked, "Can you believe that guy?"

The zone manager instantly asked, "What guy?"

Neither the cashier, the two customers who were still in the line, or I wanted to spill the beans on what had transpired, so I quickly shrug my shoulder while saying, "Oh, nothing." Then the old man that had been standing directly behind the lady and I smiled at each other. Moments later, I looked directly in the zone manager's eyes and left him waiting there for a better or more problematic answer.

Leaving him like that was something I purposely did because I had never quite trusted or warmed up to him. He always addressed me as a friend but never quite seemed to want to shake my hand or even extend an outstretched one while saying so. Therefore, I assumed he was using the term in a condescending way. Still, regardless of how I felt about him, my thoughts did not last long because shortly after walking away, the vision of that gorgeous creature popped right back into my mind. Although, I must admit, to this very day, I still believe she had been bought and paid for.

CHAPTER 11

LOST

ABOUT TWO MONTHS into my employment stint at the home improvement store, a female customer, who appeared to be of South American descent, approached me and asked for help. If I had to guess, I would say she was in her mid to late thirties, but I never asked her age while pursuing the conversation either. Come to think of it, it wasn't much of a conversation. Half of it was lambasted with her apology. Still, I felt it was necessary that I tell this story because it reminds me of a not too distant past in my life.

Anyway, there were reasons why I refrained from guessing her age. One was that I always a woman's age wrong. For one, I either undervalued her age based on her face, and the lady would tell me, "Oh, thank you. You're so generous, but I'm a lot older than that. Do I really look that young to you?" Secondly, I did the opposite and added too year to her life. She would eventually say, "I'm not that old. Do I really look that old to you? Why would you think I was that old?" From there, the conversation would go downhill.

To compound the problem, in both scenarios, I've often answered, "Yes," without being given the opportunity to explain the strategy I use because of the jubilant or tyrannical state my words put women in. On the positive side, I find it hard and incomprehensible to douse a woman's jubilation with cold water. On the negative side, without having an abundance of time, I know it is hard to thaw a woman's heart once it has been hardened. It's not easy digging out from under a two-mile-thick ice capsule with a toothpick for a shovel.

Here is my strategy: I always look for wrinkles on the woman's face, especially under her eyes and on her neck. Then I take the first reasonable number that pops into my head and add seven years to it. This is how I come up with the number I often utter. As one can tell, it hasn't always worked out for me. I am notoriously wrong about 70–80 percent of the time, which means about eight out of every ten women end up getting glad or mad at me.

I even had a lady once tell me to go and "F" myself after I said she must have been born in a decade that was earlier than she supposedly hatched in. It wasn't like I had added the whole decade to her age. The number I came up with to represent her age and uttered, coincidentally made her a few years older, took her away from the eighties decade, and placed her in the seventies.

Her suggestion, however, led me to quickly say to myself, *That did not crack my list of the top one billion, but me f***ing you was number one on my priority list.*

Let's get back to our story. The lady asked me if I could help her with some flower pots that were on the wall beside the pool pumps and gazebos. They were too high for her to reach from ground level. In fact, they were too high for me to reach from that level and were close to a foot taller than she was but with a much greater wingspan.

I went to aisle three under the fence canopy and brought back a small four-step ladder, After she made her choice, I returned the ladder. I had not put the flowerpots in her shopping cart before I had returned the ladder, so I went back to help her with them. Moreover, it was part of my job to assist the customer until he or she no longer required assistance.

It was going to be a chore to get them inside, due the fact that her shopping cart was already full. It was full in the sense that she had some other bulky items in the cart that weren't properly placed and not from the sense that she had too many items in it.

It would have been a lot easier for me to go and get a flatbed cart to put the flowerpots on, but when I made the suggestion, the lady did not agree because she felt that it would influence her to buy more stuff. This is something that put her in the same category with lot of our customers who felt they were being more budget conscious if they carried items around in their arms rather than getting a shopping cart.

For those folks, my question was, "Why carry around fifteen items in your arms and under your armpits around the store?" If you are that much of an impulse shopper, go ahead and get a shopping cart, put everything that is written on your list or in your head in the cart, and then head straight to the register.

People should stop window-shopping while they're inside the store and in close proximity to many items. It is called impulse shopping or writing a check your behind shouldn't cash. Window-shopping should be done from the outside of the store, looking in through its windows at the things inside, admiring them, and then going on your way.

Anyhow, after I rearranged the lady's shopping cart and fit the flowerpots in it, she asked about potting soil and pawned her cart off on me to push. It was something I had no objection to, but it was done so smoothly, I didn't even know when it happened. We had been walking over to the right corner of the store. Then suddenly, she was in front of me holding nothing but her handbag, and I was behind her pushing an unevenly stuffed cart with gimpy wheels.

I dislike these kinds of cart because they seem to have a mind of their own, which always clashes with mine. It seems that wherever I go (the grocery store, the hardware store, the mall), the majority of carts I pick have gimpy wheels. At my store, it's no different. This really gets on my last nerve when I have to bring them back from the parking lot—the place where the one I was pushing for the lady should have been, and at the deep end of it.

While I was pushing the cart through the garden center behind the lady, I thought, *How many bags of potting soil is she planning to purchase? Where on this overflowing shopping cart does she intend to put it?*

Shortly after those questions crossed my mind, she slowed down and asked, "Which type of potting soil would you recommend?"

"Recommend for what?" I asked.

"For my plants," she replied.

The first thought that came to my mind was, *Does she think I'm a mind reader?* However, I did not say anything negative. I simply said, "It all depends." Then I asked, "What type of plants are you going to repot?"

"My miniature Japanese citrus trees," she answered.

"Why? Are they getting too big?" I asked.

"I wish. I bought some a while back, but they are not growing like they should or as it was suggested they should," she stated.

"Maybe Farmer Jane Doe doesn't have a green thumb," I said with a smile.

"Not at all. I do—mostly. I usually have pretty good results whenever I plant something, but these are just being stubborn," she suggested.

"I have never heard of stubborn citrus plants before, especially Japanese ones," I said with a chuckle. Then to make her smile, I quickly added, "People are so little and easygoing. Aren't their plants supposed to be just like them?"

My attempt at a joke, however, fell on deaf ears. At least, that's how it appeared based on her facial expression (nothing) and her next statement. "One of my friends said I should change their environment," she said.

"Hence, you are buying bigger pots and soil," I said.

"Yep. I'll do this to see if I can get them to grow," she replied. Then she asked, "Do you think that will work? Do you have any recommendations?"

It has been said that one should ever use a question to answer another question, but I forgot to ask her what other things she planned on trying. I just swung into my reply by saying, "None, off the top of my head. I don't usually plant miniature Japanese citrus trees. In fact, I've never planted anything Japanese before."

She gave me a smile along with a you-sly-devil look. Then she added, "I see."

So without hesitation I continued, "Plus, one should never brag about one's good fortune. Still, it seems like everything I've planted has grown like a wildfire, but I can't take credit for that. I contribute it to my green thumb rather than any manufacturer's miracle in a bag."

"So are you saying you don't recommend the things you guys sell?" she quickly asked.

"No, no, not at all. They work wonders for people who are not blessed with green thumbs like me. If you're one of the few like me who are, you rely less on things like these and more on your gut feeling—where, how, and when your mind tells you to plant something," I explained.

"I see. Maybe I should take you home with me," she said with a smile.

I chuckled and said, "Two problems with that."

"Why? Are you married?" she asked.

"No. One, I'm still on the clock and don't get off until 11:00 p.m. Two, I don't come cheap," I said to her.

"Wow, eighteen dollars for this bag of Miracle-Gro. I hope your services are not as expensive," she said with laughter.

"Technically, it's not eighteen, it's seventeen ninety-nine. And—"

"What's the difference?" she interrupted.

"It makes a big difference … over time," I said.

"Yes, over time, maybe. But right now it doesn't make that big a difference. Seventeen ninety-nine is virtually eighteen dollars," she countered.

"Yes. That's true. But like I said, over time, it makes a big difference. Imagine a tank being set up outside the store. Over a five-year period, every customer that leaves through these doors has to deposit a penny in it, based of course, on every item he or she purchases at ninety-nine cents. It would literarily add up to thousands of dollars at the end of that time period," I countered.

"Convincing! I see your point," she said. Then she added, "Still, seventeen dollars and ninety-nine cents is a lot to pay for a promised miracle in a bag.

"No pain, no gain, or in this case, you have to pay for the good stuff," I said.

"Would it cost me less if I took you home with me?" she asked.

I immediately thought, *Oh ho! This is the second time she has suggested taking me home. Where is she going with this?* However, I said nothing while pondering if I should fan the flame or not.

While I was pondering, she said, "I guess the Miracle-Gro is a lot less expensive."

"What the heck? Fan away," I said to myself. "Not necessarily. The price is open to negotiation.

"What's your asking price?" she quickly asked.

"You tell me what task I need to perform, and I will tell you what it will cost. Then if you disagree, we can negotiate."

"Digging holes," she uttered quickly.

"Japanese or American?" I asked with a smile.

That got her to issue a statement in her Spanish accent while laughing, "I'm done. You have too much of a vivid imagination for me." Then she added, "Are you allowed to help me put these in my car?"

"Sure! It is part of the customer service we provide. The only stipulation is, you have to bring your vehicle up to the front of the store along the yellow line," I said to her.

"Only to the yellow line? What if I am parked close to the front door?" she asked.

"The yellow line is close to the front door," I replied quickly.

"You know what I mean. What if I am in a parking spot that is close to the front of the store?" she said. Then she quickly added with a smile, "And don't say the yellow line is a parking spot close to the front of the store."

I was going to say that, but since she preempted me, I had to quickly think of something else—something that would make her feel special and keep the conversation going. So at that point, I said with a smile, "Of course, rules are made to be broken. If you are parked within the first three parking spots, I will bend them for you."

She smiled and said, "Well, thank you. I feel kinda special now."

"That's our intention here: to make every customer feel special in his or her own special way," I replied with a grin.

"That's why I like coming here. You guys are the best. Certainly better than your competition. They don't even walk you to the door after a sale," she replied. Then she quickly added, "I just hope you won't be mad at me in the end. I know that I am parked pretty close to the front of the store, but I can't say for sure if it's in one of the first three spots."

"Oh, don't worry. I will use this as an opportunity to go and gather carts from the parking lot," I said in a reassuring voice.

A few moments later, we were at the checkout register with her unevenly stacked, overflowing shopping cart—one to which I had contributed very little. All I had added to the mess were the three medium bags of Miracle-Gro soil she had asked me to put there. I had done so reluctantly. It was her cart, and I was not being paid to make a customer's shopping cart look good.

However, if I had been the one putting things in it from the start, it would not have looked that bad. Although she was in a home improvement store, her cart looked like shit. It reminded me of the women I saw in the commissary walking around with their bread at the bottom of or stuffed in a corner of their carts. One shouldn't brag, but I must say, I am praised whenever I get to any checkout register (especially in the commissary) with my shopping cart.

Anyhow, the lady paid for her stuff, and we walked outside. She walked slightly ahead of me. After about three steps into the lot, she stopped on a dime and turned toward me with a panicked look on her face. The sudden change in her demeanor caught me off guard.

"I don't remember where I parked my car," she said.

The first thing that came to my mind was a word that I don't usually call women but have thought many times. So to be honest, I instantly thought, *What, bitch? A few moments ago, you were dead certain that you had parked close to the front of the store, just not in the first three rows. Now you can't remember where you are parked?*

"Is this the first or second entrance?" she asked while I was processing my thoughts.

"Well there are three entrances," I said.

"Three!" she quoted.

"Yes! It all depends on where you start your count from," I told her. Then I added, "This is the garden center entrance. The main entrance is in the middle of the store over there, and further down is the lumber center entrance."

"Well, I know I did not come in through that one—at least I don't believe I did. So it must be one of these two," she said pointing.

Seconds thereafter, she began to scan the side of the parking lot adjacent to us, and before too long, I heard her say, "I see my car. I'm a lot farther away than I thought."

She could not have been more correct about being farther away than she had thought. I followed her in the direction of her supposed car. However, the closer we got to the end of that side of the parking lot, the more her direction changed. Plus, she was moving in between cars so fast I could hardly keep up.

Before too long, we were traveling through the portion of the parking lot adjacent to the front of the store. A few minutes later, we had visited just about all of the cars on that portion of the parking lot to no avail and, if I may add, with no slowing of her stride.

When we traveled over to the lumber center's side of the parking lot, I shouted out to her, "Are you sure we are on the right side?"

She ran back toward me and said, "I don't know. I think so." Then she added, "Please don't be mad at me. I just don't remember which side I came in on. I am about to move and stopped by to pick up a few things for my new place. I parked my car and ran inside."

"That's okay. If your car is out here, we'll find it," I said to her.

"I hope so. I already paid for all this stuff. I need something to put it in so that I can take it home," she said before taking off again.

Within the next ten to fifteen minutes, we went on to crisscross the entire parking lot three times and were on our fourth time when two things clicked in my mind. They weren't the things that should have clicked in my dumb-ass mind. I thought, *Since you are moving, do you have stuff in your vehicle right now? Even better yet, what color is your vehicle?*

Answers to those questions could have narrowed down our search, not to mention stopping us from looking stupid as we zigzagged the parking lot like nincompoops. My mind tagged her statement, "I hope so. I already paid for all this stuff. I need something to put it in, so that I can take it home."

I started to wonder if she really had a vehicle. Was she just being friendly and nice to me in the store so that she could come outside and play the my-car-just-got-stolen trick on me. Then I would sympathize with her and give her a ride home. Then I would become the next missing person because out of niceness, I got chained up in someone's basement. Moreover, for all I knew at that moment, she could have been playing a trick like the guy who had jacked me in a Walmart parking lot a few weeks earlier for two dollars.

Even though it wasn't a lot of money and he did not literally pulled a gun on me, he walked up to me while talking on his cell phone and asked me for two dollars. He wanted the money because his car had supposedly run out of gas in the parking lot, and he had no way of getting back home. He said that he had lived across the waters. In Virginia, this meant under or through one of the tunnels that led to the other side where a person could put his or her feet on dry land once again.

I gave him the two dollars without a thought, and he walked over to a red two-door car that was parked near my car. However, by the time I drove off, he had left his car and was nagging someone else with the same sappy-assed story I had fallen for. I supposed that two dollars hadn't been enough money to put gas in his vehicle, which should have been able to use any mount of gas to get it going.

What really stuck in my craw was that a few days later, we were discussing generosity in one of my classes, when I mentioned the Walmart parking lot guy to one of my classmates. To both our amazements, she said that a few days earlier, the same guy had approached her in a nearby Kmart parking lot with the same story. She had handed him money to put gas in his car. It must have been only enough to get him from the Kmart to the Walmart parking lot about half a mile up the street.

Still, I don't want to stray too far from the lost-lady story. However, I have to mention this: Ironically, a few weeks later and in the same Walmart parking lot at around 1:30 p.m., a red beat-up, four-door vehicle pulled up in the parking space beside my vehicle as I was getting into it. The lady driver and her female passenger jumped out in a hurry, and while the driver was unbuckling a little baby boy from his seat, the female passenger ran up to my door.

"Sorry to bother you, but my friend and I just got back from the emergency room with her son, and we are out of gas. Would you happen to have any spare change you can give us?" she said.

Now, this could have been another sappy-assed story, or worse yet, the baby could have been used as a sympathy ploy. In whichever case, I would have donated like I usually do when I have change and people on the street ask me. Yes, I give at times, and if they use it for a reason other than the one they tell me, I leave that up to them and God. Unfortunately, on this particular occasion, I did not have any change. I had paid for my things with my debit card but had used it as a credit card because people had been warning me to start doing so. They have said that it's the best way to keep your pin number secure from would-be crooks.

I did not get any cash back from my transaction, and that was what I explained to the ladies. I never thought about offering to take them over to the Walmart gas station and fill up their tank for them. So I felt bad as I drove away without offering to help them, whether their plea for help had been genuine or not. I feel even worse now, when I think back on how one of the ladies held up the dirty little boy for me to see, as if to say, "See, we are not lying." We eventually found her blue, two-door car in the shade of one of the trees and on the side of the parking lot she was certain she had not entered the store from. Coincidentally, we had walked past it several times. Although, I must admit, I don't think either of us had paid much attention to the spot where it had been sitting.

Upon recognizing her car, she issued what must have been the understatement of the year and could very well be in the top ten for the current decade. "I am using my car to help with my move and don't think there is any room in the back, so you will have to put the things in the front seat," she said without hesitation.

Her car was so packed, some of the items in her shopping cart jumped out and tried to run back into the store. If she drove with her windows closed, she would not have room in her vehicle for five minutes of life-sustaining air inside of it. Still, she begged me to put the things in the car for her and not to leave before doing so. Then she squeezed herself into the driver's seat and said, "Put it wherever you can."

Luckily for her, the good Lord was granting nincompoops with cramped car miracles that day, otherwise, she would have been SOL! But her miracle enabled me to get the items she had purchased into the vehicle. As equally or even more dangerous was the fact that she had little to no vision out the passenger's side window. Good motorists knows how important being able to see that blind spot can be. At least the windows (well, on the driver's side) could be rolled down to let some air inside to sustain life beyond the parking lot. She couldn't roll any windows on the passenger's side down without losing some of her possessions.

When she drove off, I thought about her four biggest worries. The first wasn't really a problem. She didn't have a stick shift, so all she had to do was put it in drive. Still, she was going to have a hard time moving even that stick in any position.

Secondly, her best bet was to hope it did not start raining between leaving the store and getting home. If she had to close the windows, she was going to die before she made it home.

Thirdly, and what should be her biggest concern of all was her inability to see any of her mirrors, except the one on her left side and her rearview mirror. In fact, her vision out the front windshield was hardly bigger than a nineteen-inch television. I could say with 95 percent accuracy that a twenty-five-inch screen would have pretty much blocked her view.

Finally, she needed to try to avoid the smallest pebble on the road because if she ran over a single one, the trunk of her car was going to pop open. The part of her miracle that enabled me to get the three medium bags of Miracle-Gro into it did not leave any room for even the slightest impact. One could actually hear the trunk cracking to unhook before she even drove off.

The only fortunate thing for her was that she wouldn't have to worry about an open trunk blocking her rearview mirror. The forty eleventeen pieces of items she had inside it had already taken care of that for her. However, if it came undone, she would have to worry about it blowing off and worse, causing an injury or accident.

Other than those, I have not thought or worried about her since then. I just chalked her up to another lost nincompoop (which I can sometimes be myself) who had entered my life for a very brief moment and then had left me with something I could take away from the encounter. Still, I was so hot after she had driven off, I went back inside without taking in a single cart, even though it had been for that reason I had said I would follow her out to her car, beyond where I usually go.

For all that effort I had exerted to get the things into her car, she had driven off without even offering me a tip or better yet, a thank-you. She had driven off like she had been upset about being lost and without the common decency of a thank-you.

CHAPTER 12

THE TEARS IN
HER EYES

ONE WEDNESDAY MORNING a few weeks after July 4th at around 8:50 a.m., a lady walked through the garden center door pushing a shopping cart she had picked up on the nearby curve. She was about five foot, five inches and looked like she was in their mid-fifties to early sixties, give or take a few years. Her silvery-blondish hair was up in a bun, and she was dressed like someone in the medical industry—more like a nurse's aide—and was wearing comfortable-looking, off-white sneakers. Of course, I didn't know for sure what her professional status was, but it had to be medical because my mother had been in it for the better part of thirty plus years. She usually dressed exactly the way this lady was dressed.

I could also tell that her silvery-blondish hair was long by the size of her bun and the loose strands hanging down by her right ear. However, it was hard to say if those strands were there through her deliberate action or from a difficult time at work. At that moment, I wasn't yet sure if she was coming or going to work. Whichever was the case, she tried to place the strands behind her ear a few times while walking into the store and during our conversation. Like a female tennis player on the court, a second later, her hair would come undone spontaneously. Then she would lift her right hand to put it temporarily back into place.

I said good morning to her as she approached the doorway, and she promptly responded in kind with the glimpse of a warm smile. Due to that, I thought about asking her right there and then, if I could help her, but I decided against it, which was against company rules. Although she was within the ten-foot rule for such a question, she had barely entered the store, and I believed she needed some time to look around, even though that is not what the ten-foot rule dictated and I could get written up for breaking it.

About two minutes after the lady had gone inside, I made amends when two gentleman in blue work clothes stepped out of a white van labeled "JohnMend Lawn & Garden Services" and started their approach for the same garden center entrance. I said good morning to them when they were within the ten-foot radius. In fact, the one on the right almost beat me to it. He had already extended his greeting of "Hi" when I cut him off with, "Good morning. How are you guys today?"

After a few steps in unison, both responded in kind. Then the one on the right asked for directions to the additional mulch, weed suppression liners, larva rocks, and large cement blocks. Before I answered them, I thought, *Guys who are shopping know exactly what they want, which makes for an in and out shopping experience.*

"The additional mulch is in the back of the garden center to the left, the lava rocks are on aisle two toward the back, the weed suppression sheets are on the right side of aisle five, and the large cement blocks are on the far side of the store next to the lumber section," I said to them.

After a short strategy discussion between them, the one on the left asked if they could pay at any register, and my answer to them was, "Yes. Yes, you can."

"Thank you," they both said and proceeded ahead into the store.

I followed them into the store with a two-tiered green cart a departing customer had dropped off at the door after taking the two hanging plants she had purchased at the register. I had not made ten strides into the store when I heard the resource manager saying what sounded like my name over the intercom. However, I did not respond because I was not sure if it was my name or someone else's. Several people who worked at the store had names similar to mine.

I think my hearing was going too because I always got confused whenever similar names were announced over the intercom. Furthermore, I realize that lately, people have had to repeat things to me before I catch the full extent of what they are saying, especially if they are far away.

Anyhow, like I said, I paid the announcement no mind on account of two reasons. One, I wasn't sure if she had said my name. Two, I was quite interested in seeing her because she had become an ugly person to me lately in terms of attitude.

Since her attitude had changed toward me, I decided to play the ignorant card. If this had occurred right after I had started my employment there, I would have rushed to see what she wanted without a thought. She had been so much nicer to me then, plus she was a gardening addict like I was (She was a bigger addict to be exact). She had always given me pointers on what and what not to do or on how to grow the best-looking plants. She was a dynamite looking little woman for her age and had the prettiest toes I had even seen.

Now things were different between us, and I didn't know why. To be honest, it really didn't bother me, except that she would play a role in my future employment with the organization. I must admit that that part had me on pins and needles and made me a little nervous to see her because it getting near cutting time according to the store manager.

However, with the intercom announcement pushed to the back of my mind, I went in search of someone to help or for something to do. Usually this early in the morning and on a weekday, my greatest responsibilities were helping customers and the head nursery lady with the British accent. I was pretty sure it was not from Great Britain based on what I had gathered. I was told she had been born and bred in New Orleans. Regardless of this, she sure sounded awfully like a Londoner and was a royal pain in my ass.

I am not the only one who disliked her. The guy who took me under his wing for training purposes (recently fired due to faults of his own), the retired navy lady (also recently fired on account of the nursery lady), and the lesbian chick (who constantly told me that she did not think the nursery lady liked her even though she was a good worker, which was absolutely true) didn't like her either.

I mentioned a while ago, that the resource manager had raved about the lesbian to me when I had been going through the initial employment training, even though I had no idea who she had been talking about at the time. Still, from all the raving heaped on her by the resource manager, I had been impressed long before I had even met the young lady.

The first time I met her, I came away with two conclusions. One, she had good work ethics, meaning the resource manager hadn't just been blowing smoke up my ass. Two, this lady had to be a lesbian or at least bisexual. There was no way on earth she was straight.

The first time we met, followed by the first couple of conversations we had, I must admit, I thought I might have been wrong about her sexual preference. That was before she revealed the problem she was having with her partner to me. She said "partner" and not "boyfriend." Before she told me what type of relationship she was in, I had already confirmed my earlier suspicion. When a man or a woman uses the word "partner" in or during a conversation, he or she is 99 and 44/100 percent talking about a person of the same sex that he or she is in a relationship with.

Anyhow, as for my strong dislike of the nursery lady that I expressed earlier, I really meant it. I think she came off as a prick 90 percent of the time. She genuinely acted like someone who was sleeping her way to the top, except in her case, the totem pole was not very high. Her standing was only second in line for the head of the garden center management—the lawn and garden manager. The garden center manger wasn't going anywhere because he had been there since Moses had been a child, and now Moses was a grey old man. The only position this guy had been promoted to since being hired was lawn and garden manager.

The two were close, however, and most times she acted like she was the one inside of his pants or who picked out the pants he wore in the mornings. But then again, she probably acted that way because she had the store manger's ear when it came to plants. I don't think she was in his ear constantly for any other reason or plan than riding him to get somewhere. It would take someone really desperate to sleep with him. He absolutely looked like Nemo's father. In fact, if it wasn't for the fins and the tail, Nemo's daddy would present a better portrait than the store manager.

To digress, I worked my way to the far corner of the store, to what I liked to call the Mulch-R-Us section. I did so by means of aisle five and traveling by the outer reaches of the store along the end of aisles four, three, two, and one. I then crossed to the far right of reduced plants and other damaged items and into the corner where the mulch aisle formed its L shape. It was a long and unusual route, but there was a reason for it.

Even though I cannot actually say with a straight face that I was looking for the guys in blue I had directed to that area earlier, it could be used as an excuse. In reality, I knew I had not seen them anywhere on my side of the store, which led me to believe they had gone on the other side to check on the large cement blocks they had inquired about. So with no one in sight for me to help, I started to look for damaged products I could re-bag and mark down at a sale price.

After re-bagging two bags of red mulch, I marked them down from three dollars and fifty cents to one dollar and seventy-five cents and put them on a flatbed cart nearby. I then walked three storage blocks down on my left to where the Canadian mulch was stored because I knew that those bags usually burst easily. Sure enough, four busted bags were waiting on me to do my thing, so I started to do my thing—discount damaged items for customers' satisfaction.

Between bagging the second bag and starting on the third, I looked behind me. Coming down the lane was the lady dressed like a nurse's aide. She was slowly pushing her shopping cart and looking this way and that as if she was comparing prices. When I saw her, I stopped working and waited in anticipation for her to get closer to me—somewhere within the ten-meter radius or so. The moment she was within the prescribed radius or thereabout, I said, "Good morning again. You look like you're a bit confused."

"Good morning," she replied as she drew closer. "Do I?"

"Just a little," I said. Then I asked, "May I help you with something?"

"Well, I don't know what I am looking for," she said with a slight grin.

"That's not good," I replied with a smile.

"I know," she said.

"First, I need to make you aware that you are in the rattlesnake territory," I said with a wry grin.

"Ah!" she exclaimed with a subtle look.

"Just kidding," I quickly responded. "I assume you are looking for mulch since you are in this area."

"I am, but I don't know what I should get," she responded.

"Well, give me an idea, and I will help you get to your destination," I told her.

"I wish I knew where to start," she said with a smile.

"Okay," I responded. "How about we put our heads together and come up with a solution?"

"Great. Let's try that," she said with a smile.

"Okay. First of all, my name is John, but some people call me "*JEL*" which is my initials or short -- which I wish more did. Welcome to the garden center," I said with outstretched arms.

"Hi, JEL. My name is Gloria," she responded.

"Hi Gloria, may I be of some assistance to you?" I asked with a smile.

"JEL, I certainly hope so. I am here looking for mulch but don't know where to begin," Gloria stated.

"Gloria, you've come to the right place, and to make it even better, you're in the right section," I said in return.

"So this is a good start, eh?" Gloria said.

"Absolutely!" I exclaimed with a smile of my own.

"You seem like a person who knows his stuff," Gloria stated.

"Not really, but hopefully soon, I will have all facets of this place down pat. But until then, there are many others around here who know more and that I rely on. Still, I am willing to part ways with the little I've learned the past three months," I said to her.

"Thank you. That is more than I probably know ... for sure," Gloria said.

"Tell me, Gloria, do you know what brand or color of mulch you are looking for?" I asked Gloria.

"Not so much the brand. Probably anything that's not too expensive or reddish," Gloria stated with a smile. Then she added, "Not too cheap where it fades two weeks into the summer."

"Not too expensive. Well, we have some of those, and they are guaranteed to hold their color for a year, just like the more expensive brands," I stated.

"That sounds good," Gloria said.

"But unlike our plants, they do not come with a one-year money-back guarantee," I stated with a smile.

"I didn't know that. Your plants have a one-year money-back guarantee?" Gloria curiously inquired.

"Yes, they do. If you buy a plant from us and it dies within one year of purchase, you can bring it back with your proof of purchase, and we will refund your money," I explained.

"Wow! That's nice," Gloria said.

"It is. The customers seem to like it," I suggested. Then I jokingly added, "We are not the best in that department though. I once heard of another store who took back a dead Christmas tree well into the following year."

"Wow," she responded. Then she curiously asked, "What if I cannot find my receipt?"

"Good question. You're still not totally out of luck. If you paid with a credit or debit card, all you have to do is give us the card number, and we can look up your information in the system," I informed her.

"Well, that's very nice to know. Although, I doubt I'll be in need of purchasing any plants soon. If that ever changes, I'll certainly come here first," Gloria replied.

"Certainly. Just keep us at the top of your list unless you intend to return your Christmas tree in the middle of June. Other than that, our money-back guarantee covers plants, flowers, shrubs—anything perennial," I further informed her.

"Thanks. You seem to know more than you first suggested," she exclaimed.

"Well, I have retained a little of what my coworkers have explained to me three or four times," I said with a smile.

She took it with a smile as well and nonchalantly looked down at her watch, which indirectly suggested to me that she was in a hurry. So I quickly changed the subject back to her mulch search by saying, "Unfortunately, there is no such guarantee for mulch. If you lay some down today, and it rains tomorrow and washes it all away, you must replace it at your own expense. Let me show you what we have in terms of mulch that really holds its color and is kind of heavy too."

"Not too heavy," Gloria said quickly. "I have quite a few trees to do and don't have help."

"Your husband is not of the gardening variety?" I asked.

"I used to be able to depend on him for all of the yard work, but he hasn't been outside in the past three years," she replied.

Let's be honest, when the last part of her comment crossed my mind, my first thought was, *Holy shit! I might be talking to a killer here. This grandmotherly, innocent-looking, gardening lady, who is here to by mulch and is dressed like a nurse's aide to boot is the last one anyone would suspect of a heinous crime.*

When I coupled this with the fact that an individual had already come to buy mulch so that he could bury his dead cat, I was even more convinced that she had done something bad to her husband. Still, I never let the expression inside me show its true feelings on my face. I just echoed, "Three years," in a somewhat surprised tone.

"Yes! He has been wheelchair-bound for the past three years, and it has taken its toll on me," Gloria explained and instantly choked up.

The sight of tears in her eyes sent me to a different world immediately. I went from thinking of her as a husband killer, to feeling sorry for her husband, to empathy for her, all within a few seconds. I spontaneously gave the woman, whom I did not know from Eve and whose name I had just learned ten minutes earlier, a huge hug.

Without hesitation, Gloria reached out in return, and we embraced for about fifteen seconds. There was one scruffy-looking black man and one middle-aged white woman hugging in one of the far corners of the home improvement store like they were best friends or lovers who were happy to see each other. In some kind of weird way, it reminded me of the song *"Just Walk on By"* by Jim Reeves.

A few seconds before the hug ended, I whispered in her ear, "Everything is going to be all right." I did not know that or the extent of her circumstances, but I did know that she was in pain and needed some reassurance, so I said it.

"Thanks. I needed that," Gloria said.

"You're welcome," I replied. "Let me help you so you won't be late for work."

"I just got off, actually," she said.

"Well, go home and get some sleep and come back later," I said to her.

"I would love to, but it's not possible right now. I work at night and tend to my husband during the day, so it's either now or no other time during the day," Gloria said.

"So when do you sleep?" I asked.

"Here and there," she said. "The last three years have been hard--very hard. I've had less money, less sleep, and less time for me. If it wasn't for my little job, I don't know how we would make it. The little that my husband gets from social security is not enough for us to get by on, and I have more than a handful of years to go before I am qualified myself."

Gloria choked up again, and it made my eyes water as well. So I had to step away from her to avoid showing it. I guess she thought I was moving just to move, so upon pulling a tissue from her handbag, she wiped the tears from her eyes and pushed her cart to follow me.

I immediately had to devise a plan to dry my own eyes without alerting her, so I quickly turned to my left, which was away from her, and bent over to straighten a stack of garden soil. It provided a good cover because in the motion of bending down, I was able to slide my left shirt sleeve across my eyes. That action took away most of the built-up tears in my eyes and allowed me to gather my emotions for my next question.

"Do you have any kids?" I asked.

"I have two, but they are all grown up. They hardly ever come around though. They are usually busy with their own families," she replied.

"How old are they?" I asked while standing back up.

"They are both in their thirties, but I hardly ever see them and see even less of my grandkids," Gloria candidly replied.

"Wow! That's not cool," I uttered, even though I was aching to ask if she and her kids had a falling-out. I never really ask what happened, but later in the conversation, something was revealed to me, which allowed me to develop my own theory.

Up to that point though, we had not discussed much more about the mulch she had come to purchase or any of the additional items I had been trained to entice customers like her into purchasing and did think it would happen anytime soon. After a few more steps, she said something revealing to me, which later became my theory of why her kids had abandoned her.

Gloria was forthright with her next statement, and it came out of her like she was a woman who had something she was aching to share. She let it fly unfiltered.

"I wish I had stayed with my first husband," Gloria said out of the blue.

"Come again," I instantly said.

"When I think about what I am doing now and all the things I have gone through, I wish I had stayed with my first husband. We were only together for eleven years before we got divorced," she said.

When she said, "only," I really and truly believed she had regrets pent up inside. So at that moment, I asked Gloria, "Where is he now?"

"He passed away a few years back. He was only forty-eight," she sadly stated.

"So sorry to hear that," I said.

"I probably helped drive him to his heart attack," Gloria said.

"How do you figure?" I asked. "They can happen anytime and to anyone. You just never know."

"I don't think he ever quite forgave me for leaving him to go to my current husband," I heard Gloria say before my mind interrupted my concentration on her explanation and sent me wandering and developing my own theory of the transaction between the kids and her.

Somehow, I don't think your kids have forgiven you either, popped into my mind and temporarily blocked the sound of Gloria's voice. To this day, I cannot say with any certainty, how many of her next words I missed, but when I was able to focus back on her speaking, I heard these words coming out of her mouth, "We got married young; right out of high school. Then I took a job as a secretary. I worked at it for two years before spending the next ten as my boss's secretary and … his lover."

I don't know what I was expecting, but I certainly had not expected to hear those words from her. They absolutely threw me for a loop. Then to add insult to the injury, while I was standing there processing my thoughts, I heard Gloria say, "I guess you are wondering if I cheated on my first husband, eh?"

"To be honest, Gloria, my mind is processing that right now, based on your timeline of marriage, staying faithful, cheating, and divorce that you just laid out for me," I replied.

"I did," she said openly. "He offered me more at the time than my husband could, and we've been married for twenty-nine years now … but it hasn't been easy or good. I have put up with more crap from him in our first ten years than I would have in a lifetime with my first husband.

As I stood there speechless and amazed at how easily this lady let her life's secrets loose to a practical stranger, Gloria carried on unfiltered and un-coached. "I lived through his infidelities, mental and emotional abuses, lies, cover-ups, and a whole slew of other things. I am still by his side taking care of him."

At that point, I wanted to ask if she had seen the movie *The Diary of a Mad Black Woman* by Tyler Perry, but I swallowed those words and instead begged the question, "I guess the grass is not always greener on the other side, is it?"

"Not always. But a good painter knows how to brush the strokes to make the beginning of the forest look green without revealing what's inside of it, especially when there's nothing growing there," Gloria said with a touch of sadness.

"I guess sometimes we mistakenly take the trees for the forest, eh?" I asked.

"Exactly!" she said in agreement.

"So who takes care of your husband while you're at work?" I asked as we stopped by the area where the Scotts Nature Scapes red mulch was stacked.

"No one, really," she replied. "He is pretty much drugged up and in bed sleeping before I leave for work each night. By the time he's up and ready to be moved around in the morning, I'm already home."

"Wow!" I echoed instantly. Then I suggested in an inquiring manner, "That's living by your skinny, skin, skin … isn't it?"

"In a way it is, but what else can I do? I don't get any help from anyone else," Gloria stated. Then she quickly added, "My boss pretty much knows what's going on and has given me the okay to leave if the need ever arises."

"How about your neighbors, can't they look in on your husband for you?" I curiously asked.

"Our closest neighbors live about a block away. Other than in church on Sundays, I really don't see much of them," she informed me.

"That's not very neighborly!" I said.

"Well, everyone is busy in their own little world these days," she suggested.

"Yes, but that shouldn't stop people from being neighborly," I replied. Then I asked out of curiosity, "Where do you live?"

"I live in Smithfield," she replied. Then she asked, "Do you know where it is?"

"No, I don't, but one of my coworkers, whom I don't like, is from Smithfield.

"Why do you dislike him?" she questioned.

"He gets on my last nerve and twists every fiber in my body," I said.

"Wow!" she said.

At that point, I continued on, "He's the only eighteen-year-old person I ever met with a major receding hair line. Moreover, he's only been here three weeks longer than I have, yet he acts like he's my immediate supervisor. He makes these condescending comments, such as, "You served longer in the military than I've been alive. Now you're in college, and I just graduated from high school, and we both work at the same place … but I'm sure you know a whole lot more than I do and have been to a lot more places than I have."

"Wow! I hope you do not feel that way about everyone from Smithfield," Gloria said with a forced smile.

"Not at all," I quickly responded with a smile. Then I just as quickly asked, "How many trees do you have to lay mulch around?"

"Quite a few," she quickly said.

"How many is quite a few?" I asked.

"Well, our whole backyard is covered with trees, but I am only going to do the ones my husband used to mulch, which is still quite a few," she explained.

"Would you like some help?" I asked.

I guess my offer caught her off guard, and she stopped in her tracks and closed her eyes ever so briefly. So I immediately thought I had offended her. However, when she reopened them, they were filled with tears. She choked up as she said, "Thank you. That's the best gesture anyone has made to me in a long while."

"You are welcome," I said.

"Not even a member of my church has offered a helping hand, even though many of them are aware of the struggles I've been dealing with the last few years," Gloria stated with a very sad and disappointing tone.

I have to admit, it broke my heart to hear what she said about her congregation, and it made me silently wonder, *How many lost souls does she attend church with? That is not the example that Jesus set. Who are they preaching to and whose lead are they following?*

I said nothing to criticize the congregation in front of her. I just moved in and gave her a big comforting embrace—one she wholeheartedly opened up her arms to receive and clutched me like I was a long lost friend. While standing there embracing her, I thought, *This is some of what she needs from her shallow-hearted congregation. How can fellow members of your church congregation be suffering like this and you don't see it as a sign to help? Worst of all, how can you be aware of the suffering of others and just turn a blind eye toward those individuals? Have they ever thought about what Jesus would do in this situation?*

It is absolutely amazing to me, in the most negative way, how people can willingly and without regret turn their backs on their families, friends, fellow neighbors, strangers, or in this case a fellow church member in need. Still, other than my hug of sympathy, I did not say anything aloud because I've learned over the years that most stories have two sides to them.

This was not to say, I did not believe in her. I did because of how genuine she seemed. However, I've been fooled before. If it happened there, it would not have been the first time and most likely wouldn't be the last either. I know of a situation right now where I'm being played for a fool, but that's a story for another time and place when I'm satisfied it has been completed.

So let's get back to Gloria. After my genuine and sympathetic embrace ended, I offered her my phone number. At first, she must have thought that it was something fake by the expression on her face. She reacted the same way most people so when they ask for my phone number.

When I start off with my 860 area code, they somehow always put 757 down and look at me strangely or tell me that I have given them too many digits. They act as if now that I'm residing in this area of the country, I can't have a phone number with a different area code. She did as well. However, I immediately put her shadow of a doubt to rest by telling her it was a Connecticut area code. I also told her that she could call it while we were standing there so she could see that it actually worked. However, she passed on that idea.

I took that as an indication she did not feel secure about giving out her number. Therefore, to further put her mind at ease, I did not ask for hers in return. I just told her that if she ever really needed my help, she could call and leave me a message. If she did, and I did not answer the phone, she had to say who she was (like the mulch-buying lady from Smithfield) because I would not answer unknown numbers.

Gloria agreed to my high demands, and we walked over to the damaged products area. There, the conversation turned toward me, beginning with why I had a Connecticut phone number but was living in Virginia.

At first, I jokingly said to her, "At least I'm not living in West Virginia. I don't think they get any kind of reception in that state. The last time I drove through Morgan Town, people were standing on top of the highest peaks they could find, trying to pick up reception for their TV rabbit ears."

My attempt at a joke struck a chord with her, and she began to laugh. From there, I went on to give her a brief overview of my situation. I told her about how I had been in the military stationed at Langley for the last handful of years. I shared that I had recently retired and that I was going to school on the 9/11 GI Bill. I was trying to figure out if I still wanted to work or stay home and work on my writing addiction, which had brought me limited (very limited and in the red) success with hopes of making it one day. I was disappointed that I had to share the money with a wife who didn't deserve a dime more than what it took to raise two kids and so on and so forth.

It seems people can always sympathize with me during that part, especially if they knew how a person could be married yet desperately lack or miss the feelings of everyday human interaction at home. I also realized that each time someone mentioned going to school on the GI Bill, he or she was always congratulated or told, "Good for you." This comes out of the respect. That program has been good for America and Americans. It is something people can easily associate with because many have had direct contact with it or know someone who has benefited mightily from it—one of the best social safety net programs the government has ever instituted.

It also comes from knowing that in today's world of a do-nothing congress, it is one of the best and greatest legislations ever passed when we had a functioning three-body group of governmental servants for the people. A lot of the credit should be given to Virginia's Senator Jim Webb for working the new 9/11 GI Bill into a law so that members like me, who did not take advantage of the old version for one reason or another, could still afford to go to school after their military career ended.

There was a turning point in the conversation about me, which happened shortly after I had explained that I was working part-time to help foot my bills while waiting on the Veteran Administration to process my disability compensation payments. This reversed the trend of the conversation.

"Why have you stuck with your second husband after he put you through so much hardship?" I asked.

"Because I had two teenage kids and did not want to make the same mistake twice," she replied.

"Well, it wouldn't be a mistake if you actually went back to your first husband," I said.

A pause ensued, and during it, I nonchalantly asked, "He would have taken you back, wouldn't he?"

After a few more seconds of silence on her part, she finally said, "You can't really make up the lost time after hurting someone. You can only forgive and move on. together or alone. In our case, we went in separate directions. He never actually forgave me, but who could have blamed him. For the majority of our marriage, I cheated on him, even after our kids had been born."

On that note, I thought, *Who is the real father of her kids?* However, I did not say anything or change the expression on my face. I stood there and listened to the rest of her story to get the full context, and she was happy to oblige me.

"All those hours I had to worked late and all those work trips and meetings I had to attend out of town, were all a cover for my infidelities. Most of the time, we didn't even leave town. We were in the office, in one of our cars parked somewhere, or locked away in some shanty motel room on the outskirts of town or in the next town over. Other than the few extra dollars that would get shoved in my pocket as if I was a damn prostitute, my actual paycheck never got any bigger," she said as her voice cracked.

"Wow! You must have been a firecracker in your younger days," I said with a smile. Then I quickly added, "Not that I'm saying you don't look good for your age now, even though you haven't told me how old you are. I assume you are you are over fifty."

"No, it not ladylike for a woman to tell her age," she said with a smile. Then she added, "I will give you this bit of advice though, if a man and a woman are together, it is not hard to pick out the one who is cheating or trying to end the relationship."

"How do you do this? I asked.

"Sonny, John right?" she asked with a sly grin and a nod.

"Yes, but you can call me anything if you school me one-on-one about a cheater's telltale signs," I glowingly replied.

"Sure," she said. Then she added, "Take this from someone who has lived and experienced it. Once someone starts working later at a normal job, that's a sure sign of cheating. When a person starts coming up with excuses not to do the things he or she usually did before, that's a sign of cheating because someone else is now filling your space in that area. Once a person starts coming up with …"

At that point, Gloria paused for a moment to look me over as if she wanted to add something but did not quite know how to put it. I was not quite sure of what it was, so I egged her on, and she continued after a few apologetic words.

"I'm not a racist or anything, and I don't want to offend you or your people, so I'm going to say this in the most upscale version I can rather than how my folks used to say it. Once your significant other starts coming up with more excuses than a negro going to jail, then you can bet the house, something is going on."

"Wow," I said somewhat shocked. Then I immediately added, "I didn't know that."

I honestly couldn't say if that was the reaction Gloria expected out of me, but we both stood there in silence for a brief moment until I set her mind at ease. I told her that she was the second person in the last six years that I'd heard use that term. The first time I had heard it, the real term had been expressed and it hadn't been from someone I had expected would say it, even though blacks are the ones who mostly use these words. I mentioned this in my 2005 book, *The Bathroom Comedian*. Moreover, the place and setting where I had heard it had been the least likely place in the United States or associated with the United States government I had thought would use it.

It was between two black United States army captains in Germany. I was an air force noncommissioned officer in a non-recognized joint army/air force unit. My black company commander told my black captain boss that he came up with more excuses than a "nigga going to jail."

Long before then, as I have said in *The Bathroom Comedian*, those words will always be very disparaging to me. But as disparaging as I think the words are and were, it was the funniest thing I heard that day ... and it was true. When my captain boss didn't want to do or participate in something or to break a promise he had previously made, he was like my wife when it comes to sex: He would find every reason under the sun why he should be counted out or could not do it.

After explaining that to her, I said, "Really?" in a curious way to get her going again,

Gloria continued on. "No doubt," she said. Then she let me in on three more clues, but one is little too sexually explicit in nature, so I'll keep that one a secret. She said, "When two people are apart, such as on a business trip or not living together, and one is constantly going to sleep soon after the workday is done or returning phone calls at one, two, or even three o'clock in morning when they supposedly suddenly awoke from their sleep, that's a sure sign of cheating. I played it with my first husband, and I lived it religiously with this bastard I'm killing myself to take care of right now."

She then paused before using her pointer finger to count off another number before continuing on. "And if your other half says he or she is going through a lot of personal problems right now and does not want to include you while supposedly working through them, then that's another sign something else is going on."

"Yeah? Like what? I said.

"Well, they are either cheating on you or have found someone else that they would like to replace you with. We—I say we because it came up in my first marriage—use personal problems to slowly and peacefully ween ourselves from the person we are with so the ending will look more mutual than one-sided. They will even say and do little things now and then to help you keep that false sense of hope while they've completely detached themselves from you. It's a mind game. We women have become experts at it."

"So you're saying I shouldn't believe the hype, eh?" I asked.

"No, John, not for one minute," Gloria replied. Then she paused and added, "If you are married, you can seek counseling to try and work things out, but normally once the damage is done, it's very hard to put the pieces back together again."

"So you're saying it's not even worth trying then?" I asked.

"Of course. Everything is worth a shot. But here is where the difference between men and women really shows up," Gloria said.

"Why is that?" I asked

"Well, when a man cheats on a woman, he expects the woman to take him back no matter what. But when a woman cheats on a man, he considers it a violation of his property and doesn't want to forgive the woman or take her back," she stated.

"Wow!" I said.

"Yes. Problems in relationships can still be worked out. but mostly in marriages though, to try and save them. But when you're single and dating, now that's a whole different story. Once you've seen the signs, and they are starting to mount, it's time to cut your losses and run because you've become the third wheel," Gloria said, "whether you want to admit it or not."

"And things will only be said and done to appease you, eh? I immediately said.

"Yep! You're catching on," she quickly said. Then she added, "It's only a matter of time before you get left behind wondering how you could have been so blind or asking yourself what did you do wrong. For the most part, if any you get any answers at all after it's over, they will be about things that didn't matter when you guys first got together but have now become a problem. If you look back, you will see that they only became a problem when your replacement entered the picture."

"Wow. I did not know all that ... well, I probably did but never really paid it much attention," I said.

"We will lie. Believe me, especially women will. I'm one of them. We will cry bloody murder, say you're crazy for thinking or saying the things you are saying even though we know it's true. We will tell you, you are just making up things, being paranoid over nothing, and even ask you what kind of a girl you think we are," Gloria said. Then she laughed and added, "I even remember way back in the day, one of my cousins used one of her sister's kids to slowly wind down a relationship she had going with a guy when she found a replacement for him."

"Yeah," I said. Then I curiously asked, "How is that?"

"Well, months after things took off with the new guy, she told the old guy over the phone that the reason she stopped hanging out with him was because she did not want her kids to see her living that way. Of course, she didn't have any kids. She was just using her sister's kids," Gloria said after a short pause.

"Ah, something else I can be on the lookout for," I said with a smile.

"You certainly can, especially if this is something the woman decides on her own and never bothers to discuss it with you or mention it to you until months after the fact. When you are in a meaningful relationship, you and your partner discuss everything that may impact that relationship, positively or negatively. One person decides and tells the other about it months later after the other starts to wonder why things are not the way they used to be," Gloria said.

Then she shook her head and added, "No, no, that's a sign that you've become nothing but a pawn in an otherwise two-person relationship, and you'll be used until the time is right for them to dump you. This will happen before the fool in you catches on or when the other person decides she has gotten everything she can get out of you without having to give up any of herself, if you know what I mean?"

At this point, I just shook my head either in agreement or because of the fact that she was telling me all these tell-tale signs. She continued, "Because as hard as it is for you to believe, some women who cheat, only do so with one other guy. Once they start doing things the two of you used to do with another person, it will be hard for that person to do them with you again. They will try keep you close but at bay for as long as possible and until the relationship fizzles out. You will notice if you ever get a kiss from that person again before it ends, which is the most you'll ever get while the keep-away game is being played. The kiss or kisses will not feel the same. They will be more of a lip service and nothing more."

"Wow, I'm sure glad you came here today and decided to impart some of life's wisdom to me," I said to her.

"Well, consider it a lesson learned and don't you ever forget it, regardless of what any of your future companions tell you," Gloria said with a motherly smile. Then she asked me how old I was. I hadn't told her yet. In fact, I deliberately had not told her. Now I gave the question a deaf ear as we walked around the garden center. Still, she did not mind answering my questions.

I later asked her how her first husband had discovered that she had been cheating on him, to which she replied, "I guess he was paying more attention to my pay stubs than I was giving him credit for."

"Oh," was my only reply.

"He sure was, and he kept it all inside, mainly because he loved me and his kids more than anything in this world and wanted to hold out for hope," she replied. Then she added, sometimes holding on to such hopes, is just a fool's paradise and a chunk of coal that leads to a broken heart."

Shortly after that answer, she asked if I could keep an eye on her shopping cart so she could run to the other side of the store. I obliged, and she dashed off while glancing down at her timepiece. But the bounce in her steps as she bolted for the other side of the store told me she was feeling better than when she had first come into the store. That made me feel good and filled my eyes with tears ... the tears I now referred to as my start-of-things-to-come-this-week tears.

Later that week, on July 27, 2011, I went to the personnel office for my first of six interviews. Out of the eleven advertised job openings I had applied for, I had supposedly only made the cut for six, even though I had already been working there. That should have told me the odds were stacked against me. Besides, I was also told in prior conversations that current part-time summer-hire employees would get first dibs on all jobs after the summer-cut open positions.

Therefore, the limited numbers of cuts I was told I had made did not bother me much, mainly due to all the praises I had been receiving since my April. Because of this, I had assured myself that I would be retained in one of the open positions I was about to interview for. Therefore, I went into the session full of confidence, especially knowing in the back of my mind how the process worked: First, one interviewed with the resource manager before moving on to one of the various assistant/zone managers' interview session if the individual makes the resource manager's cut. After interviewing with the assistant/zone manager, you moved on to the store manager, if you made his or her cut.

The store manager and three assistant/zone managers seemed to like me. The fourth one worked at night, and I did not have much interaction with him.

Before the start of the first interview, I was finally told which six positions I would be interviewed for. The fact that the one garden center slot was not among them should have but did not bother me at the time. In general, I like the garden center: I loved plants but I disliked working in the sun so much. I wanted to work inside more but not too far inside.

During the third of the six open slots I was being interviewed for, I found out that the resource manager was no longer a fan of mine. Midway through the interview, we suddenly and ceremoniously had to reexamine the hours I was available to work, due to my ongoing schooling.

She already knew about these hours when I had first been hired. Back then, she had no problem with it at all. In fact, she had praised me for going to school and had told me they would be happy to work with me and around my class schedule, as long as I let them know what my hours would be before the start of each semester. In good faith, I kept up my end of the bargain.

However, now it was a big problem because the lady stopped in the middle of the interview and said to me, "I see that on your application you list that you can work anytime, but aren't you lying when you say that because you actually can't?"

I was so stunned at her questioning that I could not even utter a word in my defense until after she said aloud, "Potential employee is not reliable for this position."

I am not quite sure if she actually wrote that down on the application form, but what I do know is that the rest of interviews with her did not last long at all. So when the last one ended, I walked out of the HR office thinking, *My gosh, the dang woman has really turned against me. For what, I don't know!*

I went back to the break room and waiting to be told that that was it for me. However to my surprise, I made her cut for three of the six positions she interviewed me for. Therefore, I was told to wait around to see if any of those assistant/zone managers could do their bit that day. Luckily for me, I did not have to come back a second day like some had to for part two of their interviewing process.

After all three assistant/zone managers interviewed me, I went back to the break room assured I would see the manager for all three positions. So I sat down and began to calculate in my head which one of the positions I should take when the offer was made. I even began to giggle inside when the manager was paged over the intercom system.

I was more than sure I was going to blaze through his portion of the interview process because I still remembered the questions he had asked me the last time and the answers he had wanted to hear. The moment he entered the break room, I got up with excitement and motioned in the direction of his office before he actually told me where to go. However, without his usual friendly greeting, he coldly said to me, "No. This way. We're going to do it in here," while pointing back to the personnel office.

No doubt, it was an odd and unusual move then, but at the time, all I was thinking was, *This is just a formality, so we don't need to use the manager's office. The personnel office is perfectly fine. The HR manager is still sitting there, so we're they're going to ask me which position I want,*

I walked in and stood at the far end of the office in my usual military at-ease position. I was facing the store manager and his personnel manager. Then the manager closed the door and looked me directly in the eyes, but the personnel manager didn't. She just kept her eyes glued to the applications on top of her desk. There was a momentary pause before the store manager started.

Without any opening comments, he said, "John, it has been a pleasure to have you as an employee, but as of this moment, your employment with us is terminated. You can finish out the rest of the day if you would like to, but at the close of business tonight, your services will no longer be required."

Needless to say, I was stunned beyond stunned. However, while standing there motionless and stunned out of my mind, I overheard a banging in the room around me but could not tell where it was coming from. For a brief moment, I actually thought it was my heart trying to jump out of my chest because I had not been expecting the words I had just heard. It was hard to fathom because for the first time in my life, I had been slapped across the face with the most disappointing job news I had ever gotten.

I knew employment there was temporary because it had said so on the initial documents I had signed back in April. However, it was now the end of July and I hadn't been let go yet. So yes, I thought my continued employment there was assured. It was also bolstered by all the raving words of praise I had received and how much everyone wanted me to stay.

After the disappointing news, the store manager opened the personnel office door to usher me out, but I was so overcome with sorrow I could hardly move. It was also then that I heard the biggest bang of all, followed by a loud "Here!" This was the scariest moment of all because I actually felt my heartstrings being tugged and thought they had jumped out of my chest and were saying to me, "Here, we jumped out of your chest. You better catch us before we fall."

I looked down and thankfully realized it wasn't my heart but the hand of the personnel manager banging her desk to get the store manager's attention. The store manager had jumped the gun because apparently I had made one of the three assistant/zone manager's cuts. So my feeble walk to the open personnel office door was interrupted when the manager unceremoniously invited me to his office for one final interview.

In all my life, I have never been fired or even let go from anything before, not counting the times when I willingly gave up on a few things that I had set my sight on. To further illustrate this, even though I was not the best athlete at certain games, I was never the last one chosen—second to last maybe, but never last. Therefore, this was a stunning turn of events, to say the least. I had gone into it knowing it had been temporary at best. But when my expected termination date passed by and all the other temporary hires around me got canned and I wasn't, it gave me a sense of invincibility.

You were looking at a twenty-five-year veteran of the United States Air Force who had never been written up once. Out of reasons beyond my control, I had been given two partially bad reports out of 100. So 98 percent of the time while I had been in the military, I had been rated with a maximum 5. Therefore, I felt I had to impress them enough to keep me. So when the unexpected had happened, it had jolted my system, more than I had ever thought it would. Still, it looked like I was about to be given a second chance—a presidential turkey pardoning.

Ironically, after we sat down in his office and even though he did not have that same glow to see me as he had when he had first interviewed back in April, I thought he had basically asked me the same questions that he had back then. Of course, I had basically given him the same answers that I had back then.

Then he threw an unfair monkey wrench at me. "Why do you want to work in the hardware and pluming department? What do you know about those areas?" he unceremoniously asked.

To be honest, I did not have a prepared answer for either question, but I quickly said to him, "Sir, I don't know much about each of those areas, but I am willing to learn just like I did when you first hired me for the garden center, which I didn't know much about."

The interview ended abruptly then, and the manager said to me, "You will hear from us in a couple of days after we've interviewed the other candidates. Make sure to turn in your stuff before you leave tonight. As a matter of fact, don't even finish out your shift, just go ahead and turn in your things now and leave."

I did exactly as he asked but with a heavy heart. I had never been fired from anything before, even though technically, it wasn't a firing because my employment had been scheduled to last only two months. Still, the way I was let go sure felt like a firing. When I took all of the buildup into consideration and his indirectly saying, "You are fired," I felt totally depressed. In some weird way, I kind of understand more keenly what Gloria was feeling, even though when she came back from the other side of the store, she had a different glow in her eyes.

I asked Gloria if she was okay, and she told me that she was fine. I then escorted her through the checkout line, pushing her shopping cart for her to her vehicle where I loaded the five bags of mulch into the back of her little pickup truck. Right before she got into her truck to drive away for good, she thanked me for everything and gave me a tremendous hug. Yet during the hug, I felt a sense of sadness on my part and knew it could be seen in my eyes as well. It also showed in hers when the embrace was over, and she entered her truck with tears in her eyes.

Just before Gloria put the truck in drive, she said to me, "Don't forget the lesson on cheating signs I told you about."

"I won't. I will keep them in mind," I replied.

"Good. But don't allow them to be the focal point of future relationships. Live your life but keep them in the back of your mind as pointers to explain why humans start behaving certain ways. That way you can start preparing yourself for the end or the hurt and disappointment that will certainly come in the end," Gloria cautioned.

I have kept her advice in the back of my mind since then. The most burning thing on my mind then was who had ended the relationship between her first husband and her, but I didn't quite have the heart to ask her that. I just stood there and watched her wipe the tears from her eyes once again and put the truck into drive. The last thing I remember saying to her after that was, "Don't forget to use my number if you need my help." That was the last time I saw her.

I must say that after she left though, I immediately started to apply the lessons and pointers she had given me to past relationships I had had. All the signs applied to the only girl who ever broke my heart back in the summer of 1995. That affirmed that the lady's pointers were 99 and 44/100 percent accurate. I will never stop applying them because more likely than not, I will be correct in my assumptions about cheating and cheaters thanks to the woman from Smithfield—Gloria with the tears in her eyes.

CHAPTER 13

PSYCHO

ONE SUNDAY EVENING around 7:30 p.m., during the summer of my discontent, she walked into the video store alone and unannounced. It was ninety minutes before closing, and she entered with a smile on her face, as if she was about to start some trouble. On two accounts, I really didn't care because I was going through a living hell. First, it had only been a few weeks since the only woman (Samantha) who ever really tore my heart apart had left me bleeding inside. It had really hurt like hell because I had fallen deep and quick and had thought it would have been the next big thing. When it finally died after about three months, during which I was the only one in love, it hit me like a sledgehammer times a thousand hitting the broadside of a shaky building.

In 2011, I thought, *If I had only met Gloria sixteen years earlier, I would not have been so blindsided.* I also told myself that sixteen years late was better than nothing because I was more prepared for stuff like that. The fact of the matter was that her pointers have rang true in me ever since then, even in breaking down other people's descriptions of their significant others' behaviors.

Secondly, without a doubt, this lady was a sight for sore eyes on the average man's click-o-meter. The funny thing was that she turned out to be a close acquaintance of Samantha, which I found out later. However, at that moment in time, I did not know who she was from Eve or whom she knew or did not know. I thought she looked fairly good and had my brains pumping especially because of what she was wearing.

She was dressed in knee-high white short pants, a sky-blue blouse/shirt, and a casual white loafer with ankle-high socks. Her hair was not quite shoulder length, and the radiance off her exposed skin seemed to make the shining lights in the lobby even brighter. To tell the truth, I felt a connection to her immediately and wanted nothing more than to start up a conversation with her … and yes, to see where it would go. But I was never a fan of quick pickups. I quickly erased that thought from my mind and started to look at her as a customer in the establishment where I worked and not a bag of my favorite chips on a rack at a convenience store.

Upon entering the store, she stopped briefly to look up at the movie we had playing on the nineteen-inch television high up on the wall. Then she proceeded straight into the middle room where the six months or older movies were on display. However, she did not spend a long time in that room. She was out of it in a New York minute and headed toward the new release room on the left side of the store.

Out of pure curiosity, which I heard usually kills the cat or lands its butt in hot water, I left the counter to get a closer look at her but not before grabbing a handful of new releases that were on hold for a loyal customer. I immediately started to hope like hell he did not show up that evening to pick up his movies. In complete disregard for his unfettered loyalty, I proceeded to the room with his on-hold movies to act like I was about to put them where they belonged. As faith would have it, she was standing with her back to me and in front of the spot where the newest releases were usually placed.

I said hello to her and then asked her to excuse me while I intentionally tried to reach around her. To be fair, she did not actually move. She just gracefully leaned to her left while asking, "Is that a new release?"

"Yes, it is," I replied.

"New, new?" she uttered while leaning back to her right to retake the latitude she had given me.

In doing so, her right forearm gently grazed the side of my face, and it was like being shocked with some good electricity, if there is such a thing. Still, I played it off and only responded to her inquiry.

"One of the newest ones. It was just released on Wednesday," I replied.

"May I have it?" she asked. Then she quickly added, "But only if it is good."

"Ma'am, I don't know if it is good or not because I haven't seen it. But so far, the reviews coming back from customers are very positive," I said.

"But you said it's only been out since Wednesday," she said.

"Yes!" I echoed.

"Well, there can't be that many in favor of it then," she continued.

"That's very observant of you," I responded.

"Thank you," she said with a smile. Then she added, "It pays to be these days."

"Without a doubt, and you are partially correct," I said to her. Then I immediately added, "We have six copies of the movie, so using the limited number of days it's been out is not a good outlier to determine those who are for or against it. But we haven't been able to keep it on the shelf either."

"Okay, would you recommend it?" she asked.

"Well, not from the standpoint of seeing it myself but based on the feedback from other customers I would," I said while handing it to her in a showy fashion.

"What if I don't like it? Will I get my money back?" she asked while taking it from my hand.

"I don't know. This is not a personal recommendation," I said.

"Does that mean you don't believe it's as good as they said it is?" she inquired.

"Not exactly. But you are asking me to guarantee the true grits of something I personally haven't seen, and that's hard to do," I explained.

"So I don't get my money back if it's not good, eh?" she prodded.

"Okay then, what do I get if you like it?" I countered.

"That's not how it works. You can't answer a question with another question," she quickly said.

"Okay, fine," I said before she continued on.

"Besides, I am the customer, and the customer is always right," she said with the warmest of smiles.

"Or in this case, gets whatever she wants," I suggested with a smile of my own.

"So do I get my money back or not if the movie is not good?" she asked again in response. Then she added, "Or at least get my choice of another movie in return?"

"Okay. I can't give you your money back, but I can guarantee you a free movie if you do not like this," I told her.

"Fine. I'll keep it," she quickly said.

"And that's where it ends, eh? I don't get anything in return if you happen to like it?" I asked. Then I quickly added, "Even if you like it, you won't admit to it so you can get another movie."

"No, that's not true. I will tell you if I like it or not," she said with a smile.

"Okay then, so what do I get if it turns out to be a good movie?" I quickly asked.

"I don't know. I'll think of something," she remarked.

"Wow! That doesn't sound too hopeful," I replied with a smile.

She slightly tilted her head to one side, smiled back at me, and asked, "So what's your price? What are you after?"

Jokingly I said, "I don't know." Then I quickly added, "Can it be more than the cost of a three-dollar movie?"

"Maybe," she said with the biggest of smile.

"Well, in that case, I'll let you think of something," I said to her.

"That's not fair. I told you what I wanted in return if I did not like it," she stated.

"Yes, but you are the customer, remember. And you said the customer is always right. Besides, if you want them to keep coming back, you have to give them what they want, or in this case, determine the end result," I said to her.

"Okay, but don't be disappointed with what you get," she said aloud.

"I won't. Beggars can't be choosers," I replied. Then I stepped away with the other two movies in my hand and added, "If you'll excuse me, I have to get back to the front before someone walks off with my cash register."

"What about those you are holding? Are they any good?" she asked. Then she quickly added, "First of all, are they new? And secondly, are they any good?"

"Yes, they are new. I heard that one is a waste of your money, and the other is a waste of your money and precious moments of your life that you can't retrieve," I said while walking away.

"Wow!" she said. Then she asked, "Do you have any suggestions, other than the one I'm holding?"

"Have you ever seen *The Shawshank Redemption*?" I asked while drifting toward the front of the store.

"What?" she shouted in return.

"Give me a minute. I'll be right back," I stated.

Moments later, I returned. After comparing a few movies, all of which she rejected, I started to secretly pay more attention to her aroma than the quality of the movies I was trying to help her pick. Not long thereafter, she said to me, "You are a lousy critic for someone who works in a video store," and headed off to the back movie wall of the room, shadowing the big glass window.

We were now about twelve to fourteen feet apart, on opposite sides of the room, with our backs to each other. Soon after arriving at the movie wall, I heard her say, "How about this one? Do you have an opinion on it?"

I walked over immediately, carrying the movie *The Shawshank Redemption* in my hand, and peeked over her right shoulder at the movie she was inquiring about. To be honest, I cannot say I can recall the name of the movie in question. But I'm inclined to say it was *Casual Sex*, but it's only because that movie had been burnt into my mind from a previous incident, which occurred about eighteen months after I began my employment at the video store.

The incident occurred one Saturday evening at about 9:45 p.m., while my coworker J. B. and I were bored out of our wits. It was probably one of the slowest Saturdays we had ever experienced. Then two American Caucasian ladies (more than likely military dependents/wives) walked into the store and temporarily blew our minds because they were dressed in barely there outfits for a hot July's summer evening in Germany. As they approached the checkout desk, one of the ladies said, "We are looking for *Casual Sex*!"

"Can you tell us where to find it?" the other spontaneously added.

Needless to say, J. B. and I knew they meant the movie *Casual Sex*, but we laughed at the way they had asked their questions. Additionally, the fact that the two ladies were complete strangers to us and were dressed added to the oddness of their questions at first. So even they thought it was funny and simultaneously tried to correct themselves by saying, "No, no, we meant the movie *Casual Sex*. We would like to rent it." It turned into a not-so-much the first lasting impression you'd want to be remembered by.

Now the customer I later dubbed as "Psycho." As I said before, I'm not quite positive if the movie she had inquire about was *Casual Sex,* or not. I also don't remember what I eventually did with *The Shawshank Redemption* movie I had been holding because the next turn of events was beyond my imagination. Because when I walked up behind her, the aroma from the distillery on her neck sent my mind into a different dimension. Assuming she was married, I said out loud, "Holy Toledo, lady, why did your husband allow you to leave the house by yourself that way?"

"What way?" she quickly responded while turning around.

"Smelling so good … like a Victoria's Secret perfume factory," I said.

"Do you like it?" she responded while facing me.

Before I had the opportunity to answer, we briefly looked into each other's eyes and then our lips locked. As the movies we were holding fell out of our hands and onto the floor, she basically pulled my tongue from my mouth into hers. It was like we were long lost lovers who hadn't seen each other for years, even though we knew nothing about each other. At least, I knew nothing about her.

Several weeks later into our psychotic situation, I found out through something she said that she knew about me through her German friend and former neighbor Samantha. Apparently, Samantha knew that the psycho lady had needed somebody to hang out with until her husband returned from his deployment to Bosnia. So Samantha told her about this nice guy whom she had just broken up with who worked at a video store. So her coming into the store that night was no accident. But I did not know this yet.

Kissing her, however, was as refreshing as getting a cool drink of water after walking across the desert sands for three full days. In fact, in order to give her kisses full justice, I must paraphrase the words of my all-time favorite singer, Mr. George Jones. Her kisses were as smooth as "Tennessee whiskey," and her lips were like "strawberry wine."

She kissed me like she owed me money, more than a million dollars to be exact. It was one thorough tongue-pulling, everlasting kiss. It lasted for about ten minutes or more and certainly no less. Thank God, it happened late Sunday evening when the customers were few and far between. We only pulled apart once when the echo of the store's front door opening reached the new release room. Otherwise, we might still be kissing today because it was the most fantastic first kiss I've ever had. Nothing since or before then has even come close.

Needless to say, I went back to the customer service counter and quickly disposed of the intruding customer. Happily for me, she had only been returning movies, which made her leaving a lot easier than I could have asked for. To be honest, she tried to ask about new releases, and even though it was not right, I only allowed her to try to ask. Before the words completely rolled off her tongue and out of her mouth, I replied with the big fat lie of, "No," to every question she tried to ask. Nothing was in, and nothing was due back until the next day, the latter of which was true, but I just wanted her gone so that I could rejoin my kissing game with the psychotic stranger who knew more about me than I knew about her.

I wanted the lady gone so bad that I almost pinched her backside off when I closed the door. She felt the near miss too, and quickly turned around to give me a what-the-hell-is-wrong-with-you-tonight kind of look.

If you asked me if I was in a caring mood at that moment, I would flat out tell you that I was not at all. It was bad customer service, but at that moment, ignorance was a bliss. She had come in and interrupted something great and had me thinking that for damn near as old as I was (thirty-something), I was on the verge of having my first one-night stand. That was starting to sound very appealing considering how Samantha had done me. I didn't find impregnating a woman married to another serviceman and an avid club-scene guy (as the psycho lady herself later revealed) to be appealing.

Unfortunately though, I could not immediately rejoin the kissing game because I believed that the lady I had prematurely shoved out the store had cursed me. As she was driving off, two other vehicles pulled up, and a third was not far behind. The first guy came in to return movies. The second guy, however, came in with two empty hands and headed straight in the direction of the pornography room. The third was a lady who returned two movies, one of which was porn, and then headed in the direction of the porn room as well. However, she didn't waste any time.

In less than five minutes, she was back with two red tags. I don't know if she was embarrassed to find someone else in the room and therefore hurried up and grabbed something quickly or not, but whatever the case may have been, I couldn't tell and didn't ask. She came in and acted like a man going shopping anywhere: She knew exactly what she wanted, went directly to it, grabbed it, and head for the nearest checkout register. I was all too happy to oblige. I checked her out so she could go home and do her thing.

Quickly, in a hurry, or embarrassed could not be said of the second person though. He shopped like a woman. It took him damn near close to fifteen to twenty minutes to find what he was looking for. For a man with some burning lips waiting in the new release room, that was forever and a day. However, after he made his choices, I could have labeled him a "horny SOG" because five of the six tags he brought up to me were red. Since I don't judge, I just hurried up and checked him out so I could get back to the kissing game I had recently started.

After the gentleman left, I moseyed on back to the new-release room to pick up where I had left off with the psycho. Without a word, we continued like our intention was to make our mark in the *Guinness Book of World Records*. In fact, I would be hard pressed to say that she had moved an inch from the spot I had left her in twenty or so minutes earlier. It was as if she had stood exactly there with open arms waiting for my return. So the game began again and went on with only short two to five seconds breaks in between. This went on unimpeded for the next fourteen to twenty minutes or more.

Neither one of us seemed to be worried about the time. I prayed that no more intruding customers would show up. My prayers were answered because nobody came after that, which kept us going nonstop. It was damn near eight minutes past closing time when we finally made our way to the front of the store. Still, that did not stop us from abusing each other's faces, necks, and any parts above the shoulders (mostly hers) that our lips could latch onto.

We finally stopped long enough for her to open a movie account in her name, which allowed her to check out three movies. Then I closed out the books for that night and secured the money in the insurance office safe while she waited patiently for me like a lovesick fool. Moments after I was done, we were back at the kissing game again. However, it was during the account application process that I found out a little more about her.

I found out that she was married to a soldier who was down range (in Bosnia at the time, and six months after he got back, he'd be on his was to Afghanistan for a one-year stint). I also found out that they had a four-year-old daughter whom a neighbor was watching while the woman was in the movie store kissing on me or allowing me to kiss on her. I later found out four troubling things about her that her application hadn't revealed.

While I stood at the counter talking and listening to her (mostly listening), I thought that one of us must have been a little bit psycho for carrying on this way. We barely knew each other. I understood her actions better when she revealed that she had been horny for four months. I also chalked my actions up to a man who was trying to cope with a massive broken heart (caused by one of her friends, although I did not know that at the time).

After I turned out the lights, she began to lead me toward the front door. The moment we got close to it, I reached down with my free right hand and grabbed her firm buttocks. It surprised her, and she quickly spun around without letting go of my left hand, which drew me closer to her. So I pinned her against the glass door, which I figured she wanted, and we kissed mercilessly for about six minutes. Then we broke apart for a breather, which enabled me to unlock the door. After this, we excitedly moved to the other side of the door and picked up right where we had left off, kissing on the way down the two steps and to the hood of my vehicle, which was parked close to the front entrance.

By the time she lay back on my hood, the bag with the tree movies she had been holding fell to the ground, and we went hog-wild. I knew if the hood of my white Grand Am SE could speak, days later, it would have said, "I actually thought you guys were going to get busy on top of me." But we never got to that point because after about twenty more minutes of hog-wild making out, she pushed me away and jumped off my hood, saying, "Oh, I got to go. My daughter is at my neighbor's. She's gonna kill me."

She entered her car faster than a NASCAR driver and sped away from the parking lot before I could say, "Don't forget your movies." Before I picked up the bag with the movies, something must have snapped in her psychotic mind. She hit the brakes and threw the car into reverse so that she could come and collect her movies. She snatched the bag and was gone without even a sad goodbye. So thinking that was it and that it had been fun while it lasted, I slowly walk toward the store and up the steps to finally lock the door.

The following evening, which was a Monday, I made it to the video store at around 5:05 p.m. The first thing my boss said to me was, "You just missed your guest."

"What guest?" I curiously asked.

"I don't know her name, but she knew yours," my boss said to me.

"Jennifer, I wear a green badge with "John" printed below the words 'Night shift supervisor.' Everyone that comes in here knows my name," I responded.

"Hey, I'm just saying that she waited here over three hours for you," my boss replied with a clap of her hands.

"Three hours?" I shouted. Then I added, "Who is this psychotic person who waited three hours for me when I don't come to work until five?"

"You tell me," my boss exclaimed. Then she added, "She arrived here shortly before two and left shortly before you arrived."

"Why? Did she say what she wanted?" I asked.

"No! Only that it was important that she get to talk to you," my boss replied.

"Are you sure she wanted to talk to me and not J. B.?" I asked.

"Hey, don't get me involved with this one, mister," J. B. said with a smile.

"No, she didn't want J. B.. She asked for you specifically," my boss said.

"That's all she said?" I asked.

"That's all. She returned three movies and asked what time you came to work," my boss said.

"Three movies?" I curiously asked.

"You know her?" my boss quickly inquired.

"See … that's your puppy," J. B. interjected with a big-ass grin.

"Not really, but it might have been the last customer I had last night," I said.

"You had or you checked out?" J. B. inquired with his playful smile.

"You tell us what you meant," my other night-shift partner R. C. said while he threw his right arm around my shoulder and briefly pulled me close to him.

"Okay, you are just adding gas to the flame," I said as I slid away from R. C.'s grip.

"Okay! I don't wanna know what's burning or about to be burnt," my boss said while tossing up her hands. Then she added, "Just tell me you are not in trouble. Are you?"

"Trouble?" I shouted.

"Yeah, trouble. Too many women," my boss Jennifer said.

"Yep, that's him," J. B. shouted quickly and ducked behind our boss.

"Man, be quiet. You know I am a one-woman man," I countered.

"Yeah … one at a time," R. C. interjected immediately and ran to the lobby's side of the counter.

"Dang, you two are in rare form today, aren't you?" I said applying one of J. B.'s favorite phrases to use.

My boss continued on, saying, "Unexpected pregnancies? Fair warnings because the husband discovered that his wife was cheating on him with you?"

"No, boss, not that I'm aware of. I'm as clean as a whistle," I said quickly.

"Ready and wishing to be blown, right?" J. B. and R. C. interjected simultaneously.

"Oh, really guys," Jennifer said before they all burst out in laughter at my expense.

After the laughter died down a little, our boss said, "So I'll have nothing to worry about when I go home tonight or come to work in the morning?"

"Come on, Jennifer. This is me you are talking about— not R. C. or J. B.," I countered with a sly smile.

"Hey, that sounds like the pot calling the kettle black. I do not use this job to chase skirts like some people I know," R. C. suggested.

"Neither do I," was my reply. Then I quickly added, "But some people I know don't have to chase them. J. B., the women come in here chasing you."

"What?" he said with a laughter.

At that time, our boss Jennifer was standing there with a look that said, "So this is what goes on when I leave you two here in the evening."

To reassure her and tug at her heartstrings at the same time, I said, "We are perfect gentlemen between five and seven. But once 7:01 rolls around, you should see all the freaks that walk into this place looking for the American whose German is more fluent than the Germans themselves."

"Oh, your funny," J. B. said with a laugh.

"He's right. Your German is really smooth," our boss added.

"So smooth, this place is like a rock concert after seven. Women walk in here and toss their underwear over the counter at him," I added.

"Okay, that's too much information," our boss said with a smile.

"I see that John's in rare form today, isn't he R. C.?" J. B. asked with a smile, before he kind of answered his own question simultaneously with R. C..

"Yes, he sure is," both of them said.

"You know me," I said with a smile.

"Too well, mister, too well!" J. B. implied with a broad grin and a shake of his head. After this, he added, "And the way you turned this on me was masterful on your part."

"Thank you," I said as I pointed at him.

"Yes, you did turn this on J. B., didn't you?" our boss said.

"When you were the one some psychotic woman came here looking for," R. C. added.

"Guys, that's not nice. We don't know anything about her, and the one who does is not telling us anything about her," our boss said.

"Yes, but she stood here for three hours waiting for him after she was told he didn't come to work for another three hours," R. C. quickly stated.

"Yes, that was a little bit strange, wasn't it? my boss asked.

"Psychotic, if you ask me," R. C. added.

"I don't know what you guys are talking about. There's nothing to worry about," I said with a smile. Then I added as I was walking away, "It's probably just someone I promised to hold a movie or two for."

"Well, that could be true. You do make a lot of those promises," J. B. added.

"Yes, that's another thing. Will you stop doing that? Every day someone walks in here saying that John told me he was going to hold a movie for me last night. Most of the time when they show up, there's nothing here for them," my boss interjected.

"Jennifer, I can't help it if those people are idiots. If they didn't come back that night, they can't honestly expect the movie to be sitting here for them the next day, do they?" I questioned.

"Well, explain that to them," my boss suggested.

"This is a moneymaking business, Jen. Economics 101 says we make money when we rent movies out, not by holding them for forever and a day for idiots who might or might not show up," I replied before stepping to the customer service desk to collect eight movies a lady was returned.

After that, the weekend's movie-return rush began. Military and civilian personnel who worked on all the bases and posts in the Kaiserslautern military community were now leaving work and stopping by like to drop off their movie rentals. So my buddy J. B. and I, each manning a cash register, and the young lieutenant, who understandably always came to work thirty to forty-give minutes late, got busy dealing with the rush.

It's not that we were caught off guard. We expected a rush every Monday, Wednesday, and Saturday. That's why we always had three people working in the afternoon until closing on those days. Our other coworker R. C. had not been scheduled to come in that Monday. He was only there dropping off movies. His wife, who also worked there, had rented over the weekend.

Wednesday was new release day. Saturday started the weekend where customers could rent any eight movies for the price of six, and they were not due back until Monday before closing. So most Americans and some Germans came in and took advantage of that on Saturday. The real movie buffs also came in on Sundays and got more on top of that. This created crazy Mondays because sometimes, one person alone would return anywhere from a few movies to over a dozen movies.

Anyway, as the mad rush started, my boss made me promise that she wouldn't have to drag her pregnant self out of bed to come down to the store later that night and that everything would be the same when she came to work the next morning. I agreed to all of this, which caused the puzzled look on the lieutenant's face. Of course, she did not know what was going on because she came to work, as I said before, understandably late as usual.

I was also extremely glad she hadn't been there for the whole scenario. Although she had only been working there for less than two weeks, she was already a regular. She was also a newly minted lieutenant in the army struggling with bills she had compiled before joining and an individual I had to salute when in uniform.

However, outside of the military and while working at the video store, I was her boss, thought she was adorable, and had really, really developed a liking for her. In fact, I thought she was the most adorable thing to ever come out of Texas. She was fifteen years my junior, young and green to the world, and struggling like hell to make it on her own. She didn't seem to be getting any help from her well-to-do family back in Texas.

Anyhow, after that initial surprise, I surprised her again by taking another jab at my buddy J. B. as our boss was waddling out the door. "Don't worry about a thing, boss, as far as my deeds are concerned, but don't be surprised if when you arrive in the morning to open the doors, you find a slew of babies in baskets on the front step with notes reading 'Have you seen my daddy J. B.?'"

Jennifer just looked back at us over her left shoulder and said, "You two have issues," and kept on waddling.

247

The lieutenant was frozen in her tracks with a don't-know-what-to-say look on her face and some movies in her hands. However, the blood in her body finally started to flow again when J. B. laughed and said, "Lieutenant, he's really in rare form tonight ... really rare!"

For the next two and a half hours and up until shortly after eight o'clock, things stayed busy with massive movie returns and a few rentals. I had more money in my drawer than J. B.. I believe I had less than or close to $300. However, because of the slowdown, J. B. and I were able to fully jump in and helped the lieutenant put away the mountain of movies she had. We did this while virtually customer-free, right up until about nine o'clock when a string of nine customers showed up in a matter of minutes. To my surprise, one of those customers was the lady from Sunday night—the same one who had waited three hours for me.

I don't know when she arrived, but I know she was the last of the slew of customers to enter the store. I believed she had arrived there and had waited for everyone to leave before entering the store. But when she walked in and didn't see me behind the counter, she came to the back and found me. J. B. and I were in the newer movies room in front of the newly released movie wall hanging up returned movie tags when she entered, which was somewhat of a surprise. I certainly had not been expecting her, so I did a double take when I saw her. She, in turn, looked at me and said, "I need to talk to you now—outside," and walked away.

"Uh-oh! Never seen that one before. That don't sound good," J. B. immediately said. Then he just jokingly added, "Should I call the MPs?"

I walked away saying, "Nothing I can't handle," but thinking to myself, *What if this woman is really psycho? What is the lieutenant gonna think when she sees me following an unknown woman outside?*

I followed the lady outside and around to the side of the building, which faced toward the front entrance for vehicles but away from the store's front entrance and the sight of anyone inside. As soon as we were at a comfortable distance, she turned toward me and said, "You listen to me and don't say a word until I'm done. What we did yesterday can and will never happen again because it was wrong. Wrong on two counts. One, I was wrong for allowing it to happen. And two, you were wrong for doing it. Moreover, it was wrong to do to my husband, who is in a faraway land serving his country—our country."

At that moment, I interrupted her and said, "That's three counts so far."

"Did I say not that you should not say anything until I was done," she responded in a sterner voice.

I immediately shut my yap and went back to doing as I had been told. I listened. Still, that didn't stop me from thinking, *Wow! Maybe, I should have had J. B. place that call to the MPs after all. You are the one who said two counts, and now that you are on number three, your intent is to get mad when it's been pointed out that you are terrible at simple arithmetic?*

So she rambled on. "On that count it was wrong. And think of my daughter … it was wrong to do to her too."

At that moment my mind totally closed off to what she was saying and told me, *What the heck? Weren't you the one who left your daughter at your neighbor's home to go to a video store and kiss on a stranger? This woman is really psychotic.*

The next thing I heard out of her mouth was, "Do you understand?"

"Fully!" I replied, even though I could not tell you what question she had asked. Then I added, "I hate to break up this little scolding, but I have to get back inside now. It's less than an hour away from closing, and we have a lot to do."

"That's fine, as long as we have an understanding that it can't happen again," she stated.

"Got it!" I replied as I turned to walk away.

However, after my third slightly nervous but brisk step (I expected her to use something on the ground to clobber me over the head with while my back was turned), I heard, "That's it? It's that simple for you?"

"Lady, no means no for me ... so does stop, over, and done," I said as I drifted away. Then I added, "For all that it's worth, you were the best damn kisser I've ever come across." I went back into the video store with a sense of relief. The lieutenant did not know where I had gone, and all J. B. softly said to me was, "Glad to see I won't have to file a missing person's report."

We worked without uttering a word about what was clearly in my mind—an over and done chapter in my life. If I might add, the next forty-five minutes to an hour went more smoothly than it ever had on a Monday night, until about 10:15 p.m.

Upon making sure all her returns were put away, the lieutenant asked if she could leave because she had to meet with a board in the morning and wanted to go home to get her gear in order. So without any hesitation, I told her she could go and wished her the best of luck, even though I did not know if she was the one meeting the board or she was a sitting member of one.

Back then, I wasn't quite up on the army process. It wasn't until my second assignment back to Germany when I had been assigned to a joint unit that I became fully aware of some of the army's comings and goings. Still, that's neither here nor there. I liked her so much, I would have let her leave even if I knew she had been lying to me. Besides, her work was done, and J. B. and I were busy adding up our money at the registers This left her standing guard, which was not necessary.

Ten minutes or so after the lieutenant left, J. B. and I finished our books, and I took everything to the insurance office to secure it. Then we both headed for the exit door. Upon looking outside, it seemed just like any regular weeknight. There were only two vehicles on our side of the parking lot, as it mostly had been around closing time. It was just J. B.'s and my vehicle. His was parked closer to the front door this time, and mine was parked further away, This was the opposite of what normally happened because I usually arrived at work before he did.

As J. B. was opening the door to his vehicle and I was walking by my front bumper to go around to my driver's side, we noticed a vehicle turning off the B40 (the German thoroughfare that separated the base across the street from where we worked) and into the entrance of our parking lot. It caused J. B. and I to momentarily stop what we had been attempting to do and look at each other. Figuring it was another customer returning a late movie, J. B. threw me the rock before I had the chance to do it to him.

"I'll let you handle this one and give them the bad news, killer," he said as he jumped into his vehicle and cranked the ignition.

"Thanks. Thanks a lot," I said, but I doubt he had heard me because he was already leaving like a bat out of hell.

The vehicle pulled up to the left of mine, and before I could go, the female driver jumped out and loudly said, "So you like my kisses, eh?"

"We are closed, ma'am," I sarcastically said.

"I figure that, but you didn't answer my question," she uttered. Then she asked, "Did you like my kisses or not? Did they leave you burning with wonder?"

I was temporarily at a loss for words. Wanting to be polite and truthful, I just couldn't find the right combination of words that would say it the way I wanted to but at the same time, not give her the wrong impression. So as I was standing there vigorously searching my mind, she picked up where she left off, and I couldn't continue searching my mind.

"So the cat got your tongue now, eh?" she inquired while drawing closer to me.

At that moment, I said to myself, *Run, boy, run. Get in your Grand Am SE and drive like heck.* But it was as if my feet had been cemented to the video store's parking lot and my right hand was welded to the handle of my car door. As she drew even closer to me, she added, "Earlier tonight, you basically said my kisses should be placed in the Smithsonian museum, and now you can't tell me if you meant it or not?"

"I, I, I … that's not," I muttered before I finally put a sentence together. "I didn't quite say that. I said that you were the best kisser I had ever met."

"Well, I appreciate the compliment," she said as she buffered my grill with her sweet smelling breath, before placing a wet, juicy kiss on my lips.

My mind said, *Back away*, but the ground wouldn't allow my feet to move. They felt as if they were really cemented to the parking lot, but now the door handle was gracious enough to release my right hand. As I gained control of its use again, I used it to pull her closer to me, which made the kiss even longer and more passionate than it was probably intended to be. She didn't resist—neither of us did, so I might have been wrong about that assumption.

Still, as we stood there kissing like long-lost lovers against my car, I couldn't help but think, *One of us is psycho, and I haven't yet figured out if it's her or if it's me, but one of us is definitely crazy—possible both.*

We abused the outside of my Grand AM without ever touching each other's lower private areas and then migrated to the hood of her car and abused it as well. We probably abused it even more than mine because each time I tried to untangle my lips from hers, she would just wrap her legs around me and pull me back down on top of her and the car's hood. We kissed so much that it felt like we were running out of spit to swap and my lips were beginning to chafe. It went on for a good forty-five to fifty minutes after J. B. had left.

Just as it had on the previous night, something clicked in her, and the kissing stopped. However, this time before she left, she read me the riot act of how bad what we had done was and how we should never let it happened again because we were betraying a whole slew of people by doing what we had. Then she was off. When I came to the video store on Tuesday for work, I fully expected to be fired.

Amazingly though, when I arrived on Tuesday at around 4:47 p.m., all was well. I was still employed, and she hadn't shown up there. Furthermore, the rest of the evening went like a typical Tuesday. It was eventless, and more importantly, the psychopathic lady never showed he face, which was a relief times two. More comforting though was that I would be off Wednesday and Thursday. The following three days brought relief when she did not show up and I heard nothing from or about her. The same could be said of the following Monday. Other than an unusually large volume of returns that four of us (J. B., R. C., the lieutenant, and me) had a hard time handling, it was pretty eventless. I was off that Tuesday.

When I came to work that Wednesday, which was a new release day, my boss Jennifer said she wanted to talk to me, and no, I was not worried. I figured it had something to do with the business, and since I was the night-shift supervisor, I was technically the assistant manager. She probably wanted to update me on her pregnancy. However, the look that was developing on Jennifer's face made me a little bit nervous until she said, "The lieutenant more than likely will have to quit because of her work schedule among other things, so we hired someone to replace her."

I said, "Cool beans." Then I asked, "Who is it?"

"Her name is Crystal, and she starts on Friday," Jennifer said. Then she asked, "Are you cool with that?"

"Of course I am," I said at first. Then to deflect my sadness of the lieutenant leaving, I added, "Why wouldn't I be?"

"We figured you'd be mad at us for hiring Crystal to replace the lieutenant," Jennifer said.

"Oh, no, not at all. The mission comes first, and if her the military needs her more, so be it. Yes, I hate to see her go, but we will still have her as a reliable customer," I stated before heading from the back office up to the front.

The lieutenant and I had to work that night. We had never talked about her leaving so soon after her employment had begun. We were all in Germany because of our military mission, and in my mind, that should always come first. What had bothered me though, was my boss asking me if I was mad about her hiring Crystal to replace the lieutenant. It tickled me even more when she asked the question again as she was leaving for the day.

If truth be told, I wanted to ask her why she kept asking me that, but I let the opportunity slip by without uttering a word. Still, my night did not end badly because I finally got the invitation I'd been waiting on for almost a year. The lieutenant invited me to her house for dinner, which was scheduled to take place during the weekend they were due back from the field. The only unfortunate part was that she had already issued one of our other co-workers' and self-professed ladies' man, Maximillian Whitehead an invitation too. He was one sorry-ass self-indulgent human being.

I was off that Thursday though, and when I arrived at the video store on Friday, my heart skipped a beat. In fact, it skipped several, due to the fact that the psychotic lady was standing at the video store entrance and was grinning from ear to ear. So I started saying to myself, This can't be good. This is bad—bad, bad, bad. Oh, Lord, please let this be a dream, a bad one no doubt, but at least I will wake up from it."

I nervously walked past her without saying a word, and as I was doing so, she said, "You are a rude boss. Is that any way to treat your future employee and co-worker?"

I did not pay much attention to what she said, or it just did not register because I said, "Whatever?" and kept on walking.

As usual, I went inside and collected my cash register's money for the night and set up my till for Friday evening's business. I chose a different register that was to the far right so I could see who was entering more easily. I would swear afterward that I had not held a conversation with the psycho lady. She had disappeared from the front door. Now I was in the position to see clearly if or when she returned and what she was carrying.

However, shortly after that thought crossed my mind, my boss, who was sitting at the desk in the L-shaped movie display cubby counting her till, said to me, "Did you say hello to your newest troop member? She was standing outside waiting when you arrived. You have to train her tonight on the register because the lieutenant is not going to be here and R. C. is running late."

"No, I did not see anyone at the front door when I was coming in," I replied when suddenly out of nowhere the psycho chic wheeled around the counter.

"I'm ready to be trained," she said.

So as I was looking at her, my facial expression said, *What the fuck? This woman has really lost it.* I heard my boss say, "I'm pretty sure you already know each other, but

John, this is Crystal. Crystal, meet John, the night shift supervisor."

Undoubtedly, I was stunned beyond expression, and all I remembered saying was, "Crystal … Crystal. Your name is Crystal? You are Crystal. Crystal. Your name is not Crystal, is it?"

"I thought you guys knew each other?" my boss asked in an informative way.

"Yes, we do," Crystal quickly said.

"Yes, we do, kind of, sort of," I replied quickly. Then I just as quickly asked again, "Your name is Crystal?"

"What are you, an echo? Yes, her name is Crystal," my boss interjected from her sitting position.

"Ah … wait a minute," I uttered as I jumped to the membership card box. Then I added as I frantically searched through it, "You wait a freaking minute."

"Sure!" both Jennifer and Crystal simultaneously said.

Then my boss got up with her wobbly self and moved closer. I supposed it was to see what my malfunction was. So I looked over at them standing next to each other and rambled on. "Good, stand there next to her. That's not the name she put on her application the other night, and I can prove it," I shouted as I was still frantically searching due to the fact that I had not remembered what last name she had used.

"You're right. I put down Ruthy," Crystal said.

Without paying much attention to what she said, I uttered in response, "Exactly." Then I added, "What's your last name again? I need it so that I can see what name you really put down on your application card."

"John, I just told you it's Ruthy," Crystal said.

"Last name, girlfriend," I said in response.

"Horton," she said with a smile. Then she quickly added, "Ruthy Crystal Horton."

"Horton, good. Wrong box," I shouted and flipped the lid to the A through M box open.

"Anything else?" Crystal asked as I was closing one box and opening the other.

"No, Ruthy," I said. Then I pulled her brand new application card from the box, which had about nine or ten movies logged on it and said, "See, her name is Ruthy."

"That's what she told you, John," Jennifer said with a puzzled look on her face.

"Ruthy … not Crystal," I said while shaking the card before stopping briefly to glance at it once more. Then I said, 'What the …?"

"Yes, I know. My name is Ruthy, but I hate that name, so I mostly use my middle name, which is Crystal, except when I'm filling out paperwork. I think it's only appropriate that you use your given first name when it is required," Crystal explained.

"Yes, but you've been renting movies?" I shouted. Then I added, "Look."

"I have a membership to do so, don't I?" Crystal asked.

"Yes, but you've used it on one, two, three, four, and five different occasions since you opened an account," I shouted.

"Yes. My husband is deployed, and I need something to occupy my time," she said.

"But I thought you haven't rented any movies since that first time," I shouted.

"It's obvious I have," Crystal said.

"But—" I uttered before my boss chimed in.

"She comes in during the day to rent movies."

"But I haven't seen her since that first night," I said.

"She comes in during the day, John," My boss said again. Then she quickly added, "You're in the military, so you work evenings during the week, remember?"

"Yes, but nobody told me she had been coming in here to rent movies when I wasn't here," I stupidly said like it was any of my concern.

My boss gave me a strange look and then turned her attention in Crystal's direction. Crystal shrugged her shoulders as if to say, "Why are you looking at me?" So my boss turned back to me and curiously asked, "Am I missing something here?"

"No, no, no," Crystal and I simultaneously shouted. Then I added, "No!. Nothing to see or miss here."

"Okay," my boss said with a puzzled look on her face. Then she wobbled off and added, "I can count on you to handle everything and to train her until R. C. gets here—if he ever gets here—right?"

"You have my word," I said to my boss as she wobbled past the counter.

"That's what I'm afraid of," she jokingly said.

"Come on, boss," I said in return.

"Just kidding," she smirked as she drifted away.

About fifteen minutes later as my boss was wobbling out the front door next to the lady from the insurance office, she said, "You two be nice to each other."

"We will," both Crystal and I said simultaneously as if we had rehearsed it.

"And be nice to the customers. Remember, customers pay our bills and are always—" my boss added before I interjected.

"Not right," I shouted above her voice.

"Okay, assistant manager," my boss shouted as she chugalugged down the two steps.

"Night shift supervisor," I shouted not, knowing if she had heard me or not.

"I heard that," my boss's faint voice echoed.

"I didn't know you were the assistant manager," Crystal said immediately. Then she just as quickly added, "Aren't you in the military though."

"Night shift supervisor," I said as I pointed to my name badge without entertaining her question.

About ten minutes later, it was as if someone had opened the flood gates because people started to return movies left and right. It went on nonstop for about two hours, give or take a few catch-our-breath spots in between. It was so steady, I could hardly talk to R. C. when he called around 8:05 p.m. to let me know that it would be pointless for him to come to work for one hour. He was supposedly just getting off and still had to go home and change. By the time he made it to the store, it would be nine o'clock or close to it. So I told him not to rush and that I had it. Little did I know how much I was going to get it.

Crystal caught on fast. Of course, she had turned into a regular customer and had probably figured out the routine, which hadn't been hard. So with little corrections here and there and while running into each other as we put away or retrieved customers' movies, we did not spend much time socializing. But later that night after everything was done, she followed me to the insurance room to watch me lock up the night's take. However, she did not come all the way inside the room. She just leaned against the door while I proceeded inside. For the life of me, I just thought she wanted to take in some of the closing procedures and therefore, didn't pay her any attention when she stopped at the entrance. But she made my knees wobbly the next time I looked in her direction.

I honestly cannot say with any certainty what happened to Crystal's bra, but after I locked up the night's deposit in the insurance manager's desk and looked up, Crystal was standing at the door with her top wide open. I had to grab onto the desk to keep from falling. The scene was a shock to my system because even though we had spent about five hours kissing, I had never gone past her shoulders. Sure my hand had accidentally passed over her breast once or twice (well, several times), but up until that moment, I could not tell what they were like. I didn't know if they were firm or just felt that way when we heated up and the pointing of her blinkers distorted their true worth.

I must say, there were no distortions going on. To this date, Crystal had the firmest and most spectacular set of ta-tas I have ever seen on a woman. She did not need to wear a bra, period. Wearing one was just for show and tell, and what she was showing and telling me at that moment, would have made an old man wish for his younger days. As I was bent over holding on to the edge of the desk with my eyes planted firmly on her chest, she said to me, "Hello my nightshift supervisor and assistant manager, would you like a go at these?"

While I stood there speechless and admired her bodacious set of ta-tas, she continued on, "The cat's got your tongue now, eh? You know you've always wanted these, so let me move closer to see if I can use them to loosen up that tongue of yours."

On that night, while she had me take a crack at second base about a billion times, I developed the most burning desire to have sex with her. Yes, we had spent many hours kissing, but I had never had such a strong desire to have sex with her until then. This was due to many things.

One, I had never been a one-night-stand kind of guy. In fact, I had never had one in my entire life, so when we had first kissed, I had not expected it to go any further than that. Our second and subsequent times spent kissing, I had been thinking the kisses were so good, neither one of us should take it to third base and probably ruin the heavenly kissing relationship we had developed. Thirdly, I was thinking maybe she was only blessed with good kissing abilities and that the rest of her body was not all that great. In fact, one night after one of our kissing spells, I had put her into a scenario some guys in Korea had described about Korean women when I had been there many moons before that night.

They had said that one of the rarest things in the world was to find a Korean woman blessed with all three appealing assets: good looks, a nice ass, and great breasts. Finding a woman with one of the three was not very hard; two of the three was like finding a diamond in the rough; all three was like one in a million.

Therefore, when things pushed us further than the kissing game (which I wasn't pushing), I just chalked it up to great lips, a terrible second base, and an awful cookie. But seeing her boobs for the first time that night instantly changed my mind and brought the burning desire to get to third base and soon. The way we were carrying on that night, I felt sure that the pants were going to drop soon, and we were going to leave a wet spot on the insurance manager's desk.

This psychotic situation continued for another two weeks like this. We always got to second base but no further. Every day heavy petting took place, but the opportunity to go past second base never really presented itself, or we didn't make the opportunity happen.

She even came to the store right before closing on days she did not work. It was also on one of those days that I found out she knew R. C. because her husband was in the same unit as him. In fact, R. C.'s wife (one of the prettiest women to ever come out of the state of Connecticut) had recommended Crystal for the job.

Still, this customer who had turned fellow coworker would rock my world with supercalifragilisticexpialidocious kisses night after night, but would find a way to leave each time I thought it was going go to the next level and before giving me the invite I thought would definitely take me to third base.

In the middle of our third week of working together, I came to work one evening prepared for another night of after-work petting because I knew I would be working with Crystal. However, moments after I greeted my boss, she told me that Crystal's daughter was running a high temperature and that Crystal wouldn't be in that night. R. C. would be coming in for her. I was a little disappointed, but at the same time, it was no big deal.

R. C. was also my buddy, and I took it as an opportunity to find out a little more about this psychotic woman. However, R. C. did not divulge much that night except that her husband had been shafted for the deployment he been going to go on because he should not have been sent so soon after getting to their unit. He had been coming from a stateside assignment. Still, I later found out through Crystal that the reason R, C. didn't talk much about her was because he liked her and was a regular peeping tom at her building complex, which in a way was not hard to explain.

Anyhow, as I said earlier, that night I had received the invite I thought would lead me to test out third base. Even though she did not come to work, she called later that night and asked me if I could rent some movies under her name and drop them off at her residence on my way home. So I agreed with anxious pleasure in mind, even though I did not know where she lived. When I got to her building, it was just like any other military unit in a housing complex. They have since changed it, but back then, they were stand-alone buildings, which were three- to four-stories high with twelve to sixteen family apartments inside them.

I pulled into one of the two vacant visitors' spots in front of her building and walked into the far right stairwell, which serviced apartment 1-D, and knocked on the door. It did not take her long to answer it. I expected to be greeted with some of our usual tongue-waggling, mouth-watering kisses, but it did not happen. Still, I followed her down the hallway past the bedrooms and bathrooms and into the living room. To my surprise, the first thing that caught my attention was that her living room and kitchen lights were on and that she did not have any curtains up. You could stand anywhere in her kitchen or living room and look up at the buildings on the hills above hers. More disturbing was the fact that everyone in those apartments could look directly into hers and see everything she was doing. That tripped me the fuck out.

Let me be fair, 90 percent of the lights in the two buildings that looked directly down on hers were out. Plus we were on a military instillation where anything out of the ordinary was not that abundant. However, over my years in the military I had known of military personnel (husbands) who had come home to surprise their wives and had gotten the surprise of their lives—a naked man jumping out the bedroom window. So things that went on outside did happen on military instillations as well. It was like my grandmother used to say, "You can get the pig out of the mud, but you can't get the mud out of the pig." Moreover, the people in the buildings that overlooked hers did not have to turn their lights on to observe everything that was taking place in her living room or kitchen. Because her lights were always on each time I visited and she was incline to turn them off even though she had no curtains. It was as if she wanted it to be open seasons 24/7 and did care the slightest bit what passerby's, peeping toms, nosy neighbors, or anyone in between thought.

Upon taking the movies from my stubborn arm, she invited me to come and sit down on the couch beside her— an invitation which under normal circumstances I would have gladly accepted. I wanted what was going to happen, but my mind and legs were more concerned with what the prying eyes were going to see, so I stood still the first couple of times she invited me. It wasn't until after the fourth or fifth invitation that I finally made it to the couch beside her. I couldn't keep my mind and attention off her un-curtained windows and a living room that was lit up like the moon. When she felt the nervousness in my kisses, she asked if I would feel more comfortable in the bedroom, to which I gladly said, "Yes," and was up off the couch before she was.

My trip to her bedroom took some getting used to. I had to get use to the fact that she did not have any curtains on her living room windows and did not think that was strange, even when I brought up the subject of peeping toms.

"Without any curtains on your windows, how can you accuse someone of being a peeping tom?" I asked.

"Just because I don't feel like putting any curtains up doesn't give others the right to look into my living room whenever they choose," Crystal replied.

"But isn't it an open invitation if you don't do something to stop people from looking inside?" I asked.

"No. I don't go to their homes and look through their windows," Crystal replied.

"Forgive me for saying this, girlfriend. They don't have to come to your place, the people in the other buildings just have to sit in the dark and observe everything that's going on in yours," I replied while hoping I did not upset her.

Those in-between-talks bedroom kisses were starting to get good. When I told her this, we stopped temporarily so she could reach behind to unhook her bra. So obviously, after the words had left my mouth, I started to think, *Oh, man, you just fucked up.* But to my surprise, the bra still came off during her reply.

"That still doesn't give them the right to look into my apartment whenever they want to," replied Crystal. Then she added, "Besides, nobody can force me to hang up living room curtains if I don't want to. It's my prerogative."

Then like a fool, I asked, "So why did you put up bedroom curtains?"

"Because I don't want people who are passing by to look into my bedroom," Crystal replied quickly. Then she added, "Are you trying to piss me off or did you come in here to make out?"

From that moment on, it was heavy petting for me. Most of the talking between breaks were done by her. We kissed constantly for the next hour or more. I did not make it to my hopeful destination that night, but I did gain a lot more info than I knew before. That night was when Crystal informed me as to why Samantha had broken up with me. She also told me that some of her neighbors had described someone resembling R. C. sitting on the hill and looking into her apartment.

Apparently, she believed it was him because it happened on some of the days when she had invited the short kid over that R. C. had introduced her to. According to her, R.C. liked her and knew that she was a little lonely but couldn't directly approach her because she was friends with his wife. Therefore, she believed he had introduced this guy to her, hoping she wouldn't like him so that he could swoop in and rescue her. But she and the guy had hit it off to the point that they had made out on her couch the last couple of times he had come over. Since R. C. had all of a sudden stopped talking to the guy, she figured he was really the one her neighbors had seen.

As I was processing those bits of info, the fire in my kisses started to flicker, and my once strong, over-burning desire to have sex with her lost some of its luster. She also felt it and asked, "Are you getting tired, or was it something I said?"

Well, the chapter in *The Bathroom Comedian* named "Kids Say and Do the Damnedest Things" couldn't holds more truth than it did at that moment. As I was lying there on my right elbow across the pillow from her searching for an answer, out of nowhere, we heard her daughter at the bedroom door calling out "Mom."

In true mother fashion, Crystal jumped off the bed, taking the pillow with her to cover her upper body while rushing to the door and telling me to get down. I did the best I could while still on top of the bed. I did not wait around for us to get back to where we had been. I had too many things that my mind hadn't fully digested yet, and I figured her daughter waking up offered me the perfect opportunity to slip away, and I did. Plus it saved me from having to lie to her. So after she and her daughter had been gone about ten minutes, I quietly slipped out of the apartment. I was glad we hadn't even exchanged numbers so she couldn't call me while I was driving home. She certainly couldn't call the store because no one was there at the time.

The next evening, she came to the store with her supposedly sick daughter to re-rent the movies I had taken to her the prior night because she hadn't had a chance to watch them. She also used the trip as an opportunity to inquire as to why I had left without saying goodbye. Of course, she extended another invitation for me to stop by after work that night, and like a damn fool, I accepted. This happened in spite of the fact that I knew she had not put up any curtains in the past twelve hours. I guess I felt more at ease knowing she did not mind going into the bedroom if I were to show any displeasure with us sitting being fully exposed to the world. If I was able to keep my thoughts to myself, I might be able to make it past second base. So once again, I ended up at her apartment thinking, *This is the night I get to sample third base*, despite how I felt about the things she had told me the prior night.

Like a typical guy, I arrived there with one thing on my mind, even though the night before that the fire, my kisses had turned into a flicker, and my once over-burning desire to have sex with her had lost some of its luster. I now figured that I was in a race against time (well against another guy) to make it all the way with her first. So with sex being so apparent, who wouldn't have regained his lost appetites? This was especially true of a person who thought the way I did—that we were going to skip the couch and the whole living-room-peeping-tom-avenue altogether and head directly to the bedroom. I certainly did or at least had overlooked what the signals had tried to tell me the day before: Stay away from this psycho.

However, like the prior night, she once again invited me to come and sit down on the couch beside her. The difference, of course, was that I went there after the first invite this time, figuring we'd be heading to the bedroom soon thereafter, when the words, "I'm so tense. Would you mind giving me a massage?" left her mouth. I quickly jumped off the couch and headed in the direction of the bedroom. It was as if I had not even sat down on the couch at all. I was floating away on air while saying in my mind,

Oh, yeah. First, I'm gonna start on her back, and when she turns over I'm gonna work some magic on her front to make her open her legs and let me slide in. Of course, the typical guy in me was on his way to la-la land in his one-track mind.

It's hard to say at this time if I was moving too fast or if she was moving in slow motion. When I looked back at her, she was still sitting on the couch, but her shirt was gone and her pretty golden-tanned back was toward me while the front of her was directly facing her un-curtained windows. When what her neighbors might be looking at hit me, all I could think was, *Oh Lordy, Jesus H. Christ, she is gonna get arrested for indecent exposure, and I'm gonna get arrested for being in the presence of another service member's half-naked spouse.*

However, before I could say anything out loud or make any moves to shield her breasts from the neighbors possible prying eyes, she lay down on the couch and pointed backward, saying, "On one of the shelves in the hallway closet there's some massaging oil. Grab a bottle."

On my way back to the couch with the bottle of massaging oil, I started to wonder, *Other than her obvious neighbors, who else might be lurking outside looking at us? R. C.? The little guy R. C. introduced her to?* I called R. C.'s friend little because when R. C. introduced him to me a month or two later, he was barely taller than a midget. I was thinking her might be out there as well. The scariest thought yet was, *What if her husband is out there?* As I said before, I've known husbands who have come home early from deployments, or knew they were coming home early and did not alert their wives to that fact due to the element of surprise, only to be surprised themselves. I also personally knew one individual who went on deployment with me and left our home station in my vehicle with me, but did not spend his last couple of nights in town with his wife and five kids. He spent it with his girlfriend and her two kids, who ironically happened to be his wife's best friend.

I picked him up on the evening of the going-away party, which his family and his girlfriend were throwing for him, to drive him halfway across the country so he could say goodbye to his parents. However, our road trip did not begin that exact night because I dropped him off at his girlfriend's house and picked him up two days later to finally head out of town. This had happened some eight years earlier, so by the time Crystal's situation came around, I was well versed on some of the things that went on between military couples. So it wouldn't be unheard of to expect Crystal's husband to come home early. With all those things weighing on my mind, my terrible massage turned into a death spiral. She must have sensed it too, even though I had not given her a massage before.

"No way. You're that bad at giving massages," Crystal said to me while raising her head up.

"I am," I replied quickly.

"No way anyone is that bad," Crystal interjected.

"But I am," I countered.

"No way," she quickly added and then said, "Your fingers aren't even moving. It's the window, isn't it?"

"Ah," I echoed.

"It's the window that's making you nervous. Let's go in the bedroom," Crystal suggested.

We walked to the bedroom after she spun around and flashed one of those unimaginably firm breasts at me. While we were in there, my massaging technique got a little bit better, but it did not qualify me to apply for any massage parlor jobs. Still, I spent ten minutes or so on her back before she rolled over and flashed her gifts at me. Her bedroom was dimly lit by the lamppost's light, which shone through her window's curtains.

Of course, like a typical guy, I began to spend more time focusing on her gifts more than any other parts of her exposed upper body, so much so, I could tell I was getting to her because the massaging became a sideshow and heavy petting took its place. During the course of some of that I would slide my hand inside the back of her pants as far as the unbuttoned pants would let it travel so that I could squeeze however much worth of her butt I could grab.

We did that for about thirty minutes. During that time, she mentioned wanting to have sex with me but was not sure if she was ready for it yet. Of course, being the typical guy, especially one who knew he had a competitor, I would try to ask, "What time is better than the present time? And why wait? What if tomorrow never comes?" It was during one of those cynical guy's questions of mine that she said, "Wait a minute," and jumped off the bed.

She flicked on the bedroom light and immediately started to rummage through the top drawer of the dresser. In my mind, she was searching for one of her husband's condoms to give to me so we could finally do the nasty. But to my second surprise of the night, she pulled out a picture and rushed back onto the bed beside me. So now I was thinking, *What the heck?*

"I know you've never seen my husband, but let me tell you how we met," Crystal said while shielding the picture behind her.

"Okay," I said in response while pushing myself up on my right elbow.

"We met in a club about six years ago near my hometown. He had just gotten stationed there," Crystal said.

"Okay. That happens," I interjected.

"He was supposed to be my last one-night stand," Crystal added for my third surprise of the night.

"Your last one-night stand," I echoed. Then I quickly added, "That doesn't sound too good."

"You're right, it wasn't. That's why I was going to stop; I used to go to the club every weekend looking for a one-night stand," Crystal said. Then she asked, "You're not mad at me, are you?"

"No, my dear, I'm not mad. I've never had one myself, but one thing my grandmother taught me was to never judge people unless you've walked a mile in their shoes," I said.

"Wise woman," she interjected.

"Many people have said that about her," I quickly stated. Then I added, "She also told me to never throw stones if you lived in a glass house. Therefore, I can't fault you on your previous life when I never asked you anything about it, but I'm here in your bed hoping to have sex with you."

"Fair enough. Your grandmother taught you well," Crystal said. Then she continued on with her story. "My idea was to break the trend of me having one-night stand upon one-night stand. I was doing this because I did not want to commitment to anyone. So I had sat down and

273

thought about it long and hard. I told myself I would do it one more time, one more weekend, and then no more. While I was at the club, several guys approached me, and I turned them all down.

I was about to leave the club thinking, *Damn, I did it.* On the weekend I had planned to do it one last time, I had not taken anyone home with me. But right before closing time, I told myself that that had not been the original plan. The original plan had been to leave with someone so I would get it out my system for good. So obviously, I had to turn find someone who was still there but whom I hadn't turned down yet. So I looked around until I ran into a fresh face I hadn't ever seen in there before, and I picked out this guy."

It was time for surprise number four of the evening. She boldly laid the picture on the pillow before me. It was such a surprise that I literary jumped off the bed while she was saying to me, "I took that picture while he was asleep one day."

The first thing that surprised me about the picture was that the guy was naked The second and most surprising aspect was that he had an anaconda lying on top of his left leg (well, I initially thought it was an anaconda). So I said, "Matthew, Mark, Luke, and John, girl, the man has an anaconda snake where his dick is supposed to be."

"Right," she laughingly said to me. Then she added, "It's big, isn't it?"

I could not answer, but at that moment, I lost every desire to ever have sex with her—ever. Because this white guy had a dick about fifteen inches long (I would assume it grows to about thirty-five when it's hard) just relaxing on his left leg while he slept.

Don't get me wrong. I'm not a cock blocker or a dick watcher by any means, but I did spend nearly three months in a military training barracks with fifty-one other guys. We ate together, marched together, studied together, cleaned our shoes and weapons (guns) together, slept in the same room together, and showered together. So, yes, I had the opportunity to size up fifty-two dicks for a few months, whether I wanted to or not.

I've said many times that I was not blessed in that department the way I was hoping to be blessed. I still have to give thanks because I saw some big guys (body-wise) that I thought for sure would be packing, but they had nothing more than mere belly buttons. When looking at them, I used to say to myself, *Only God alone could carry out such a practical joke on another man and get away with it.*

On the other hand, within that same group of guys, I saw a few dicks that made me jealous, including two white guys that were later stationed with me at other bases. Also, within that group of guys, we were all amazed that the person with the biggest dick we had ever seen was someone who wasn't even in porn movie. It belonged to a black guy from Morgantown, West Virginia. His dick was so big that when the rest us got up several times in the middle of the night to take a piss from all the water we drank during the day, he would remain asleep and his dick would go to the bathroom for him.

That was the most manly manhood I had ever seen until Crystal showed me the picture of her husband's. His shit was so huge that it could not walk anywhere for more than two steps without getting tired. It would either have to be pushed around or would have to slither around like an anaconda to get from point A to point B. It is a little farfetched, I know. But there's no way to humanly describe the volume of this guy's manhood. To think of that man having sex with a woman would totally kill your desire for having sex with that same woman, and it did.

Crystal also told me that whenever they would do it, he couldn't get it all the way inside of her but that he didn't mind. I on the other hand was thinking, *I don't know how the hell he gets it in his pants.* Still, her saying that to me did not ease my mind or relight my desire one bit. She further drowned it with ice water when she told me that the only reason she still talk to the kid that R. C. had introduced her to was because he was packing for his size. He was nothing compared to her husband, but he was very manly for being so short. That told me he already gotten to her or that she had touched his stuff, which was more than she had ever done to mine.

In the weeks that we had been lambasting each other with mouth-watering kisses and she had allowed me to travel to second base while giving no resistance when I would grab her butt from inside her pants, she in turn, had never physically put her hand on my little friend. Yes, it had gotten excited quite a few times. Well, both of us (my little friend and I) had gotten excited on numerous occasions and rubbed up against her. She had even pulled both of us so close to her crotch area (while fully clothed of course) that I had felt I had experienced the best lap dance I had ever had. But not once had she ever grabbed my little friend or even asked to see him. So her describing her other friend's (my competition) manhood in detail made me think twice.

She was married for sure then and her one-night-stand days might have been behind her (according to her), but I thought that she was still out to get her kicks. Again, I'm not here to throw stones, so I won't take issue with this. However, I did take issue with her seeing or wanting to see more than one person (not counting her husband) at a time. I excluded her husband because people can be in love but not love the sex or are having sexual problems. Although after looking at the size of her husband, it was hard to imagine that was happening, other than the fact that he could never get it all the way inside of her. But other than that, I don't see where there could have been problems. The man's stick was so huge, it didn't even have to come alive for him to have a good time.

In addition, I did not know what kind of a relationship they really had. Therefore, even though her significant other counted as a person, I did not include him in the numbers game. But when her intention became to date multiple people at the same time, that's when I had a problem. I dislike the use of condoms with a passion and always feel out someone before I do "the do" (sometimes too long for my own good), so that I don't become involved in a sticky situation I do not want to be entangled in. This does not negate the possibility, however, that it only takes one dip of my stick to engulf me in two worries: creating an unwanted pregnancy and catching a disease. It makes it less likely if I get to know the person first.

Things between Crystal and I changed that night. I never got back into bed with her. The closest I came was sitting on the edge of the bed while she detailed more of her life story to me. I have to admit begrudgingly that I did glance at the picture of her husband and his manly manhood a few times. The man's shit was like a sequoia tree. People talk about mistaking the tree for the forest. Well, if his dick was a tree, it would have been a whole forest by itself. As I said, things were never the same between his wife, Crystal, and me after that night.

We worked together, on and off, for about three more weeks. I use the words *on and off* loosely because she started to miss work on a regular basis, so I figured she was spending more time with the little guy R. C. had introduced her to. A tell-tale sign for me, even on the few days she came to work when I was working, was that our interactions were not the same. We did share a few more kisses during then, but they weren't anything close to what they had been before. Since that night, it seemed that she always had to run home because she had left something at undone before she came to work: clothes in the washer, clothes in the dryer, or dishes to wash. She even used being tired and wanting to get some sleep as the reason we could not spend much time together.

When people are cheating, it is amazing how they always use sleep as the excuse. I guess they figure that no one on earth could be mad at a person who just wanted to get some sleep. Well, it all depends on what kind of sleep you are talking about, especially when sleep was never a big thing before but has now become a top priority.

Gloria had told me to look out for that because that was how cheaters covered their tracks. People claim to be asleep when the bill collectors come, the phone rings and they don't want to answer, and they are trying to hide their cheating ways. She was absolutely correct in her assessments because I was watching it play out right before my eyes.

I did not hold it against Crystal. We even had one more, big sexual encounter a few weeks after that night.

Early on when we had first met, one of the few things we had discussed was letting my kids hang out with her daughter because they were in the same age group. Therefore, we had arranged for this to happen during on an upcoming weekend when I had known I would be in a babysitting bind. She had planned on watching the kids that Sunday for me.

On the Friday of that weekend (I believe this had two weekends past when she had shown me the picture of her husband's ding-a-ling), I had asked her if it was still possible for me to drop my kids off. Of course, she had said yes but hadn't come to work that Saturday, so I had never had a chance to reconfirm it. I had figured that if things had changed, she would have let me known by sending carrier pigeons, building a bonfire, calling the store, sending a message through R. C. or his wife, or even showing up in the store parking lot unannounced like she used to so that she could tell me.

When none of those things had occurred and Sunday came, I got my kids dressed and drove them to her house with their day packs at 9:43 a.m. I had to open the video store at 10:00 a.m. The drive from her house to the store was about seven minutes, so that game me about ten minutes to play with. Of course, her vehicle was there when I arrived, and as usual in those days, there were no doorbells, so I had to knock on the door and wait. However, after several knocks and waits later with no one answering the door, I started to get irritated, especially as my kids looked at me as if to ask, "Aren't we going to have a babysitter today, Dad?"

The looks of dejection on my kids faces and the fact that it was creeping closer and closer to ten o'clock caused my next knocks to be even louder. I probably even spoke a little French under my breath during that time. After about five or six minutes of knocking, I heard Crystal's voice from deep inside her apartment hallway saying, "Wait a minute. I heard you. I'm coming." About twenty-vie seconds later, she made it to the door. When she opened it, she could tell I was visibly upset, so she immediately started to apologize and greet my kids.

It was during her apology, I realized she had a comforter between her legs and kept trying to stuff more of it between her legs. Despite my frustration at the time, I had to ask about the attention grabber she presented to me.

"Crystal, what the hell is that?" I asked as my kids took off into the apartment they had never been in before.

"Sorry. I meant to call, but I didn't have your number," she said.

"Call me about what?" I quickly asked and then added, "You have the store's number. You could have called and let me a message."

"Sorry. They are here now, I can still babysit them," Crystal said as she stuffed more of the comforter between her legs in a wiping fashion.

"Are you sure?" I asked.

"Yes, it's not a problem," Crystal replied.

"Are you sure they won't be interrupting anything? 'Cause I can take them to the store with me until I figure something out," I suggested.

"No, no, they are fine. It's just that my husband came home late last night," she said.

"What? He's here?" I questioned softly.

"Yes," Crystal said.

"Now?" I asked.

"Uh-huh!" Crystal uttered.

"Why didn't you call to let me know?" I asked like a fool. Then I added, "Come on kids, Ms. Crystal has things to do."

"No, stay," Crystal quickly said to the kids. Then she said to me, "They are fine. We already took care of business. That's why I have this between my legs."

"Ah?" I said.

"My husband and I were working on a quick one before you got here," Crystal explained.

"Oh," I said. Then in a half-shouted voice I said, "A quick one? I've been knocking for almost six minutes."

"I'm sorry. I know. But we had just gotten started when your vehicle pulled up," Crystal said.

"When I pulled up? That was almost twelve minutes ago," I said.

"I know. He wanted to stop, but I'm the one who told him to hurry up and get it off," Crystal said with delight.

"I see," I echoed.

"And now I have stuff running down my legs. That's why I'm dragging this around with me," she explained. Then she added, "But we are done for now. He's very tired from all the traveling and is probably asleep."

"Are you sure?" I confirmed again. Then I added, "I can take the kids with me."

"No, they are fine. Go on or else you're gonna be late. I'll just go and clean up and then go upstairs to get my daughter."

I walked away thinking, *A quick one that lasted almost ten minutes? That man is not human. Ten minutes for me is like an eternity. I'm a regular three-to-five-minute guy. Ten minutes for me would include a nap, especially if I was with a woman who didn't believe in cuddling after or before sex, such as my current wife.*

Well, she's the only woman I've ever met who's like that. In our relationship, her attitude is like a man's (all about himself), and my attitude is like a female's (want to be held, before, during, and after sex). After almost fifteen years, I still can't get her to change her sexual wants, needs, and desires so that they match or come close to mine, and I'm the one who is twelve plus years older. That definitely makes for a sucky relationship, especially when I think of couples like Crystal and her husband.

A week or so after her husband came home from his deployment, Crystal finally quit her job at the video store and went back to being just another regular customer. And once again, the movies that she rented would always come back two, three, four days late, even though she only lived about seven minutes away. I did not mind sticking here with the hefty late fees.

I wouldn't say we became best of friends, but over the next couple of months, Crystal husband and I got to know each other better. Still, I'm always worried that Crystal might tell her husband about the kissing relationship we had had or he might suspect that something had gone on. I also did not know if he had ever found out about the little guy R. C. had introduced her to, and to be honest, I really didn't care as long as her husband didn't find out about me.

After those initial first months, the closeness that we had gained started to fizzle out. This was because of work and the fact that I had met another customer named Bettina, the one I dubbed Trench Coat.

CHAPTER 14

TRENCH COAT

O N A WARM summer's day—no, I was not on a train bound for nowhere I was standing beside my coworker Maximillian and behind the video store counter of our part-time job when my next strange encounter walked into the store. It had been two weeks since he (Maximillian) and another coworker had been caught by the military police in the back of his vehicle at a well-visited local German lake. They had both been naked from the waist down, and her strapless top had been slid down to her navel, exposing even more of her. Coincidentally, both of them had been dependents who had been married to two military personnel in two different branches of the service.

Despite this recent incident, Maximillian showed no signs of slowing down. During the wasted time we spent bullshitting away, he spent nonstop on the recently hired, financially strapped second lieutenant. She was a cutie in her own right, well more than cute. I dubbed her as the most adorable flower that had ever come out of Texas. But she was doing something I had never seen a military officer do before—working at a second job. Up until that time, I had only come across one other similar situation when I had been stationed at Grand Forks Air Force Base, North Dakota from late 90s to the early turns of the new century.

In this lieutenant's case, she was fresh out of college, still a virgin (according to her), and away from home for the first. She owned nothing more than a bed, a table, and a thirteen-inch television in her apartment and was bogged down with enough bills to make the pope set the Vatican on fire. Of course, our big-time player and coworker Maximillian was 99 and 44/100 percent sure that she was in love with him and that he was going break her into the world. So the race was on between him and me as to who was going to save her and who was going to break her into the ways of the world.

Every subject we touched on, Maximillian, the ladies' man, somehow or another found a way to bring Lieutenant Lucas's name or something about her into the conversation. Well, that was until about 4:40 p.m. when a wonderfully nice-looking young lady who was about five feet, three inches tall walked into the store and smiled at us.

Although neither one of us had ever seen her before, both our hearts skipped a beat. But other than the smile she threw our way, nothing else was expressed as she drifted into the back of the store to the new release section. It seemed she had been there before but only when neither one of us had been working, which was rare for me. For the six years plus I worked there, I had only been off for a total of 407 days, which equated to about sixty-seven days per year.

Anyhow, while the young lady was walking by, we could tell that she was packing from the way her extra-long coat was proportioned from the waist down on her backside. It also sent a signal to Maximillian's head that the young lady liked him over me, and he was quick to point that out. Of course, I did not pay much attention to what he was saying. I only wished him the best of luck when he decided it was in his best interests to rush to the back and lend the young lady a helping hand, if she needed it. More importantly, I wasn't about to tell him no when we were in a customer-service business—a happy customer is a returning customer, and a returning customer spreads the word to other customers. So I joyfully watched him go sailing off to the back of the store.

To this very day, I have no idea what took place when Maximillian went back to help the young lady. However, about ten minutes after Max had gone, he came back with a big smile on his face. I took it for all that it was worth—nothing to me. Plus, months later, when I took into account what our coworker had been caught at the lake doing, it told myself and others that their relationship had fizzled out and gave me pause for thoughts. From my understanding of what the young lady had told me and from what she relayed to others, Mr. Max was only into self-satisfaction. He didn't care a dang about you as long as he got his own. What his partners wanted and needed were none of his concern during sex and after his needs were filled. Beforehand, Max would talk the game that true love seekers dreamed about. You just couldn't let him get his first, otherwise, you would be left high and dry.

Now, there is no denying the fact that on the first day, Maximillian had the first laugh, but like my grandmother (Delsithia) always told me, it's not always the one who laughs first that has the best laugh but sometimes it's the one who laughs last. At this point, I didn't know yet whether or not, in this case, my grandmother's scenario would be right or wrong. But one thing I could and would tell everyone was that she was hardly ever wrong in my book and in general.

When the young lady came back with the movies she wanted to rent, she went to Maximillian's register to open her membership. Even the following evening when she returned them, Maximillian got to check her movies in. When she left the counter area and headed to the back to look for more movies, she turned back and flashed another smile like she had the day before. Of course, Max thought it was all for him because he was the shit, something he pointed out by opening his arms as if to say, "I am the man!" after she had finally disappeared. Then he pointed to himself and made a check mark in the air with his right index finger.

I believe the following evening was a Thursday. One thing I know for sure was that Max was off work and I was working with J. B. when the woman came in to return her movies. Of course, when she walked in and did not see Max, she momentarily paused until J. B., with his usually friendly self, greeted her, "Hi, welcome to American Video." Of course, I, who had seen her twice before but had never spoken to her, rudely did not say anything to her again. That was what I assume drove her to the far end of the counter and to J. B.'s side to return her movies. He gladly obliged and encouraged her to go and pick out some more. She was more than happy to after flashing another glimpse of her pearly whites like she had on the previous two day.

It did not take her long to come back with three tags, one of which J. B. tossed to me and said, "How about a helping hand here, bro? That one is on your side."

I caught it, and within two small steps backward, I was hanging the tag on the hook and pulling the movie from its spot. While I was doing that I heard the young lady softly whisper to J. B., "Helpful? Does he even talk?"

"Talk? Who C. C.?" J. B. asked in return.

"Yes, him," the young lady said softly as I was returning with the movie.

"Oh, ma'am, he's a regular record player when he gets going," J. B. said to her. Then he added as I handed him the movie, "Isn't that right C. C.?"

"Ah?" I said as I pretended not to know they were talking about.

"That you are a regular record player once you get going," J. B. said with a smile. Then he said to the lady, "That will be eight dollars, ma'am."

"Maybe, I should have grumpy over there pay for my movies for not acknowledging me the three times I've been in here so far," the lady said to J. B. aloud.

"Hey, that sounds like a challenge to me," J. B. laughingly said. Then his instigating self quickly added, "So what do you say C. C.? Are you going to accept the challenge or are you going to be Chicken Little about it?"

"I notice that you are a non-talker, but—" the lady said before J. B. interrupted.

"It's the quiet ones you need to worry about," J. B. quickly interjected.

"I heard that somewhere," the lady added. Then she asked in a begging tone, "But is he also a cheapskate to boot?"

"Sounds like the lady is calling your bluff," J. B. added.

"I didn't remember making any bet," I said.

"Oh, look at that. He speaks," she said with a smile.

"Oh, ho, you've gotten him started now," J. B. said jokingly.

"Yes, he speaks. For a moment, I thought English was your second language," the lady said with a smile.

J. B. instantly started to laugh and then the lady joined in. During their laughter at my expense, J. B. turned toward me and said, "The lady doesn't have all night, C. C. Are you gonna take care of this bill or not?"

"You know what J. B.? You annoy me," I said while reaching into my pocket. Then I pulled out some money and handed him a ten-dollar bill while saying, "Here, keep the change. You might need it for your trip down 40 Mark Strasse later tonight."

Of course, that was never the case. It was just one of our video store's running jokes. After the lady had gone, J. B. laughingly said to me, "I hope she doesn't know any better because that was a bad one, C. C., for a lasting impression."

I said, "I know, and I was happy to apply it."

"I think she likes you, C. C.," J. B. said with a smile.

"I don't know what gives you that impression, but you can have her," I replied.

"Shit! My wife would kill me," he replied.

"You're right. She'd definitely do that and more," I said to him. Then I added, "She's been in here a lot lately. What have you been doing?"

"Being a good boy," J. B. replied quickly.

"Good boy, shit. It's kind of hard to teach old dogs new tricks, isn't it?" I plugged as one of the first sergeants from a unit that was located close to the store walked in with his movie returns.

"Fellas, how is it going this fine evening?" the first sergeant asked.

"Fine, first sergeant," J. B. replied.

"Wonderful first shift," was my reply. Then I quickly added, "Did you make the sergeant major list, bud?

"Maaan, those communist bastards overlooked me again, but I'm gonna get them next year. This will not happen three years in a row. You mark my words," the first sergeant said as he was walking away from the counter.

"We'll be watching for it," J. B. and I said simultaneously.

"You best believe it will be on there," the first sergeant replied. Then as he opened the door to exit the store, he added, "Hooyah!"

After the door closed behind him, J. B. and I just looked at each other as if to say, "Lord have mercy on those guys at PT in the morning. Thank God we are in the air force." Then we went back to our store-attendance business. He grabbed the tags of the next customer checking out movies, and I continued to collect returns and put them back in their rightful place. When things died down, he jumped right back to the lady who had helped to give me a hand.

"So, you don't think she likes you?" he asked.

"Nope. I think she likes Max, and he believes he's already got her in a bag," I stated.

"Max?" J. B. said with a little surprise to it. Then he quickly added, "That SOB thinks every woman likes him. He's after the lieutenant. He just messed up with what's his name's wife. He thinks he's army chic and that Brown wants him as well. Now he thinks this girl likes him too?"

"Well, that's the impression he gave me," I said.

"Impression is one thing. Action is another," J. B. countered quickly. Then he added, "You've heard what what's-his-name's wife said?" J. B. asked.

"Denise?" I quickly interjected.

"Yes, her. You heard what she said about him, right?" J. B. continued.

"Yeah. She told me specifically that he wasn't a woman pleaser. He's only into self-satisfaction. He doesn't do anything extra to make sure a woman gets hers, but he'll whine like a little baby for women to do stuff for him."

"That's exactly what I've heard," J. B. implied. Then he asked, "She told you that herself?"

"Yep. Right her on the front steps a few days ago when I asked her about all the other rumors swirling around," I said to J. B.

"Yeah, I heard some other shit too. Is it true?" J. B. curiously asked.

"Honestly, she didn't admit much more to me other than she probably won't be here much longer with her husband," I said.

"More like not taking personal responsibility or at least some of it for what's swirling around," J. B. interjected.

"I couldn't have said it better myself," I added before continuing on. "But whatever the case may be, she and Max are both playing the blame game right now. Apparently, one of them gave the other one something, and it got passed on to her husband. And now he's steaming mad ... to the point where I heard he that threw her out and is looking for this person named Max so that he can have a fist-to-fist conversation with him."

"So he don't know it's our Max?" J. B. asked.

"Apparently not," I said.

"Man, this is some hot stuff," J. B. said with a laughter.

"You can say that again," I added quickly. Then I said, "I heard he also found out about the lakeside incident and is trying to get a copy of that police report so he can get Max's last name."

"Man, he's gonna get to Max one way or another, eh? J. B. laughingly said.

"The fortunate thing for Max is that his wife is in the air force, and she uses her maiden name, so that's going to make it harder for him to find Max. Plus, the military won't just release that kind of information to him, even though it involves his wife. They are smarter than that," I explained.

"True, true. We who are in the air force are smarter than that," he added before collecting four blue tags from a customer.

The next day was Friday, which meant that J. B., R. C., and I would be working. The first two people would work at the registers, and the last saddle would work with movie returns and retrievals and in customer assistance. The day also meant the start of the usual long-weekend haul for me—eight plus hours at the video store, which were added to my the eight I had already spent in the air force office.

Saturday was a full day at the video store (9 a.m. to 12 p.m.). Sunday was another full day (10 a.m. to 9 p.m.). I did this with pleasure because I loved working, serving, and dealing with customers, even the psychopathic ones. I got to meet and know some very interesting people, such as the lead members of the group La Bouche. In some small way, I helped make some of these people famous because I knew them before the world really knew of them. I also handed La Bouche's CDs to anyone who would take one while working in the video store, before they ever became a household name.

I met Jerry, the main personality on Armed Forces' Kaiserslautern Network (AFKN), in the Rheinland-Pfalz, Germany, who regularly stopped in to get movies and to chitchat with me. He even invited me and another coworker, the army's Master Sergeant Borgess, to the radio station dozens of times. He also introduced us to one of his coworkers, Mrs. Deborah Kennedy, who did the voice-overs for most of the station's commercials and advertisements. She was married to an air force officer, who was between the ranks of captain and lieutenant colonel. I don't quite remember exactly which one it was.

But I could say with certainty that next to my all-time favorite lady (the real Ms. America 1983), she was the most elegant lady I'd ever seen in pictures or in person. That Mrs. Kennedy was so elegant, the few times she visited the video store, the place felt like it had turned to cloud nine. Sergeant Borgess and I instantly turned into schoolboys with puppy-dog crushes during her visits. If we happened to have the radio on in the store and her voice came on, everything would stop on a dime.

Those, however, were not the only ones I was fond of. I remembered and also cherished meeting non-so-famous people, such as the army's First Sergeant G, whom I would hold movies for because he was one of our most loyal customers. I can forget my very own coworker, the army's Sergeant R. C. He probably could and would have been the most famous of them all because he made the store a place where many who knew him or at least knew of him.

I love the military and serving this country at home and abroad. I would also discourage anyone from serving. Except for that damn fool friend of mine, R. C. because if he had waited another year or two before signing on that dotted line, I probably would not have met him. Still, he would have been famous beyond his wildest imagination. Besides, he was married to a bombshell from my home state, and that was good enough for me.

However, R. C. signed up with the army way too early in life, and it kept him from his original life's pursuit. But this made his life's story and his encounters with me interesting.

Of course, there was Karina, the packing lady in the trench coat who thought I was a non-talking cheapskate and the one I delightedly greeted when she returned her movies that Friday evening. I even offered to help her pick out some new movies, if she thought she might need help while R. C. checked in the other ones she had just returned. She, however, did not take me up on my offer, and as usual, she came in and was ready to check out in less than five minutes. The only difference was, this time she came to my line as if she wanted to prove that J. B. had been right, which made me think I was being set up. I also became more suspicious when she said, "Are you going to pay for these, too, tonight?"

However, right before I could say, "Sure," she told me that she was joking and that maybe next time I could offer to do so before she asked. I gave her a slight grin at that suggestion, and right before she took the movies from my hands, she softly whispered, "You can call me sometime if you would like to."

The invitation totally caught me off guard and riled up my suspicions again. It was as if J. B. was part of the setup to prove that he was right about her liking me. So after he left without even acknowledging me, he said aloud, "She told you to call her, didn't she?"

"No, she did not," I quickly said because I did not want to give him the satisfaction.

"You're lying," he said with his big gap-toothed grin.

"Okay, she might have said something to that effect," I admitted with a gap-toothed smile of my own. Then I jokingly added, "But I'm not going to. I don't want anything to do with what Max is passing around."

"You're right. One has to be careful these days with people like him, lurking around and trying to go after any and every thing that moves," J. B. suggested before adding, "By the same token though, I don't think I have a chance with this girl ... what's her name, Karina? She has the hots for you, regardless of what you say or the attention she has shown to Mr. Eraserhead, Max."

"Right! Mr. Fastmover himself probably slept with her already, and he's just probably trying to get back there to prove a point. They could just be toying with me to see if I'll try and jump into the mix," I replied. Then I added, "But either way, something smells fishy here." After which, I started thinking, if Karina was another friend of Samantha's and it was just now her turn to take her crack at me due to the weak state of mind Sam left me in.

"No way," J. B. said, as if he had pinpoint accuracy with what he was saying.

"No way, what?" I asked as I woke up from my wonderland.

"No way Mr. Eraserhead has gotten a crack at Karina," J. B. said with surety.

"But he could have. Anything is possible," I said with a smile.

"Possible. But I'll bet every dime in your wallet that it hasn't happened," J. B. said with one of his laughs.

"My wallet?" I immediately asked. Then I added, "Why *my* wallet?"

"Because you're the one who's gonna luck out, not me," J. B. replied with more laughter.

"Luck out? Not me, homeboy," I replied with a smile. Then I added, "Lady Luck is not coming my way, bro."

"Boy, the race is on, and you're ten miles ahead," J. B. said.

"Right. More like ten miles behind and drifting further behind," I said to J. B. Then I added, "Moreover, I'm not even interested."

"You just let me know how the little filly is once you've roped her, okay?" J. B. said and then walked away.

"Right. This is where this cowboy rides away, or in my case, walks away," I said to J. B. and headed off to the back of the video store to put up a handful of the movies I had stockpiling on the table behind us. However, in the middle of my eighth trip, my coworker J. B. called out to me, "Hey, I think you have a visitor."

However, before I made it back out to the lobby, which I wasn't in a hurry to do because I wasn't expecting anyone, I heard a familiar voice say, "After I left here to gather my kids, I thought about you guys and stopped by Popeyes across the street to get you guys something to eat. So I hope you guys like what I got you."

Then as I put away the last movie I had been holding and headed back toward the lobby, I heard the voice adding, "Gotta run. I left my kids in the car outside."

Upon entering the lobby, J. B. held up the bag foo from Popeyes and said, "See, I told you she like you."

"Whatever, man," I said to him. Then I added, "If anything, she likes both of us. I think I heard, "food for both you guys," come out of her mouth."

"That's because she didn't want me to feel bad. Who am I to refuse free food," J. B. said.

"I do when I didn't ask for it," I quickly said.

"Boy, get over here and take this food before I whop you with this bag. It's store-bought. It's not like she went home and cooked the food and you can't tell how clean here place is," J. B. said while shaking the bag at me from across the lobby. Then he added, "I know you are funny like that. You find it hard to eat food from other people."

"Oh, be quiet. I trust people," I said with a lying smile.

"Yeah. But not their home-cooked meals," J. B. countered.

"Sure, I do," I added.

"Yeah, just as much as you trust a rat with cheese," J. B. stated. Then as I opened my mouth to counter his remarks, he added, "Boy, shush and bring your ass over here and come get this food."

"Man, I don't want that thing. She probably brought it thinking Max had showed up here," I said as I moved closer to J. B. and the bag of food from Popeyes.

"Boy, shush and come get this food," J. B. said. Then he sat the bag down on the movie table in the back, started to go through it, as he called out the names of the stuff inside.

"There is a twelve-piece bucket of chicken. Boy, she's really trying to fatten you up. Dirty rice, Red beans and rice, biscuits, lots of honey, Popeyes' utensils, plenty of napkins— mostly for you, Messy Marvin, and a note saying that you should be more nice and speak more to your customers."

All that J. B. said about the bag's contents was true except for the note. As soon as we started to eat, I realized something was wrong. Before I could open my mouth to mention it though, the front door swung open and the lady rushed in with two drinks in her hands, saying, "Sorry, guys. I forgot these. I noticed them after I pulled up in front of my apartment."

She put them on the counter and dashed back out the door as we were both thanking her. Then J. B. turned to me and said, "That's what you were gonna say, weren't you? That she didn't bring us anything to drink." I smiled, and J. B. said with a smile, "You're something else. Eat the freaking food and be quiet."

"Me?" I said with a mouthful of food. Then after a few more chews, I added, "You seemed to be the one doing all the talking," and then kept on chewing.

Needless to say, the food Karina brought us really hit the spot. There were two pieces of chicken, two biscuits, and half a tub of red beans and rice left when J. B. and I had finished, and it never made it home with either one of us. R. C. devoured it when he finally showed up for work later that evening. He was like a starving beast and didn't even wait to change out of his military clothes into the civilian attire he had been carrying on a hanger. In fact, he didn't even bother to change that night.

Most of the customers knew that he worked there but did not know his schedule, so it was as if he had stopped by on his way home from work and had stayed to chitchat with us and give us a helping hand while wasting time. He was working but unofficially doing so because he was still in his army uniform. This didn't seem strange to us because even regular customers would volunteer to help out sometimes. Many of them would still be dressed in their military uniforms. That is how the lieutenant got started working for us and how we found out she was in desperate need of a second job. However, in R. C.'s case, it was a bit unusual.

R. C. usually changed his clothes, even if he was really late and only had one hour of work to do. In this case, he had the better part of a whole shift, which had started at five o'clock (though he had been two hours late), to complete. He had not made any attempt to change. Still, we did not ask about or mention it because from our understanding through the rumor mills, things on the home front had gone south—and in a hurry. Based on the people his wife was reportedly spending a lot of time with and the fact that lately, R. C. was no longer in his usual rush to get home, one could assume it was true.

Still, we all know what happens when we assume? We makes asses out of you and me. However, for two people who worked there (though on a part-time basis) R.C. and his wife hardly ever talked to or about each other anymore. R. C., when not working, was usually in, out, and on his way home to his son, Dino, and his wife (two of the finest things Connecticut had ever produced). And whatever R. C. used to bag her in the first place, he should have bottled it and sold it. It's not that he was a bad-looking guy (not like the geek he introduced to Crystal), but his wife was smoothly fine. If she had been a wine she would have been a top-ten seller, year after year, and the state of Connecticut would have been right up there with California in every wine connoisseur's conversation.

The next few hours of the night went by as smooth as possible. All three of us were working, joking, and laughing until 9:30 p.m. when R. C. flipped the hell out. I honestly cannot recall what was said or by whom to suddenly change his grasp on the fun-filled evening we were having. I can remember that his attitude changed from joy to anger in one swoop. If you were to ask J. B., he would tell you the same thing. Neither one of us could pinpoint the change. However, we both remember him saying something out of the blue, and then he stormed off to the back to grab his clothes that he had brought in earlier on the hanger. Then he was gone.

R. C. left the store faster than a bat out of hell or one on a last-ditch effort to catch his lifesaving meal before the sun came up. There was no goodbye, no kiss my ass, no FU, no I'm going outside to cool down and I'll be right back—no nothing. He just up and left. J. B. and I were left standing there with a WTF look on our faces. I was the first to break the silence.

"Did I do something wrong?" I asked seconds after R. C. had stormed out.

"No … not that I'm aware of," J. B. replied quickly. Then he just as quickly added, "Did I?"

"Not that I'm aware of," I replied to him. Then we both looked at each other briefly before shrugging our shoulders and going on our happy but confused way. It was as if we were saying "F*** him and the horse he rode in on," and "Let's work like he was never here." However, that did not last long because as soon as we turned back to business as usual, the next gentleman waiting to be checked out opened his flytrap.

"What's up with him? What did you guys do to your buddy R. C.?" he asked.

"Nothing," J. B. answered as he took the movie tags from the guy. Then as he walked off with them and deciphered their number sequences, he added, "We were just here cracking joking and having a good time when something must have snapped inside him and sent him to pissed heaven."

The gentleman and I instantly cracked up laughing, and during the laughter, I bellowed out, "Pissed heaven. That's a good one."

"Yep, it really is," the gentleman chimed in.

"Well, thank you," J. B. said with a chuckle of his own.

"I'll have to use that sometime. Hope you don't mind?" I said in full admiration of his term.

"Don't mind if you do," J. B. replied. Then he added, "But what the heck man? What did we say or do to set him off? And then for him to storm out like his leaving was going to suck up our last ounce of oxygen and kill us for pissing him off. That's what gets me."

"He damn for sure did, didn't he? I asked.

"I don't know who set off the firecracker in his ass. I don't know about you, but it wasn't me," J. B. said aloud. Then he said to the guy checking out the movies, "Can you review these titles and tell me if they are correct?"

"I really don't know," the guy said. Then with a smile he added, "I never look at the titles. I mostly look at the pictures on the box."

"I guess titles really don't matter in these cases," J. B. interrupted.

"Blue movies are all the same," the guy continued.

"Okay, that will be twelve dollars," J. B. said to the guy.

The guy handed J. B. a twenty-dollar bill. After he collected his change and left, J. B. looked at me and said, "What the heck, man? I don't care if it's a blue movie or not, I'm gonna make sure the title is correct."

"No shit," I immediately shouted in agreement.

"Can you imagine going home, getting cozy with your girl for an evening of pleasure, and throwing in a movie that's supposed to keep you turned on, and to your girl's surprise, it's a guy-on-guy movie?" J. B. said before we both busted out in huge laughter.

"Yeah. Pole versus pole," I added during the laughter.

"Yeah. Pole vault," J. B. chimed in while we were still laughing.

Yes, we had fun at the guy's expense and ran through our memories of the many others who had rented from us and had been very embarrassed. I always wonder what's going through the customer's mind when he or she brings up a tag for a movie that stirs our (the employees') imagination.

In particular, a guy used to come in, week after week, to rent the same male-on-male movie. At least I assumed he did because the dozen or so times he came through my line, he only had one tag for that same movie. If I remember correctly, it was tag X-363, and he would leave empty-handed if the movie was out. That was something I inconspicuously scoped out because the first time he came in and left without renting anything, I decided on a hunch to check. Sure enough, the tag for it was not hanging in the blue movie room, which meant that it had already been rented out.

Anyway, later that night when we closed the store and were about to leave, J. B. suggested that one of us should check on R. C. to see if he was all right. Luckily for us, we were told what barracks he had temporarily been staying in since the dustup with his wife. Unfortunately for us, the person who told us this did not say and probably did not know which room R. C. was staying in. Even more unfortunate was that the drive to the Lanstuhl army post in Germany was out of J. B.'s direction home but happened to be the same post I was living on, so I got the short end of the stick. J. B. and I departed the video store's parking lot on the same mission—to go home—except my trip had a detour and a blind-search mission attached to it.

I drove away thinking, *I'm gonna kill this mofo when I find him because I'm supposed to be on my way home to call Karina. Instead I'm on a search mission for a grown man who came to work late, swallowed down the rest of the food Karina brought for J. B. and me, got mad for some unknown reason, and left early. Ain't this a bitch?*

Upon arriving at the barracks sometime after midnight, the fact of not knowing exactly where to start looking for R. C. hit me even squarer in the face. It was Friday night, there was a three-story army barracks with several dozen rooms to search, there were probably a bunch of young, drunk army punks there, and I did not know if R. C. was even there or which room he was staying in. Furthermore, I did not know which of the three staircases I should enter to seek him out.

Should I start my way from the ground floor up, going from room to room and knocking on each door? On the other hand, I could ask the first person I saw, hoping that he or she would know who R. C. was, even though he had only been living there a few days. I started my unprecedented search, going up the middle staircase and starting cluelessly on the second floor.

My cluelessness did not last long, however. Even though I had not knocked on door yet, upon taking a right after entering the hallway from the staircase, I heard R. C.'s voice coming through the door of the fourth room on the left.

It was the sound of pleasurable grunting from a woman after the sound of a slap. It shocked me to high heavens, and I just stood there for about three minutes listening to R. C. spanking this woman every five to ten seconds and her grunting with pleasure as he talked dirty to her during each slap of her buttocks, I assumed. Needless to say, I was surprised and entranced as I stood there. I did not move until I heard some voices entering the hallway.

At that point, I stepped away and started to act like I was looking for a particular room. At the same time, I was hoping like hell I wasn't standing in front one of the individual's door. They politely greeted me and went on by.

I raced back up to the door where R. C. was behaving badly. R. C. and the lady were still carrying on with their sexual game of spanking, scolding, grunting, moaning, and love talk. It was as if they were sitting in a chair right behind the door. It was starting to drive me wild, to the point where I was picturing doing that to Karina. But it also had me thinking that I didn't know R. C. had that in him. Months later, I learned that he had more than that in him.

I spent a good forty-five minutes in that hallway, walking away from the door each time someone would enter the hallway or at the opening sound of every door. When I left, it was well after 1 a.m., and I figured it was too late to call Karina. With all my good intentions, I probably would not have called her, even if the opportunity had produced itself, because she had not given me her number and I had not taken the time to jot it down from her application card. So I went home, took a shower, and went to bed, thinking, *J. B. won't believe this when I tell him about it tomorrow.* Believe me, when I told him, he was as amazed as I had been when I had first arrived at that door by the grace of luck.

Due to unfortunate circumstances (not getting her number; not taking the liberty of looking it up in her files at work and snooping around R.C. barracks door) I could not call Karina as I had promised. I also did not see her come to the store the rest of the weekend. But this is not to say that she couldn't have come there while I wasn't there. However, I did not check her rental card to see or look into the box to see if she had late movies. I just assumed she hadn't. I probably should have learned from the assumption I made about Crystal's trips to the store. The rest of the week passed without seeing her in the store during my shift. I was off that Tuesday, and she very well might have come in then. Nobody was obligated to tell me, so I didn't know.

When Friday arrived, it was J. B., R. C., and me again on the schedule to work, but of course, R. C. was a no-show like he had been on the previous two nights he had been scheduled to work. So of course, J. B. and I had to carry the load on what turned out to be a somewhat busy Friday in the month of August. We worked at a steady pace up until around 10:00 p.m., before the real break came.

As it grew later, we stopped and wondered if people knew they had to bring their movies back the following day. They could not get the maximum weekend special (Saturday and Sunday) because it wasn't one of those days. Many of them might as well have waited because some were leaving with up to six movies. I knew that those same people would be back the following day to cash in on the weekend special. Some would even re-rent a few of the movies they had left with on Friday. It was a circular process, which I saw repeated many times over the six years that I worked there.

After 10:10 p.m., the customers ceased coming in. It was as if armed guards had replaced the college students at the entrance of the parking lot and had taken up their posts with their weapons drawn. J. B. and I worked unimpededly until 10:52 p.m. when one last vehicle pulled up. When the headlights shown through the glass front doors, we actually stopped balancing our books and looked at each other as if to say, "What jackass is now showing here up this late on a Friday night?" However, neither one of us said anything. We just quietly went back to the business at hand and waited to see who the jackass turned out to be.

Moments later, I heard J. B.'s voice say, "Whoops. Hold off their C. C. Let me close out my books. I think you have one more customer to take care of."

"What?" was my reaction as I craned my neck toward the front door.

"Yeah, buddy," J. B. echoed at that moment.

"You're freaking kidding me," I said with a somewhat sly grin.

"Yeah, buddy. I think I'll go ahead and close up my end of the shop and leave," J. B. said with a smile on his face. Then as the individual approached the door, he asked, "You never did call her, did you?"

"No," I softly said before J. B. interrupted.

"Yeah, buddy," he echoed for the third time. Then he quickly added, "Consider me gone. Don't want any part of this explanation."

"She never did give it to me," I whispered under my breath as Karina pushed the door open.

Karina came in wearing her usual trench coat, which was buttoned up more than usual. I could however, see that she had a flowery scarf around her neck and that her boots were about knee high. However, it was impossible to tell if she was wearing shorts or a dress. Without a prop or a cue, she jumped right into the conversation J. B. and I were engaged in, as if she could read lips, had bionic ears, or had pre-dated notes of it.

"Well, that's no excuse," she said with a smile.

"Oh, shit," J. B. said. Then as he snatched his till off the counter, he added with a smile, "Don't want any part of this one, C. C. You're on your own."

"Thanks," I said to J. B. Then I turned toward Karina and said, "Well, first of all, lady, you have no idea what we were talking about."

"Sounded like she did to me," J. B. immediately chimed in with a little laughter.

"Shut up and keep on walking," I said with a smile to him.

"How rude of you," Karina said while smiling at me.

"Yes, how rude," J. B. echoed from the back room.

"Oh, shush back there!" I yelled in the air.

"No good evening or good night? Where are your manners?" Karina asked.

"Manners. Ooh, wait. They are right here in my back pocket," I sarcastically replied. Then I acted like I was pulling something out of my back pocket and said, "First of all, good evening. Secondly, we weren't talking about you. Thirdly, even if we were, you never gave me your number."

"True. But all my information is on my membership card. You could have gotten it from there," Karina suggested.

"True. Bur I don't take things I haven't been given or told to take," I countered.

"Fair enough," Karina said as she bumped up against the counter in front of my till. Then she added, "I'm running a little late, will you give me the opportunity to rent a few movies?"

"Sure. You have your usual time," I replied.

"Thank you, C. C.," Karina said and pushed herself away from the counter.

Seconds later, J. B. walked past me and the counter and gave me the peace-out sign and said, "Don't move a muscle. I'll lock the door behind me."

"Really? You're just gonna leave me like this?" I asked J. B.

"You bet. You're having a guest for dinner," J. B. said as he pulled the door open.

"Thanks," I replied.

"My pleasure," J. B. said with a smile as he exited.

J. B. then locked the door from the outside and flashed me the peace-out sign one more time. Five minutes after he had left, I still stood there waiting for Karina to bring her selections back. I was starting to wonder if she had gotten kidnapped because this was an unusually long amount of time for her. She was normally in and ready to be checked out in about three to five minutes. Since the day she opened her membership, I had never seen her take more than five minutes to make a selection. But then again, she had never come to the video store this late before, so I decided to give her a few more minutes before I sounded her time-up alarm.

After another five or six minutes, she still hadn't come from the back. I honestly hadn't paid much attention to which of the three rooms she had originally headed for. I did know that I had heard no sound come from the hallway or any of the rooms in the back. So with the front door secured as J. B.'s parting gift, I stepped went to investigate after putting my money till under the counter and on top of the active-membership box.

"Hey, lady, are you all right back there?" I shouted as I went. Then after a step or two, I jokingly added, "I know the blue room is very interesting, but you can come out now. Don't be ashamed of the tags you chose, you and I are the only ones here."

There was still no sound other than my footsteps. For a person who was serving in the military, people continuously told me that I couldn't sneak up on the enemy because I didn't know how to walk lightly. I thought that my footsteps might be drowning out the sounds in the store. Therefore, I stopped and called out again, using her name this time however.

"Karina, are you all right back there," I inquired once again. Then after no response, I added, "Karina!"

"Right here," she finally answered from the direction of the middle room, which contained the six months and older movies.

"Oh, that's where you are," I said with delight as I changed my direction from heading toward the new release room to hers. Then I added, "You had me worried there for a minute. I thought the invisible man or aliens came and snatched you up."

"No, I'm still firmly planted here on earth," Karina jokingly replied.

"Thank goodness," I interrupted.

"No, I'm still in your hemisphere. Come and see for yourself," Karina continued.

"Well, it's way past closing time and when I should be allowing anyone else in the store," I said as I was about to enter the room.

"So, are you coming to throw me out?" Karina asked in an extremely sexy tone of voice.

I could not respond because I was dumbfounded when I finally caught a glimpse of her—some twenty-five minutes after she had entered the store. She was standing in the back left half of the room in a come-and-get-me or do-you-like-what-you-see pose. It was a vision that will forever be implanted in my mind because it had me softly saying to myself, *Oh, sweet mother of Matthew, Mark, Luke, and John. Put down the fork and start eating with your hands. I don't even know if those boys had the same parents or came from the testicles of the same man, but look what we've got here.*

Karina had a sly grin on her face and tilted her head to the right. The scarf was still wrapped around her neck with both ends tossed over her shoulders, her hands were on her hips, her left leg was pointing toward eleven o'clock, her right leg was pointing toward two o'clock, and best of all, her trench coat was totally unbuttoned and was held back by her hands on her hips, exposing her clean-shaven lower area and all the glory of the rest of her frontal areas. As I stood there with Wile E. Coyote eyes, she broke the silence between us.

"You said earlier that you don't take anything that was not given to you, so will you take this if it is given to you?" Karina asked.

"Oh goodness, ma'am," I muttered before she interrupted.

"Karina," she instructed.

"Karina," I said in correction. Then I continued on, "You can have the whole video store if you want to, just leave me the tills from tonight."

After that statement from me, I remember her voice saying, "Ah-ha," before she busted out laughing. Then during her laughter, she added, "I guess that means yes."

I was still standing in place motionless like my feet were part of the flooring when Karina closed her trench coat in a flash and boldly strolled by me saying, "My kids are asleep. You can come with me if you'd like a piece of this."

I woke up then and there, and my suddenly hyperactive adrenaline had me closing up the books, the safe, and the shop and the going out the door in just a few minutes. Within nine minutes or so, we arrived in separate vehicles in front of her apartment building. There she stepped out first and looked around before giving me the all-clear signal for me to follow her. and follow her I did but not very far. Because she lived on the first floor, which for me was kind of cool and appreciated due to the fact that I didn't know what I was going into. If the need to run or jump arouse, I wouldn't have far to go to do that either.

Once we arrived inside the apartment, she told me that I should have a seat in the living room while she went and got into something more comfortable. Of course, right then and there, I started to think, *How much more comfortable can you get? Other than the trench coat you have on, you're not wearing anything else?*

Still, without uttering a sound, I sat down like an obedient little boy and waited to see what was more comfortable to her. Because to be honest, I was thinking birthday suit or at least something see-through and made of silk. However, when she returned to the living room, she was dressed in a gray Adidas sweat suit, which totally ruined my imagination that had been running wild. Again, I said nothing. I was hoping and praying she had nothing else under the sweat suit, but only time would tell.

I didn't know much about her, and when she came and sat down beside me, she could tell I was a wee bit nervous. I knew she was connected to the military somehow, but I didn't know if it was through her own affiliation or through a husband's because I had never seen her in uniform before. Those were the two scenarios I had narrowed it down to because I had eliminated the dependent of parent angle due to the fact that she had dependent kids of her own. She had said so herself the night she had brought J. B. and I the food. Still, I hadn't quite put my finger on which scenario it was, even though I was leaning more toward her being married to someone in the military.

We sat there and talked for about twenty-five minutes, but somewhere between the twenty-fifth and thirtieth minute, we find ourselves sitting face-to-face on the couch, holding hands and looking into each other's eyes at close proximity. Then that close proximity got closer within seconds until we were kissing for the first time, which wasn't anything spectacular. In fact, I would say it was downright awkward and awful. However, as we repeated it (not the awkwardness but the kisses) again and again, the awfulness became a distant memory as the kisses got better each time. Then those repeated better kisses turned into something more and led to our bump-n-grind being done right there on couch.

I personally did not expect it to go that far even though she had promised me a piece of her earlier at the store. Still, the furthest I had expected to get had been second base. I had not expected to go all the way on the first night, even though it turned out to be exciting and good for me and for her as well (as she confirmed later). In addition, the condition under which we did the do had me hoping like hell that her husband would not walk through the front door and catch us getting busy on the couch he had more or less paid for.

Still, I must add, the scariest part of the whole situation came when she invited me to join her in her master bedroom's shower, and like a damn fool, I accepted. For a somewhat cautious person, it was strange that I accepted the fact that there was no lookout watching for me. If her military-serving hubby came home and caught us together in their shower, something bad could very well happen. That was on my mind the whole time we were in there together. I dared not say the image that was on my mind throughout it, but I can say it wasn't a pretty one by any means.

On my drive home that night, I promised myself that I would never do anything so stupid again. Even though I have done many other boneheaded things since then, I have not repeated many and certainly have not repeated this one.

The very next night as it was approaching closing time, we were there ribbing R. C. over the recent stunt he had pulled. That's when, out of the blue, J. B. put a pause on it all by saying, "Oh goodness. Looks like your girl with the trench coat is back again tonight."

"Where?" I immediately asked as I poked my head over the counter.

"She's coming," J. B. said. Then he immediately asked, "So what happened last night? I've been waiting for you to fill me in on it all evening long."

"Me too," R. C. jokingly added.

"Oh, nothing," I nonchalantly said.

"Nothing? You expect me to believe that?" J. B. said with his usual casual grin.

"For real. Nothing happened," I said with a straight face.

"Well, you let me know if something happens tonight because here she comes," J. B. said with a nod toward the front door.

"Man, you can't see her," I said looking back to my left at the door before continuing on. "Damn, you're right. How the hell could you tell who was pulling up outside when it's dang near eleven o'clock at night?"

"I've got the eyes of an eagle, my friend," J. B. said with a smile.

"Dang! I guess," I replied as Trench Coat approached the front door.

"R.C., let's hurry up and get out of here. Killer has some business to tend to," J. B. said as he reached for a stack of return movies.

"So what happened last night?" R. C. asked nonchalantly.

"What are you talking about, dude?" I asked while shaking my head for him to stop it and eyeing Karina's reaction.

She looked at me with wide eyes as if to ask, "You didn't kiss and tell, did you?" I, on the other hand, just shrugged my shoulders as if to say, "He's just grasping for air." Then I too picked up a stack of returned movies and headed toward the back. I did not get to my destination of the new release room however because as I was about to enter it, J. B. tackled me at its entrance and pried the movies out of my hands while saying, "Give me those and go tend to your guest. I want details the next time you come to work … details. No kidding killer!"

After the books were closed for the night and everyone else had left, Karina, who was quickly becoming more than just a customer to me, and I started to mess around inside the half-dark store. We kept on playing until we ended up into the insurance office and on top of the main desk. I will not, however, elaborate on what took place on top of that desk, I will say that just like the prior night, she had nothing on under her trench coat except her birthday suit. I did not whisper a peep to any of my coworkers, even though they kept on prying.

Karina and I kept on meeting, mostly at the store and at least two times a week. Over the course of the following two months, I learned a lot more about her and her husband's relationship. It included the two kids she was always running to pick up from the after-school program when she got off work and had stopped by the video store to grab movies for the evening. She also reiterated that her husband was an E-6 in the air force and that he worked second shift (4 p.m. to 11 p.m.). Most days, he did not get home until five or six o'clock in the morning. She said on that rare occasions, he would come home at around 2 a.m., but that was once in a blue moon.

Referring back to my days when I had first joined the military and had gone to midnight chow after getting off at 11 p.m., I commenced telling her that getting home at 2 a.m. wasn't unusual. I had not had a vehicle at that time. In fact, I hadn't even had a driver's license and had to walk about a mile home to the dormitory after leaving the chow hall. Therefore, I withdrew my suggestion. Instead, I asked her if she thought her husband was cheating on her. I never did get a definite answer. I formed my own conclusion in one of our later conversations and forced the issue again. I did not want her to catch religion on me and stop the good thing we had going.

A few weeks short of our third month of hanging out together, Karina showed up at the store one Monday evening in tears and asked if we could talk. Of course, it happened on Monday during our movie-return rush hour when most of the movies that had been rented on the weekend were being retuned. So I told her we were one man down because R. C. had not shown up for work and ask if we could talk later. She, in turn, said she did not know if she would be able to come back but would try. Then she walked away, and I jumped back into my work of collecting and renting movies but with a heavy heart.

All evening long, I worried about why she wanted to talk to me. My first thought was that her husband had found out about us, which was partly driven by her comment of not knowing if she could come back later. I also thought about her catching religion and changing her mind about us. Both of these would be acceptable scenarios and ones I wouldn't put up much of a fight against. However, when the thought of her possible being pregnant crossed my mind, that was when nervousness set in.

At that moment, I started dropping things. I couldn't walk or think straight, and I was visibly sweating. I even gave a gentleman back the late movies he had returned, as if they were newly checked out. To top it off, I didn't even charge him late fees or rental fees.

To be honest, I wasn't afraid of pregnancy. I never had been and never would be. By then, I already had four kids. However, they had all been with the same woman, although I had been legally separated from her at the time. But the thought of getting someone pregnant out of wedlock and the fact that I was still on active duty (Married but separated—going through a divorce) was the part that scared me the most. It became dreadfully nerve-reckoning when I thought about how the military react to situation like that and as I moseyed around the store, I started to ask myself, *How could I be so stupid to let something like this happen at this juncture?*

Fortunately for me, when she came back later that evening, it was none of those scenarios I had been driving myself crazy with that evening, but it was devastating news for us. Apparently, earlier in the day, her husband had notified her of his impending assignment to Korea and that he wanted her to take the kids and go back stateside immediately to live with his mother until further notice. I found this to be a very unusual move—not the going home to stay with his mom part but the going from an overseas long tour (Germany) to an overseas short tour (Korea).

Military people are always having their spouses and kids going to live with their families when they are venturing on unaccompanied assignments overseas. It is a way to save money and to also leave your family in the hands of relatives who will fill in for you while you're away. I did something similar in the early nineties, when I went to Korea from Texas. I rented a bigger apartment within my apartment complex and asked one of my sisters-in-law to move in with my wife and our two-month-old daughter.

However, for someone, who was already overseas serving a long-tour assignment, to go on a short-tour assignment was not the typical move. Moreover, that bit of news basically put an end to the blossoming relationship we were developing. I can honestly say we never got together again after that evening. In fact, I can't remember ever seeing her in the store again as a paying customer.

CHAPTER 15

FOUR WITHIN NINETY MINUTES

A S FAR AS customers and their stories go, I made a promise to myself that I would not include any of their names, stories, or the current and other location of the company I am now working for where any customer's interaction took place. Regardless of how impactful the customer interaction had been. the main reason, this particular chapter of my life will be included in a future book (one I'm currently working on) titled "Working for W!" Why? Because many people have been encouraging me to write one, even though I have been somewhat reluctant to do so. But now, I've taken a different stand against the idea and have compiled enough good (positive and negative) material to do so – and continue to collect additional details by the minute. Especially since the arrival of my new boss.

I'm just at the point, however, where I need to get what I've already written published and to finish up other ones before adding anything else to the pile. However, as I was searching my memories for some additional good customer stories to tell, I could not help reflecting on these four short ones, which I experienced because of my current rank within one former organization. Hence the title, "*Four within Ninety Minutes*" due to the four upper-level manager's customer-related issues I had to deal with within ninety-minutes period one afternoon.

After my promotion to the position I currently hold and upon my arrival at my present location, I was warned that I would encounter a whole slew of people returning bicycles. Some would even return one or two per month. As curiosity ran through my mind, I asked "Why?" I was told that because the store was in a vacation town and the patrons were visiting mostly from overseas, they abused the store's liberal bike-return policy. When I was informed that nobody ever put their foot down about it, I decided that this year it would change. So after leaving specific instructions that I should be called the next time someone tried to return a bike, I walked away from customer service saying to myself, *I will effectively end my organization's liberal bike-return policy, which everyone is aware of and is getting abused but is not willing to do anything about it.*

The following Saturday at around 10:55 a.m., as I was getting ready to attend an eleven o'clock meeting, I got a customer-related page from customer service. I called ahead to get a picture of what to expect and was told it was about a bike being returned. Of course, that got me excited, and I headed up front as quickly as possible. Upon my arrival at the customer service area, I saw two individuals who looked like they were in their early twenties, standing off to the side next to a bicycle. I did not approach them, however, but instead walked directly to the customer service desk. As if I hadn't already known what was the issue was, I asked, "What's going on?"

One of the customer service associates, Kimberly, who disliked our unheard of, liberal bike-return policy as much as I did, said to me, "Sir, those two gentlemen over there are trying to return that bike. They said they bought it three weeks ago, but it looks like it was purchased three years ago."

"Oh really," I said before walking off into the direction of the two guys.

"Are you a manager?" one of them immediately asked in a European accent.

"Yes, I am," I said. Then I quickly added, "May I help you?"

"Yes. I'm trying to return this bike, but the lady at customer service said we're not allowed to them after fifteen days," the shorter one said.

"And that's not right because we returned another one three weeks ago when we got this one," the taller one added quickly.

"Yes. I had that one for almost a month. I was told when I bought that one in that I had up to a month to return it," the shorter one added.

"Well, actually, I give seven days on bikes," I said.

"Well, that's not what your policy says. I went on line and looked it up, and it says thirty days," the shorter one said. Then he quickly added, "I can pull it up on my phone so you can see it if you want."

"Please do," I said. Then I asked, "So, what's the matter with the bike?"

Without inspecting it too closely, I could see three eye-popping problems with it. Only one of them could have occurred with a bike three weeks old. The others had to have occurred over time—maybe over a six-year span, as Kimberly had said. I must say, she was being generous with the age she had estimated because it looked like it was at least four or five years old to me.

"The seat is loose, the chain is loose, and the wheel in the back is bent," the shorter one said.

"I'm sorry. How long ago did you say you got this bike again?" I asked while looking the bike over.

"About three weeks ago when we returned the other one," the taller one stated.

"May I see your receipt?" I asked.

"Actually, we couldn't find the latest receipt, but we have the one for the first bike we bought in early June and the one we exchanged it for after that. But we can't find the one we exchanged that one for, which is this bike. But we have everything else," the taller one said.

After pausing for a brief moment, I said, "Let me see if I have this right. You guys purchased a bike in early June. You returned it for another one some three weeks later, which you returned for this one three weeks ago. Now you are trying to return this one for your another?"

"No, we'd like to get a refund," the shorter one said quickly. Then while looking at the taller one, he added, "Right? We're getting a refund, right?"

"Right!" the taller one said in agreement.

"Oh, I didn't know that. That changes the equation," I said aloud.

Instantly I could feel the sting of burning eyes on me, and as I stood upright from my closer inspection of the bike, I said, "Did you happen to pull up the return policy yet?"

Ah, no. I'm having some trouble getting back into your website," the shorter one said. Then he quickly added, "What changes the equation? Your website does say you have thirty days to return something. I read it."

"Oh, I have no doubt. I have a copy in the policy book in the back," I said.

"You do?" the taller one asked quickly.

"Yep. I certainly do, and it states—" I replied before being interrupted.

"May we see it?" asked the shorter one.

"Sorry, I can't. It is not for public consumption. But I can tell you that it clearly states that the return limitation for certain items is up to thirty days, except for plants that are returnable for up to one year, but that's neither here nor there. Your bike in question is up to thirty days at manager's discretion. My discretion is seven days," I said.

"But the policy says thirty days," the shorter one countered.

"Yes ... at manager's discretion, and my discretion is seven days. But from the looks of this bike, I won't be able to refund your money," I countered.

"But I no longer want the bike. We've had too many problems with them," the taller one said.

"And I can't do anything with this bike because it's either been abused or it's about six years old," I said.

"So what are we supposed to do? Your policy clearly states that we have thirty days to return it. We are well within that time," the shorter one said.

"Have you actually taken a good look at this supposedly three-week-old bike you guys are trying to return?" I asked.

"What do you mean?" They both asked simultaneously.

"Well, let me make some things obvious for you. First of all, you guys have no receipt. Second, the seat is almost ripped off and looks like it's been bleached. Third, the chain is rusty like it's been sitting in a rust bowl for a year. Fourth, the back rim is bent out of shape. Fifth, the handlebar is beat up from one end to the other. It looks like it's been chasing parked walls," I stated. Then I asked, "Need I go on?"

"But I don't want it anymore. What do you want me to do with it?" the shorter one asked.

"I understand that. What do you want me to do with it?" I asked in return.

"I would like you to give me my money back for it because it's obviously broken and I'm returning it within the time allowed," the shorter one said.

"And I might be willing to do that if you had brought me back a bike in good riding condition," I told him.

"We are returning it because we can't ride it. We can't even get it to stand up on its own," the taller one implied.

"A bicycle does not stand up on its own. The kickstand is what keeps it standing, you know," I replied.

"What is that?" one of them asked.

Then the shorter one added, "I'm from Europe, and I ride bikes all the time."

"Then you should be familiar with a kickstand and what it's used for," I suggested.

"We are just interested in getting our money back for this bad bike," the taller one said.

"And I would love to if you had brought me back a good bike," I replied sarcastically.

"Well, I'm sorry the bike is not good, and I'd like to have a refund. Besides, I already have a bike at home. I don't need another one," the shorter one added.

At that point, we all momentarily paused. However, during that pause, I thought, *You should bring a bike with you the next time you come from Europe or at least read your freaking European bike manual first so you can brush up on what a kickstand is and what it is used for, dumb-ass. You all come here every summer, buy a bike that you guys abuse, and then trade it in every couple of weeks until it is almost time to go back home. Then it is returned for a full refund. Well, the bike rental agency this store has been running is official closed, at least on the days that I work here.*

However, when I realized they were supposedly waiting on me for a final answer, I shifted out of my dream world and said to them, "Fellows, I'm very sorry, but I cannot authorize the return of this bike for a refund of any kind."

"We need to talk to someone else," they both said. Then the shorter one added, "Is your supervisor around? I need to speak to him."

"I'm sorry, the store manager is in a meeting, but you are free to wait for her to get back," I said.

"What's the number of your headquarters?" the shorter one asked. Then he added, "I need to call in a customer complaint on this because you're going against your own policy."

After giving them the number to my home office, I walked away from customer service without looking back. I just left them standing there, the taller one holding the bike, and the shorter one doing something on his phone (calling or texting the home office) I presumed. No sooner than I had walked away from customer service, I was being paged back there again. Of course, I didn't mind because it was keeping me from attending the eleven o'clock meeting that I passionately disliked. So I immediately turned around in the men's department and headed back to customer service.

Upon my return to customer service, I witnessed the other customer service associate (Sarah) trying to calm an irate customer who was demanding to see a manager. Therefore, without hesitation, I stepped in and apologized for whatever it was that had made her upset and asked her to stop yelling at my associate. Without listening to who I said I was or even trying to figure out who I was, the lady said, "Don't tell me to calm down. I need to speak to a manger because this little hussy here refuses to refund me for this item I bought earlier today."

"Well, I am a manager, and I'm here to try and help you, but I will not do so until you lower your voice and stop calling my employees names," I said to the lady.

"And who are you?" she asked while looking at my chest.

My first thought was, *You fucking idiot. I told you who I was when I first approached you, and you are looking directly at my the name badge on my chest and still asking who I am.* But it was a good thing I did not put the carriage in front of the horse because when I nonchalantly gazed down at my badge, it was actually flipped over. So if an individual (customer or employee) did not know who I was, he or she would be unable to tell I was a manager without making an assumption from the way I was dressed or guessing. Therefore, I flipped it back over to expose who I really was and then apologized to the lady.

It calmed her down to a satisfactory level so that I was able to ask her what seemed to be the problem. She explained to me that she had bought a Radio Flyer for her grandson's birthday and that she had been very disappointed and embarrassed when the box had been opened at the party an hour earlier. Moreover, it had left her grandson in tears, so she would like to be get her money back and be compensated for the anguish her grandson had been dealt on his birthday.

I became highly curious and wanted to see if her grandson had somehow been presented with the wrong gender of Radio Flyer. First, I asked for the receipt, which Sarah handed to me while shaking her head in disbelief. At first, I thought she was shaking her head as if to say, "No," or "Oh no, here we go again. I did the right thing, and here comes a manager to overrule me." If the latter was what Sarah was doing, she would have been entirely justified because so often in the name of customer satisfaction, we have overruled customer service associates and have made them feel bad, even though they were doing the right thing. It was a thankless job for doing exactly what you had been taught to do.

Anyhow, I took the receipt from Sarah's hand and looked it over. It said it had been purchased at 9:39 a.m. that morning for $179.85 but at another one of our stores. Still, I didn't let that bother me because it was company policy that you could buy anything at any store, and it didn't have to be returned at that store, if that's what you chose to do. It just had to be within the prescribed return window of time.

So after seeing that everything was on legitimate with the receipt, I asked to look inside the box. As Sarah turned the opened end in my direction, I could see her close her eyes and shake her head in disbelief again. When I looked inside the Radio Flyer's box, I understood why Sarah was shaking her head. I had to step back away from it myself for a brief second.

"What's the matter? You don't believe me?" the lady asked as I was stepping back.

As I turned back to her and tried not to laugh aloud, I said to the lady, "Are you serious, ma'am? You truly expect me to believe that is the Radio Flyer you got in that box when you purchased it at the Newport News store this morning?"

"You can call them and ask them if you want," the lady replied.

"What are they going to tell me? Yes, they sold this to you looking like this?" I asked her.

"Yes. They will," she replied.

"So they opened the box and showed it to you, and you willingly walked out the doors with this pile of rusty metal instead of a Radio Flyer. Now you are trying to return it here for a full refund?" I curiously asked.

"Well, they didn't actually open the box, but they can verify that I purchased it there," she said.

"Ma'am, I'm looking at your receipt here. I can verify that you purchased a Radio Flyer at the Newport News store this morning. But the possibility of this being the one you purchased is highly unlikely," I said to her.

"What are you doing now, calling me a liar?" she asked.

"Not at all, ma'am. I'm just saying I find it highly unusual and even suspect that this is not the same Radio Flyer you purchased this morning," I replied.

"Well, if you don't believe me, it means you are calling me a liar. And I ain't no liar. I just want my money back so I can go and get me something better somewhere else that will make my grandson happy on his birthday," she said.

"Well, I'm sorry to say, ma'am, but I can't refund you for this pile of scrap metal in this box," I said to her.

"Why not?" she immediately shouted. Then she caught herself and in a softer tone added, "I bought it at one of your stores this morning, and I would like to return it for a full refund. I'm even willing to forego the compensation for my grandson's anguish."

"Ma'am, I am truly sorry about your grandson's anguish, but if you would like to return this item for a full refund, I would suggest that you take it back to the Newport News store and to do it there," I stated.

"Well, I don't feel like driving all the way over there. I live closer to this store, and that's why I came here to return it," she said.

"I understand that ma'am and sympathize with the extra driving you'll have to incur, but only they can independently verify that this bunch of scrap metal is what they sold you earlier today as a brand-new Radio Flyer," I said to her.

She did not like me calling her return a "bunch of scrap metal" and blew up at me, shouting, "You guys sold me this, and you are being rude and disrespectful and unprofessional at this moment. All I needed to hear you say was, 'Yes, ma'am. I'll refund you your money,' apologize, and let me go on my merry way. But instead, you came up here to make disparaging remarks about the disgusting and filthy item you guys sold me.

"I want nothing else to do with you. You are rude beyond compare. Your customer service attitude stinks. I want my money back, and if you won't give it to me, I need to talk to someone else who will. As a matter of fact, I want to talk to your supervisor right now. Get me your boss."

"Certainly ma'am. I'll go and get him. You have a wonderful and blessed day too, ma'am," I said sarcastically with a smile before walking off. As I did, I thought, *What a crooked bitch. It is so obvious that a blind man could see that she went home and exchanged the new Radio Flyer for a pile of crap she had at home or something she probably picked up out of the trash or from a neighbor's yard and devised a scheme to get a brand-new one at no cost … just wicked, wicked, and wicked.*

Furthermore, I was certain that once I explained the situation to my boss, Mitch, he would side with me and the customer service associate (Sarah) and not give the lady a refund. But I temporarily forgot where I was working and how nervous management could get the moment a customer threatened to call the home office and make a complaint. The term *home office* always causes them to quickly buckle and give in to the customer's demands, even when it is a blatant fact or obvious that the individual is lying and that his or her only motive is to get over on (something for free) on the store, or on the company as a whole.

Just because the organization has a liberal-return policy, crooked and unethical customers just sit around and come up with ways to get something for nothing. Because management is afraid to tell it like it is or to make tough customer service decisions, it hardly ever says no to anything. To be fair to them, the home office doesn't help. It is so leery of a little negativism, it always sides with the customer over the people who work for them (store personnel). It will order us to give away damn near a whole department to satisfy a crooked customer. It's a rationale I always equated with my funeral observation

I have not once gone to a funeral and heard anything bad said about the person who died. It's often said that the person is in a better place (indirectly meaning heaven), or it is boldly stated that we will meet that person again in heaven. However, no one ever says that the person was one of the most terrible people on earth that he or she was hell on wheels while alive, so good luck to that person in hell where he or she deserved to be. Everyone always says that the person is going to heaven and that we will see him or her when we get there.

I truly believe if all these people end up there, especially the unrepentant ones or people like these next two ladies in the bed-in-a-bag store I worked for, there won't be any room for any of the good or half-good ones like myself.

Therefore, in keeping with the tradition of talking a good game and meaning something else, being unwilling to stand up for what you believe in, or worse yet, being totally afraid to boldly tell the boss why a decision (good or bad) was made, my boss completely weaseled out. He authorized a complete refund to the lady. On top of that, he gave her a twenty-five-dollar store discount card under the title of Customer Satisfaction because Sarah and I had supposedly given her a hard time. Then he told the lady that we had only been doing our jobs and that Sarah and I hadn't been wrong about denying her a refund because we had not been authorized to make that decision at our level, which of course, was a lie on his part.

John Leslie

The icing of that whole situation for me was that the lady hadn't even taken the time to put the packing material from the new Radio Flyer back into the box with the pile of scrap metal. Then my boss had the nerve to walk with me and while being visibly upset, wanted to talk to me about karma and how it would get her in the end. Karma wasn't what I wanted to be told about then. I wanted the of karma to happen now. I wanted him to tell the woman to take her lying, thieving self out of the store, gather up that pile of crap, and shove it where the sun didn't shine ... but in a politically correct way.

Surprisingly, this wasn't the first time this had happened to me and this particular supervisor. He had done it to me on several occasions before, but he had never once said that he had done it in hopes of karma taking revenge on the individual. Moreover, I did not let his slap in the face discourage me from making tough decisions I knew I was being paid to make.

Not long after that unethical-customer experience, I was summoned back to customer service to deal with two customers over a bed-in-a-bag. Of course when the page came for a member of management to come to customer service, it didn't usually say what the page concerned. They usually said, "A member of management is needed at customer service," and then one of us would copy that page. However, it seemed like I was the only one answering any pages that day or since I had arrived at work.

This latest page came shortly after Mitch and I made V-lines away from each other in front of the electronics department. He was heading toward the hardware department, and I was heading toward the pets' department when I made an immediate left to go back to customer service.

Upon arriving back at customer service, I went around to the other side of the counter directly facing the customers as usual. Standing in front of the associate who had paged for a member of management were two ladies who had entered the line shortly before Mitch and I had finished up with the Radio Flyer customer. At the time, one of the ladies had been hugging what looked like a comforter (bed-in-a-bag) against her chest, and the other had been pushing a stroller with a three-year-old toddler in it.

Now the comforter was lying on the counter, still in its clear plastic cover, and the customer service associate was holding a receipt. Before I could say anything, she said, "Sir, these ladies here are trying to return this comforter set. She said her boyfriend bought it here yesterday."

Without paying particular attention, I could immediately tell there were several things wrong with the bag on the counter. First and foremost, I could tell the bag was for a king-sized comforter set, but with the amount of space it had left in it, one could fit two midgets and a poodle inside and still have room for half-a-dozen body-length pillow cases. That included what they were trying to return in the bag. So I immediately asked the associate for the receipt and if she had counted the number of items that had been inside the bag. Hence, some obvious problems popped up with what they were trying to return.

The customer service associate Becky looked at me as if I had lost my mind and said, as if she was from Silicon Valley, "I ain't touching that. You see how filthy it is?"

The associate was right. Still, her bluntness in front of the customers caught me off guard. However, I could not disagree with her, especially when I was thinking the same thing. It forced me to tell the customers, "Ma'am, when did you say your boyfriend bought this again?"

"Yesterday. It's right there on the receipt," the one who was not with the stroller said.

"Oh, I'm sorry," I said. Then with a bit of sarcasm I quickly added, "I thought you meant yesterday, last year."

"Last year? Why would she return something from a year ago," the one with the stroller said.

"Well, with no disrespect, ma'am, this thing looks like it hasn't been washed in a year, possibly longer," I said.

"Try ten," Becky immediately interjected.

I politely told her to let me handle it. Then I turned back toward the customers and asked, "Have you seen the state of what's inside of this bag, ma'am?"

"Yes. That's why I'm returning it," the one without the stroller said.

"Well, I don't blame you. In fact, if I were in your shoes, I wouldn't have accepted it in the first place," I stated.

"Good. I'm glad you understand why," one of them said.

"One hundred and sixty-nine dollars, eh?" I said as I moved closer to the register as if I was about to start the refund process.

"Yes," the one with the stroller said with gleam in her eyes that was about to be put out.

"Do you know what happened to the rest of the comforter set?" I asked nonchalantly.

"The rest of what?" the one without the stroller asked.

"The comforter set. It seems that several pieces are missing," I casually said.

"On top of it being filthy," Becky added.

"Becky," I said in a drawn-out fashion. Then I said to her, "Please see if you can help the next customer in line. In the meantime, I'll handle this by myself. Upon which, I looked in the customers' direction again and repeated, "'Do you know what happened to the rest of the comforter set?"

"I don't know. It's all there I suppose. I never opened it," she said.

"Well, obviously someone did. It's not hard to tell that several pieces are missing," I said as Becky gazed back over her shoulder at me like she wanted me to add something more.

"I thought she was no longer in this conversation," the one with the stroller said aloud while looking over at Becky.

"She's not," I replied. Then I sarcastically added, "Is she the one returning the comforter set or are you?"

"I am," the one without the stroller answered.

"But I'm her friend, and I'm the one who gave her a ride here," the one with the stroller added.

"That was very nice of you. You're such a wonderful friend," I said. Then I asked, "Now, can I deal with only one of you please?" After a brief pause, I continued the conversation again, "Because of the condition of what's inside of the bag, there's no way I can refund your money without all of the items included."

"Well, I don't know if any of it is missing. That's just the way my boyfriend gave it to me yesterday," the one without the stroller stated.

"I'm sorry, ma'am. I can't refund your money for this," I said.

"Why not?" the lady said in a louder voice. Then she added, "This was bought here yesterday, and now you are telling me that I can't return it. That's not what your policy states."

"Ma'am, I'm in agreement with you that something was bought here yesterday, but it was not what is now inside this bag," I stated.

"What do mean?" she asked.

"Ma'am, we don't sell anything like this in the store and not in this condition. So I suggest you get ahold of your boyfriend and ask him what he did with the comforter set that belongs in this bag," I said to her.

"Well, this is what he bought, and he bought it here. I would like a refund because I don't like it," the one without the stroller said.

At that moment, I looked at the time on the receipt and then said to her, "Okay. This says it was purchased at 4:43 p.m. yesterday. Just give me a minute to go and pull the security footage from that time to see exactly what your boyfriend purchased."

The moment I said that, both ladies immediately looked at each other. Their sudden need for a refund was not a major priority anymore. The one without the stroller snatched the bag off of the counter and said, "We have to go. I'll come back tomorrow. If we don't leave now, I'm gonna run late for my two o'clock appointment."

The customer service associate Becky was very amused at how the ladies came up with a reason to suddenly leave the moment I mentioned pulling the security camera video.

Becky actually thanked me aloud in front of the other customers. One of the people standing in line nonchalantly asked, "She wasn't trying to return that, was she?" However, neither Becky nor I responded to the unsolicited question. As the ladies were departing hurriedly, I said aloud, "I'll have that video footage ready when you return tomorrow, the day after, or any time after that. Okay?"

It was another twenty-two minutes or so before I had to answer another management page (the fourth within ninety minutes) to customer service. This one was a head-scratcher for me. I still laugh when I think about it. It had been as funny as heck when I had had to deal with it. On the other hand, it had probably not been for the man's spouse. For the life of me, I still cannot figure out why a man would drag his family to the store to put them through such embarrassment over an item that cost seven dollars and ninety-four cents. But it's a free country, and I guess people have to stand up for their principles. When something does not live up to its billing, it is worth saying so, even if one has to drag the family along for the ride or maybe to prove the point.

On this call like the first one, I was asked to call customer service before I went there … and so I did. But while talking to the customer service associate, she was whispering almost to the point of being mute, so I asked her why she was talking so softly.

"Because this is too funny and sort of embarrassing, and I'm trying not to die with laughter," she softly said through a few giggles.

"Ah, ha. Do you want to go into the cash office and have me call you in there?" I asked.

"Don't mind if you do," she quickly said and hung up the phone.

Moments later, I called her from the cash office, and she picked answered, saying to me, "Please don't laugh when you get up here 'cause there's this guy here with his wife and four kids. He's wanting to return a half-used bottle of K-Y Jelly because it was falsely advertised."

"What do you mean he's trying to return a bottle of K-Y Jelly?" I curiously asked. Then quickly added, "There's nothing wrong with that."

"It's not a full bottle. It's a half-used bottle. Half of it is gone," Adrianna said with a giggle. Then she added, "And he's looking for a full refund."

"How much does it cost?" I asked her.

"Seven dollars and ninety-four cents," Adrianna said with a giggle.

"Why are you giggling? What's so funny about that?" I asked Adrianna.

"He already used half, probably a little bit more, He brought his whole family in with him and was talking about it not living up to his expectation at the top of his lungs," Adrianna explained.

"Okay, maybe he's just a loud person," I said to her.

"Maybe. But he's waving it around and telling the other customers not to buy it because it's not what it's cracked up to be. His poor wife is standing there looking embarrassed," Adrianna said.

"That's not cool," I uttered.

"Absolutely not," Adrianna said.

"Just give him his money back and get it over with," I said to her.

"I would kill him if he was my husband. Well, first of all, he couldn't have dragged me and my kids out here to come and watch him act like fool," Adrianna said. Then she quickly but nonchalantly asked, "You do know what K-Y Jelly is mostly used for, right?"

"Of course," I quickly said to her. Then I just as quickly added, "Just refund the item and let them go home."

"No, boss. He used half, probably more. Plus he bought it more than thirty days ago," Adrianna said.

"Okay. In that case, tell him we can't refund it," I replied.

"I've already told him that, and that's why he requested to talk to a member of management," Adrianna explained.

"Okay. I'll be there in a second," I said and hung up the phone.

I left with a smile on my face, wondering how I was going to keep myself from laughing when I got up to customer service. Because even though I wasn't sure what the main purpose of K-Y Jelly was, the people I'd heard talking about it had associated it mostly with anal sex.

I certainly couldn't say that in this case, it was the gentleman's sole purpose for buying it. But if it was, I could probably envision why since he came to the store with four kids, the oldest of which was probably not more than six years old. So I thought that maybe their religion forbid contraception, and they probably weren't ready for any more kids—yet. Also, maybe he didn't believe in pulling out, or his wife wasn't particularly thrilled with the idea of swallowing, so they compromised on anal sex instead.

I am not here knocking anyone's sexual desire or for trying things to spice up there love-live. My first college professor, Dr. T. Harrell, once told me (my group) during a class discussion, "People should not knock anal sex until they've tried it." And even though, it cause me to look at her differently since that day, I totally agree with what she said. In addition, I'm not disparaging anyone for having several young kids close together in age because I was once a subscriber to that club. I had four small kids in my household at once, too. When my youngest one was born, the oldest was only six years old. The difference for me was (luckily for me and my wife) that we believed in contraception—along with everything else mentioned above. In fact, my wife then, did not have to be talked into doing things sexually. She, in fact, she would talk me into doing things. Nothing like my current wife who invent reasons, or just pull things out of thin air in order to not get involved in anything romantically or sexually.

Because of organizations' needs for customers dollars and their inability to see one bad review they will treat every customer as if he or she is always right at the expense of their employees emotions and dedications. Strangely enough, that was never something I subscribed to, but in the same token, strongly believe, for cohesiveness, when you chose to work for an institution you also chose to embrace or enforce its policy. And in my case, this was something I had to do many times when I got to customer service if the customer hadn't already given up and left.

On this particular time, when I arrived at the customer service desk, sure enough, the gentleman was still there causing a scene with the half-used bottle of K-Y Jelly in his hand. His poor wife and four kids were standing off to the side bearing witness to the spectacle he was causing. It was something that was clearly causing embarrassment to his wife, who was standing close to the Coinstar machine holding the couple's youngest in her arms. Some of the children stood on either side of her. The oldest one was close by, but he was playing a game on his hand-held system and being oblivious to the spectacle his father was dialing up. I guess he was already used to his father's overblown reaction.

I stepped up to the man, introduced myself, and asked if there was a problem I could help him solve. However, this was after I politely asked him to step out of the drama club he was trying to be a member of. From there, his summation of his problem was basically what Adrianna had told me on the phone, so I gave him the same answer she had given him earlier, "Sorry, I cannot offer you a full refund for an item that is half used and more than thirty days old."

"What do you mean you can't give me a refund?" he shouted. Then he quickly added in an even louder voice, "This is false advertisement—and you know it. It did not make my wife lubricated and easy to penetrate as it said it would."

At that moment, the whole customer service area fell into a deep silence, and you could have heard a pin drop all the way in Jamaica. Furthermore, the look on his poor wife's face silently said, "Oh, my God. I'll never be able to show my face in public again."

I (me, myself, and I) began to say to myself, *If he thought she was hard to penetrate before while using the K-Y Jelly, wait until after today. Getting into Fort Knox would be a breeze for him compared to getting into her.*

At that point however, I stopped him by saying, "Sir, if you'd like me to continue talking to you, you will have to deal with me in a more rational and professional tone of voice. Think about your wife and kids standing here. Please!"

"Who? Them? They're fine," he said quickly.

"I don't think so," I cautioned.

"Oh, well, you see this here," he said in a softer voice while waving the half-empty bottle of K-Y Jelly in my face. "This is a classic case of bait and switch. You advertise this item as a lubricant for sexual pleasure, but I applied it to my dear wife over there, on several different occasions, and it did not work."

What a fucking dick you are, I instantly thought. However, this was the only thing I sarcastically muttered, "Over thirty days!"

"What?" he quickly asked.

"Oh, nothing," I responded quickly. Then just as quickly added, "Go on. I'm listening."

"So what do you intend to do about it?" he asked

"I don't intend to do anything about it," I quickly replied.

"Mister, I at least need my money back," he shouted.

"Sir, this is you last warning. Another outburst and this discussion is over," I said. Then after a short pause, I added, "In fact, I think this discussion is already over because I cannot offer you a refund for a product where more than half of it is already used. Plus it's past the thirty-day-return threshold."

"Well, I don't care. It didn't work like it said it would, and I want my money back. Plus I should be compensated for bringing my whole family down here," the gentleman argued.

"I'm sorry. That was your call to bring them here. As for the K-Y Jelly, we did not print anything on the package, so if it did not work as advertised, you'll have to contact the manufacturer yourself," I explained to him.

"Why should I? he asked. "You are the seller, aren't you? You're just as liable as they are. Someone needs to compensate me for my trust, trouble, and anguish. So I'll ask again, what are you gonna do for me?"

"Sir, I apologize if the product did not live up to your expectation, but there's no guarantee on the back that it works the same for everyone. We as an organization did not guarantee that it would. Therefore, as I stated before, I would love to refund your money, but more than half the product is missing from the container, and it's way past the thirty-day-return threshold.

"Way past? It's only been thirty-one days. Surely one day can't make that big a difference," he countered.

"If it was only that, I would understand, but you've used nearly all the product in the container," I said to him.

"It was supposed to work, so my wife and I kept on trying. We weren't counting how many days we had it or how much we'd used," the gentleman said.

"Well next time, sir, you'll have to be mindful of those things. Now if you don't mind, I have to go, I'm being paged for another issue in lawn and garden," I told him.

"Well you go take care of your issue, you hear. Don't worry about my concern. I'll just take my business somewhere else next time. I don't come here to shop on a regular basis, but you guys just lost my business forever. I ain't never coming back here again. Come on family," he said as he latched onto the hand of the oldest child and madly stormed off. Then a moment later, he added, "You can best believe I will call your headquarters about this to lodge a complaint."

When he said that, I yelled, "Hey, wait up. You forgot to get the number for the home office. I have it right here for you." However, he never turned back around to come and get it. If he had, I would certainly have handed it to him myself ... and call them too, if he wanted to talk to them from the store. It wouldn't be much different from many of the customers who got upset inside the store for one reason or another (not particularly at me or any specific member of management but in general) and then went outside to their car and called the home office to complain.

Personally, I don't look for trouble or try to be a dick about things when it comes to customer service. I actually like servicing customers to a certain extent. Why? Because some customers are blatant with no shame in their game like a woman who once returned eight pieces (sets) of fried chicken bones and demanded a full replacement meal. My "Reflections on More than Just an Eight-Piece."

I've always said, "I will help a customer to the best of my ability, but negligence on their part does not constitute an automatic emergency on my part." That's why I put my foot down when my gut tells me someone is not being honest. I really don't mind if our home office, or business headquarters is called on me for something I thought was right, even when the customer made it seem as if I was wrong and home office mostly sides with the customer because it's a lot easier to deal with the issue at hand that way.

CHAPTER 16

REFLECTIONS ON MORE THAN JUST AN EIGHT-PIECE

S EVERAL MONTHS BEFORE I got promoted to my current position, I was summoned to the deli department to talk on the phone to a customer. Being the type of person who likes to have a heads-up on the customer situation I'm about to walk into, I naturally asked the deli associate what was the call about. She told me it was a lady calling to ask if she could return the chicken she had bought the day before (a Saturday) because it was all burnt and dried out beyond eatable. Tammie went on to say she told the lady that she could, but the lady wanted to hear it from a manager. Since Yancey wasn't around, she had called me instead.

I took the phone off hold and said, "Thanks for calling the store deli. Support Manager John speaking. May I help you?"

"Yes. Are you a manager?" the lady asked.

"Yes, ma'am, I am," I replied. Then I quickly added, "May I help you with something?"

"Are you new? You're not the department manager I've talked to before," the lady stated.

I didn't put much weight or bearing on what she said, but it would weigh heavily on me later. My response at the time was, "No, ma'am, I'm not the department manager. In some ways I'm over the department manager."

"Good," she immediately said. Then just as quickly, she rolled into the rest of her story. "My name is Denise, and I live across the water," she said.

"Okay," I uttered.

"I picked up one of your eight-piece chicken dinners yesterday, but it was so dried out and burnt, we could not eat it for dinner yesterday. I was wondering if I could return it today and get a replacement," Denise inquired.

"Certainly, ma'am," I said quickly. Then just as quickly, I added, "First of all, accept my sincere apology on behalf of the store management. By all means, bring it back in, and we will replace it—no questions asked."

"Thank you," Denise said. "So sorry for not returning it yesterday, but as I said before, we live across the water and didn't want to drive all the way back over there."

"Not a problem. Just bring it, and it will be replaced," I said to her.

"Thank you," Denise uttered again.

"You're welcome. Do you know what time you'll be here?" I asked.

Denise told me she would be in at around 1:30 p.m., and we both hung up the phone and went happily on our way. Then I forgot about it because to me, Denise was another unsatisfied customer for a legitimate reason. The case was closed or would be as soon as she came in and picked up her replacement eight-piece dinner … or would it? Is anyone ever really satisfied with getting over, getting by, having the better of, or screwing other people or an organization over for the heck of doing it?

At 1:47 p.m., I was paged back to the deli for customer relations. While walking from the front of the store back to the deli, all I could think was, *What the f*** is wrong at the deli this time?* I honestly did not think of Denise. She actually hadn't crossed my mind since shortly after I had hung up the phone more than two hours earlier. Since I had spoken to her, I had done what seem like a million things, including fending off an angry woman in the bakery department. She wanted me to write on a cake for her, and I told her that I had no experience in that arena.

"I am not a cake decorator, but if you can patiently wait another fifteen minutes, the cake decorator will be back from lunch," I mistakenly said to her. At least, I had to assume it was a mistake because she almost flew over the glass cake case at me. Then she threatened to throw the cake in my face for being rude. Moments before that, I had been in the produce back room looking for loose (singles) Fuji apples for one customer and collard greens for another. We had bagged Fuji apples in the store, but this individual did not particularly care for the bagged ones. She wanted singles as if the ones in the bag had jumped into the bag as a bunch and that made them different from the individual ones.

Anyhow, when I was about twenty feet away from the deli counter, I saw that two of the three associates behind it were laughing so uncontrollably, they had to rush to the dishwashing room in the back. The third, Tammie, was standing there holding a chicken tray and trying her damned best not to crack up. To the right of me next to the pizza and seafood salad wall, a lady looked at the items. However, the closer I got to the deli counter, the more and more it looked like Tammie was going to fall over from holding in her laughter. As soon as I made it up to the counter, she chucked the chicken tray into my hands and bent over laughing while saying, "You handle this. I can't. Please excuse me, but I think I'm gonna need a drink."

Now up until that point, I had no clue what was going on. However, I was thinking some laughing gas might have escaped behind the deli counter because everyone behind it seemed to be going out of their minds. When I looked down through the clear top of the chicken tray at the contents inside, I, too, developed a sudden urge to laugh. However, my first instinct was to inquire about it because the tray only had bones on it.

"Tammie, what the fuck is this," I asked with a chuckle.

Without even saying a word, Tammie fell down on her knees and started to laugh even harder, which in turn, brought a big I-don't-know-what-the-fuck-is-going-on-here smile to my face. Something was definitely funny here. Then through the course of her laughter, Tammie, all of a sudden, started to vigorously point at the tray in my hand and then over to the pizza wall.

Suddenly, things clicked for me, and tears, which came with full-throttle laughter, filled my eyes, but I could not let the tears or the laughter out. I just looked down at the tray one more time and then over at the lady by the pizza wall. Then I chuckled to myself and repeated the process two more times before I had to whisk myself away to the closest back room to laugh uncontrollably for a good minute. Then I put on the best steel face I could muster and walked out of the back room and up to the lady who was now standing beside the cold sandwich island about twenty-five feet away, in front of the deli counter.

"Hi. You must be Denise," I calmly said to the lady.

"Yes. Is my food ready?" she answered.

Immediately I thought to myself, *Hold your horses there. Houston, we have a problem.* But of course I could not say that, so instead I said, "Hi, I'm Support Manager John. What happened here?"

"Nice to meet you, John," Denise replied with a smile. Then she quickly asked, "Is something the matter?"

I immediately thought, *Earth to Denise, news flash. There's no chicken here, so something is wrong.* But again, it would not have been politically correct to say that, so instead I said, "As a matter of fact, yes there is something the matter. When you called earlier asking if you could have the chicken you bought yesterday replaced, you said you were making the request because what you received was dried out and burnt to the point that your family could not eat it. But there's no chicken here."

"Well, we live across the water. I wasn't gonna let my family starve to death," Denise replied.

"I understand that, but that wasn't what we discussed or I was told on the phone. You told me you guys could not eat it and asked if I would replace it, which I agreed to do," I said to Denise.

"We were hungry," Denise said in a slightly elevated voice. The she added, "What did you want me to do?"

"Not eat my the chicken if you intended to bring it back to be replaced," I said to her.

"As I said before, we were hungry, and we live across the water. What did you want me to feed my family?" she screamed.

"There's no need to raise your voice at me, ma'am," I calmly said to her.

"Okay then, when will my replacement chicken be ready?" Denise inquired.

"Ma'am, Denise, I hate to tell you, but there are eight sets of bones here. I can't see myself replacing this," I said to her.

"Well, that's not what we agreed to on the phone," Denise cautioned me.

"You're absolutely correct. We did not discuss you bringing back eight sets of bones either," I reminded her.

"Well, I'm sorry. The chicken was dried and burnt. I would like you to live up to your end of the bargain," Denise said and then just stood there looking at me.

I stood there briefly looking back at her. I didn't know what was going through her mind at the time, but I was thinking, *Bitch, you better start coughing up some chicken and glue it back on these bones if you expect me to replace this eight-piece.*

However, after both of us stood there momentarily looking at each other in a muted fashion, she finally said, "Well, since you don't intend to replace the burnt, dried-out chicken you guys sold me, I need to talk to someone above you who will. Is your boss around?"

"Absolutely. I'll go and get him for you," I said before walking off to the back room where I had been laughing my ass off earlier. Then three minutes later, I reemerged from the back room with my boss, Dave, after I had given him a rundown of what had transpired up to that point. Dave, a funny and very sarcastic guy in his own right, walked straight up to the Denise and after introducing himself, said, "I understand you're looking for some replacement chicken for these eight sets of bones."

"Yes. Your support manager over there has gone back on his words and has refused to honor the promise he made to me earlier today. That's why I asked for someone higher," Denise said to Dave.

"Ma'am, you have eight pieces or eight sets of bones in this tray. According to him, you told him that the chicken you bought yesterday was burnt and dried out to the point where it couldn't be eaten," Dave stated. Before Denise could respond, he quickly added in a sarcastic tone, "So what happened?"

"As I explained to him, we were hungry, and I live across the water. I couldn't let my family starve to death," Denise reiterated.

"I understand that, and if I were in your shoes and my family was starving, I would much rather have fed them some burnt, dried-out chicken as opposed to nothing. But that's not what you and my support discussed on the phone now, is it?" Dave said in his usual sarcastic voice.

"He agreed to replace my chicken if I brought the package back in to show him," Denise said.

"Absolutely. An eight-piece tray of burnt, dried-out chicken according to you. Not eight pieces of bones," Dave said to her.

"Well, I think you all are being unreasonable," Denise said before Dave cut back in.

"I'm sorry, ma'am, but I will have to go along with my support manager on this one. I can't honestly reimburse you for this in any way, shape, or form," Dave said to her.

"Well, that's not fair because my mother who bought a burnt chicken from Farm Fresh yesterday is there right now getting hers replaced," Denise said.

Instantly, Dave looked over at me as if to say, "Did you hear that?" Still, Denise's subconscious talking did not stop there. She followed that up by stating, "And on Wednesday when I took the kids to the drive-through at Wendy's and they were given burnt nuggets, I went back later and got replacement ones from them."

Again, Dave immediately looked over at me, but this time, he had a what-the-fuck look on his face. Meanwhile I thought, *This bitch is a scam artist.* I did not want to think so negatively about her, but moments later, she confirmed what I thought of her. Then I no longer felt bad about calling her the "B" word. However, before we got to that revelation, Dave turned back to Denise with an obvious smile on his face, and this is what came out of his sarcastic mouth. "Ma'am, I'm sorry you are having a rough go at chicken serving places. Maybe you should start going to places that serve steaks," Dave suggested. Then he added, "Ah? It's worth thinking about?"

Denise pondered for a moment but did not comment on Dave's suggestion. Instead, she said, "Hmm, I don't think you guys are being fair. In fact, I know you two aren't because about a month ago when I stopped by here and also got burnt chicken, I called and talked to the department manager, and do you know what she did?" Denise commented.

Right at that moment, I thought, *Yeah, I no longer feel bad about calling you a bitch. You are a bitch—a scam-artist bitch—a chicken-loving, stealing, scam-artist bitch.* While I was thinking that, Dave responded to her statement.

"I assume she replaced the burnt chicken for you," Dave said in a sarcastic tone.

"Yes. Yes, she did," Denise boldly said.

"Did you bring her back bones too or did you bring back burnt chicken?" Dave said.

"She told me I didn't have to bring back anything, so I didn't. And not only did she replace my burnt chicken, but she also gave me a full-course meal for four and made sure I got a twenty-dollar store gift card on top of that," Denise said.

"She did, did she?" Dave said. Then he added, "Wow," at the end.

"She certainly did, and that's what I call customer service at its finest," Denise said.

"Ma'am, you might not think so, but my support and I are two of the finest customer service representatives, not only in this store but in our market as a whole," Dave exclaimed.

For a brief moment, Denise just stood there looking at Dave without saying a word. Then after about twenty seconds, Dave broke the silence by saying, "I guess you don't believe me, right?"

"You can say whatever you want. Whatever you two are doing stinks to high heaven, and if I don't get compensated for it, I'm taking it higher. There's no reason for my mom to be at Farm Fresh getting a replacement for the burnt chicken they sold her yesterday, and I can't come here and do the same," Denise stated.

"Well, I'm sorry about your particular situation," Dave said.

So long, bitch. The fancy slot machine you played a month ago is now in the boneyard, I said to myself. Then as Denise walked away in disgust, I added in an audible tone, "Don't forget your bones."

Dave heard me and shook his head to say, "Stop it." I was quite sure Denise hadn't heard me though. However, she gave me the this-ain't-over look as soon as the words left my mouth. Sure enough, it wasn't over because some two and a half weeks later, soon after I got to work, I was paged to my manager's office. I did not think it had anything to do with Denise. In fact, she was the furthest thing from my mind.

Still, I hurried to my manager's office on the other side of the store. When I got to his office, I was told we' were now meeting in personnel. So I moseyed on next door. Its door was open when I walked up to it. I could see my store manager, my co-manager Dave, the personnel manager, another co-manager, and two assistant managers inside. So the store managers motioned to me, "Come on in, and join the party."

I still thought it was about a meeting I was clueless about. So with that in mind, I chose not to sit. Instead, I stood in the back of the room close to the exit door with my back against one of the filing cabinets. Not long after I had settled in that position, the store manager smiled at me and said, "So what's the story between you and the customer with the eight-piece chicken dinner?"

"Ah?" I uttered and immediately looked over at Dave.

"Don't look at me, mister. This is all on you. You're the one she called home office on, not me," Dave said with a big smile on his face.

"What?" I uttered. Then I went on to explain what had transpired. Yes, I was ridiculed in a friendly way for fighting a lady over a six-dollar-and-eighty-nine-cent tray of chicken, half of which was profit. I did not know until that moment how great the profit margin was on such items. When they told me how much (little) we paid for a premade cake and how much (at least 400 percent) the profit margin on each one was, I almost shit my pants right where I was leaning.

Anyhow, before the meeting adjourned, I was told that based on home office instructions, the lady (Denise) would be in that afternoon and that she should be given an eight-course meal with two large potato salads and two one-gallon bottles of ice tea as extras. I couldn't believe this, but I was told to let it go. I forced myself to do it, even when she came to pick up the items and was walked up to the register to have it charged under our customer satisfaction account.

However, right before the transaction was about to be completed, Denise looked at the two one-gallon bottles of ice tea and said to the deli associate (Ty) who was holding them, "I don't want your store-brand ice tea. I want the Milo brand instead."

It just so happened that I saw the poor young lady run to the back with the two jugs of ice tea in her hands to go and exchange them. That was when I was informed that the lady (Denise) was up front having a fit about the ice tea we were trying to give her. Believe you, me, it took every ounce of patience I had to keep me from going up front and putting my arms around her greedy scam-artist neck. Nevertheless, I called her everything imaginably bad under the sun, both aloud and under my breath. In reflection, I just despise the fact that that crooked bastards beat me over an eight-piece chicken tray.

In further reflection, in my eyes she was no better than the individual who ran out one of the side emergency doors three weeks ago with four, twenty-four-packs of Budweiser beer. It was one of the most amazing things I've ever witnessed. He had one under each armpit, and one in each hand. Even though I still wonder today how he got the second pack under his armpit, it was even more amazing to see him flying through the back room and out the alarm-controlled door. But he did and into the back of a vehicle, which slowed down to pick him up. It had been well coordinated.

As I remember Denise, I realize that she's no better than those individuals who come to the store, fill up their shopping carts with perishable items such as expensive meat, take them to the other side of the store, and put them in the pets department between dog food cans. Sometimes they even throw them into the clothes or between paper towels and rolls of toilet paper on the shelves. Let's not discount the individuals who stop by the deli and order food or pick up bakery items from the bakery and then walk around the store pretending to be shopping as they eat the food or cakes. Then they stuff the empty packages on the nearest shelves to avoid paying for them.

Even though this is a different form of stealing or scamming, Denise is no better than the guy who came in last October with his little girl and then tried to run out of the main entrance door with the biggest pumpkin we had on display that Halloween season. The question I've always asked is, "Why would you want to do that in the presence of your kids?" Why would you try to steal a pumpkin from inside a grocery store when you could easily go to someone's field and steal one if you were that desperate pumpkin. Moreover, this wasn't any ordinary pumpkin. It was absolutely the biggest one we had in the store leading up to a few days before Halloween when the idiot tried unsuccessfully to run off with it.

Upon further reflection, I realize that Denise is no better or more honest than the guy who ran out the store last week with four fifty-five-inch televisions inside his shopping cart. Yes, the items he stole might be a lot more expensive at one pop, but who knows how long Denise, her mother, and kids have been scamming. From the looks of it and the way she stated the obvious, it seems that it's something they've become accustomed to. Therefore, Denise and her family driving around and hitting up chicken-serving places for their Wednesday, Saturday, and Sunday meals is just as bad as running out the store with four fifty-five-inch TVs at once.

Additionally, she's no better than the individual who took an overloaded shopping cart of electronics out to the lawn and garden section two years ago. He was caught throwing the items over the fence to two people who were waiting in a pickup truck (One was in the driver's seat, and the other was standing in its back bed catching the items).

They weren't discovered until they ran into a little trouble trying to get a fifty-five-inch spider-wrapped television over the fence. I don't know what the deal with fifty-five-inch TVs is, but they seem to be what thieves choose.

Finally, upon another reflection, I realize that Denise is no better than the family of four that came in and legally bamboozled the pet department for over $750 in broad daylight. I said legally because even though they stole the items (walked out of the store without paying), the store gave the items to them legally. The items were placed in their hands on different occasions and over a thirty-minute time span by two different assistant managers and three regular associates. When we watched the video footage the next morning, I saw that these people (a family of four) came in with a plan and executed it perfectly. This was upon learning that a whole slew of expensive flea-and-tick items were missing from the shelves with no sales to count for it.

That family of four played the store personnel like they were yoyos. All four (I assumed it was a father, mother, and two boys who were probably in their early teens) strategically positioned themselves in the department one evening at around 6:30 p.m. when the store was down to a non-rush-hour crew. One at a time, they would go and get customer service paged to the pet department. If it was someone new who showed up to help, one of them would ask that one of the expensive dog collars be unhooked for them. Then he or she would do the same on the cat aisle. However, if the person who was spying saw someone coming who had helped them earlier, he or she would call the rest of the family, and they would leave the department or walk over to the fish tank and pretend like they were checking out the fish.

They did this on and off until all eight of the dog's flea-and-tick collars (worth fifty-nine dollars and ninety-nine cents each) were gone from one security hook and all six $52.99 cat collars of the same brand (worth fifty-two dollars and ninety-nine cents each) were gone from their security hook. Each item was stuffed in the mother's handbag on an aisle where a security camera could not see them well because of a pole with a price scanner attached to it. Then they walked out of the store like they owned the place without anyone suspecting that they had stolen merchandise in their possession (well, in the mother's handbag). They are guilty of stealing as Denise is guilty of stealing, in my eyes or in the eyes of any other decent, law-abiding customer.

Printed in the United States
By Bookmasters